D1592119

HOW TO USE THIS BOOK

1. Review pages 7 through 18.

2. Familiarize yourself with material on page 19.

3. Check out information on specific State or Possession (Index – Page 5).

4. Consult Supplement for any modifying factors.

5. For Daylight Saving Time dates after 1980 see Doane's World Wide Time Change Update.

MAPS, TABLES AND ILLUSTRATIONS

6

EQUINOXES, SOLSTICE POINTS AND MOON PHASES

VERNAL EQUINOX
March 21
Day & night are equal

Noon sun is directly overhead at
Equator on its apparent travel north

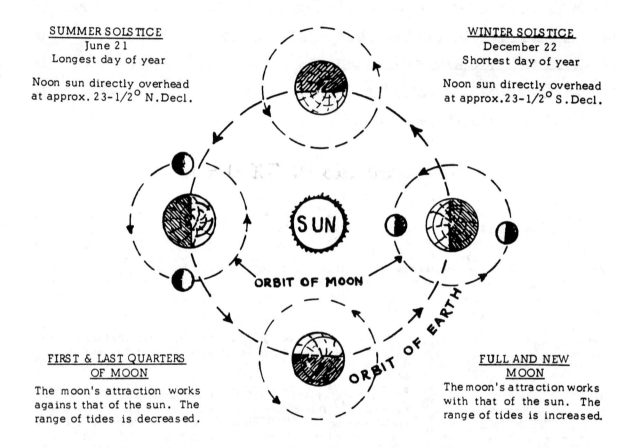

SUMMER SOLSTICE
June 21
Longest day of year

Noon sun directly overhead
at approx. 23-1/2° N.Decl.

WINTER SOLSTICE
December 22
Shortest day of year

Noon sun directly overhead
at approx. 23-1/2° S.Decl.

FIRST & LAST QUARTERS OF MOON

The moon's attraction works
against that of the sun. The
range of tides is decreased.

FULL AND NEW MOON

The moon's attraction works
with that of the sun. The
range of tides is increased.

AUTUMNAL EQUINOX
September 23
Day & night are equal

Noon sun is directly overhead at
Equator on its apparent travel south

TIME CHANGES IN THE U. S. A.

From the caveman's first awareness of natural cycles to the scientist's exploration of outer space today, man has been searching for his time-space orientation in the universe. At any point in history, we note that his search for knowledge has always been based upon observation and speculation.

Even the most primitive man was conscious of the regularity of time. He perceived an endless progression of daylight and darkness, the regularity of the four phases of the moon, and the appearance of the four seasons in recognizable order.

After centuries of watching the cycles of nature, man began to realize that motion and time were not as simple as he first thought them to be. (This thought, in one form or another, has hounded him to this day.) His consciousness broadened to relate and associate environmental factors with the events in his own life and lead to his dividing time into three parts: Past, present, and future. Since then, he has been concerned with breaking time into smaller and smaller parts.

In his efforts to solve the riddle of time he has developed a calendar; invented time measurement devices ranging from a crude sun-dial to the atomic clock; standardized time zones around the globe; and then had the audacity to confuse the whole issue by observing Daylight Saving Time on a complexity of dates.

I   THE CALENDAR

Early peoples were migratory. They "farmed" a place for awhile, then abandoned it to go "hunting" until they found their next place to farm. Having little need for calendars of days, weeks and months, they probably reckoned time by notching sticks of wood to represent so many "suns." But as language, writing, culture and knowledge advanced in ancient civilizations, the tools were at hand to speed the process of breaking time into smaller units.

After a method of counting was devised, the early astrologers applied mathematics to their knowledge of astronomical phenomena to make the first calendar. They were plagued with the same problem modern calendar-makers face today. Weeks, months and days do not square off with astronomical cycles.

Fundamentally time is reckoned by the earth's rotation on its axis in reference to the sun, a day; by the moon's revolution around the earth, a month; and by the earth's revolution around the sun, a year.

Early calendars were based on the moon, and each month started at new moon. However, the synodical month (from new moon to new moon) is just about 29-1/2 days long. The usual custom was to make one month 29 days, the next month 30, the next 29, and so on alternately. The total length would be 354 days.

As the length of the lunar year is 11 days less than the solar year (from winter solstice to winter solstice), the discrepancy mounts up. After two years the lunar year is 22 days shorter than the solar year. After three years, it is a full month short. Because the seasons follow the solar year, calendars based on the lunar year require intercalations (adding days and/or months in between ordinary calendar days and months) to harmonize the solar and lunar reckonings.

The story of calendar-making reveals the difficult problems facing early peoples. The Babylonians, Mohammedans, Chinese, Hebrews, Egyptians and Romans had a go at it, but their calendars had to be intercalated (corrected) frequently because they were lunar based. Later, the Egyptians became the first to adopt a solar calendar. But the rest of the world resisted this change until Julius Caesar took a hand.

In ancient Rome, the calendar was changed almost every year to keep step with the seasons and with the constellations of the zodiac. By Caesar's time, the vernal equinox was falling--of all places--in December, instead of in the spring. One supreme and inflexible necessity for a workable calendar is the recurrence of the Vernal Equinox on the same day each year. This is a problem even modern man has not fully solved.

History leads us to believe that Caesar was a man who knew exactly what he wanted and how to get it regardless of whose toes he stepped on. This was demonstrated when in 46 B.C., he returned from his conquest of Egypt. He resolved to make one of the biggest time changes in history --the first great calendar reform. It had not escaped his alert eye while he was in Egypt that the solar calendar was pretty accurate as compared with the lunar calendar of his own country.

For centuries the religious machinery in all countries had resisted any calendar reform, because all of their religious festivals were timed by the lunar calendar. As dictator of the Romans, Caesar not only controlled the government, he also controlled religion. When his mind was made up he never gave a thought to consulting anyone of either the political or religious groups of his day. He came home prepared to tackle the task. He brought a Greek astronomer from Alexandria, Egypt, named Sosigenes to help him. A man who wanted everything completed by yesterday, the tyrannical Caesar announced the new calendar in just one year. Correlating the calendars of the world was no small task, and it took a driving egomaniac to push the project.

First he decreed that the year 46 B.C. was to continue for 445 days (the longest year in recorded history) to allow the calendar to catch up to the sun. At the time, the Romans were still using a lunar calendar with Hebrew intercalations. But because Roman mathematicians were not as precise as the Hebrews, their calendar had become a hopeless mess, being 80 days behind the sun.

The popular solar calendar used by the Egyptians at that time was 365 days long, even though their astronomers knew that the tropical year (from solstice to solstice, or from equinox to equinox) was closer to 365-1/4 days long. This meant that every year the calendar fell a quarter of a day, or six hours, behind the sun. In four years, it was a full day behind. In 1,460 years, it would be a full year behind.

Made aware of these factors, Caesar decided to refine the solar calendar. The length of the solar year was corrected to 365 days, 5 hours, 49 minutes and 12 seconds. He adopted the first of January as the beginning of the year in place of March 25th. And to harmonize the solar and lunar

cycles, he fixed the lengths of the months as they are today. February had 28 days in common years, 29 days every 4th year, except for the century years which were to be leap years only if divisible by 400.

After the calendars of the world were correlated, these elements were added, and the Julian Calendar, named for Caesar, became effective everywhere in the civilized world on January 1, 45 B.C. Today we call this the "Old Style" calendar. The old calendar is referred to as Julian (OS) Calendar in the TIME REFERENCE TABLES.

With this frantic work done, one would assume that at last the calendar was in good shape. With the eleven day lapse of the lunar year and the six hour lapse of the solar year corrected, surely the solar and lunar reckonings harmonized by now, did they not?

Not quite! With 365 days a year for three years out of four, and 366 days a year on the 4th year, the Julian Year averaged 365-1/4 days long. Modern computations give the Tropical Year, from winter solstice to winter solstice, as 365 days, 5 hours, 48 minutes, and 46.43 seconds long. It is eleven minutes shorter than the Julian average of 365-1/4.

What does eleven minutes amount to over the years! Well, they accumulate. In 128 years, the Julian Year gained a full day. By late medieval times the discrepancy was noted by the astronomers. It had gained ten days on the sun.

The farmers did not seem to know the difference when they planted a spring crop ten days earlier. But church dignitaries were quite concerned with this state of affairs. If the Julian Year continued on indefinitely, the seasons of the year would slowly drift through the entire year in about 46,720 years. They envisioned celebrating Christmas in the spring and Easter in summer.

This would never do! The religious leaders urged another calendar reform, and astronomers of the day advised Pope Gregory XIII to correct the calendar to harmonize with the sun.

The Pope's brother, Dr. Luigi Lilio Ghiraldi, a physician and astronomer, worked out the exact requirements for correcting the calendar, but he never lived to see them operating in the Gregorian Calendar, named after the Pope. It became effective October 15, 1582 (NS) and is termed the "New Style" calendar. The new calendar is referred to as Gregorian (NS) Calendar in the TIME REFERENCE TABLES.

To set the calendar even with the sun, Pope Gregory decreed that October 5, 1582 (OS) should be October 15, 1582 (NS), thus dropping ten days.

He also decreed a change in the leap year system to prevent the same discrepancy from happening all over again in a few centuries. He added exceptions to all fourth years being leap years. Years that ended in a double 0 were not to be leap years unless they were divisible by 400. As with the Julian Calendar, the application of this mathematical expedient provides for the dropping of three whole days which would have been gained in 400 years.

Although the Gregorian Calendar has been in operation for centuries, it is still 25 seconds longer than the Tropical Year. At this rate, it will gain a full day on the sun every 3,323 years.

Important notice should be taken of the fact that the Gregorian Calendar was not adopted by the whole civilized world as was the Julian Calendar. Some countries did not adopt it until well into the present century. The Protestant world resisted changing from the Julian Year, therefore any dates listed in Protestant countries in the past few centuries probably need to be checked for changing to the new style equivalent.

When England, a Protestant nation, adopted the Gregorian Calendar at noon on September 2, 1752, the Julian Calendar was already two centuries old. It was eleven days ahead of the sun; therefore, eleven days had to be dropped. As British laws held for the American colonies, who were not yet independent, the Gregorian Calendar was adopted in America at the same time, September 2, 1752. Even though some State areas were not settled at that time, the new style calendar date appears under each State in the TIME REFERENCE TABLES.

As the centuries passed, the Julian year gained more days on the sun. The matter of calendar switches (changing OS dates to NS dates) is of the utmost interest to anyone dealing with history--such as astrologers, astronomers, biographers, historians and researchers.

When the Julian (OS) Calendar became obsolete, ten days were dropped. Immediately following October 4, 1582 (OS) the Gregorian (NS) Calendar showed October 15, 1582.

To facilitate the changing of OS dates to NS dates through the centuries, a table of correction is presented below. The necessary correction is made by adding a certain number of days to OS dates for each century in order to obtain the equivalent NS dates.

CALENDAR CORRECTION TABLE

Century	Years	Days	Century	Years	Days	Century	Years	Days
21st	2000-99	13	14th	1300-99	8	7th	600-99	3
20th	1900-99	13	13th	1200-99	7	6th	500-99	2
19th	1800-99	12	12th	1100-99	7	5th	400-99	1
18th	1700-99	11	11th	1000-99	6	4th	300-99	1
17th	1600-99	10	10th	900-99	5	3rd	200-99	0
16th	1500-99	10	9th	800-99	4	2nd	100-99	-1
15th	1400-99	9	8th	700-99	4	1st	0-99	-2

Example: April 1, 1915 OS is the equivalent of April 14, 1915 NS.

OS   April   1, 1915 - 20th Century, add 13 days.
               +13
               ――――
NS   April 14, 1915

When George Washington was born in 1732, his birthplace, Virginia, was one of the American colonies under the dominion of the British, whose official calendar was Julian. Therefore, his "official" birth date was February 11, 1732. The Calendar Correction Table indicates that 11 days should be added for eighteenth century dates to gain the Gregorian equivalent. This explains why we celebrate Washington's birthday on February 22nd.

***

II   STANDARD TIME

Because we live in a highly scheduled society in which a public time system is a vital necessity, we hurry to our appointments and take the matter of precise timing for granted. If our watch or clock stops, all we have to do is dial the telephone company for a recorded answer or listen to the radio for the broadcasting of time signals. This takes but a few seconds and on we go.

Think of what a frustrating experience it would be if we had to rely on the time-keeping that was used in the first part of the past century. Even today, no watch or clock, regardless of its skillful construction, is a precise timekeeper. Frequently it has to be adjusted to an accepted standard of time.

For several centuries the revolving earth has provided us with a time standard. However, this standard must be constantly corrected for two reasons. The earth itself has five or six different motions of its own, and the astronomical phenomena with which it is associated is cyclic in nature. Both of these fluctuations prevent precise timing.

As early as 1750 the British Royal Observatory established the mean solar day by astronomical and mathematical methods. The clock was corrected to the second every 24 hours to conform to the "standard day." However, as telephones, telegraph and other communication devices were not yet invented in the eighteenth century, there was no way to inform the general public of the correct time. It is said that the earliest known "time service" came into being in 1760, when a London widow would set her especially reliable watch each morning by Greenwich Observatory time and "carry" the time to her customers all over the city.

In America the United States Naval Observatory began to send out time signals by telegraph in 1865, and in 1904 they were broadcast by radio. But before these magnetic time signals were sent out, the people had to rely on various crude ways to set their clocks. Most jewelers set their watches to a nearby sundial and displayed this time in their shops. This was not very accurate because the sundials were based on solar, or sun, time which shows a constant seasonal change. The length of the day varies due to the speed of the earth in its elliptical orbit around the sun.

At that period publishers printed regional almanacs for the clock-makers listing the time of sunrise at various localities for every day of the year. Jewelers leaned heavily on this service for public time-keeping was based on the sun's passage over a local meridian. When the sun showed high noon at the court house, the town hall, or some other important place, it was noon all over town and the surrounding areas.

To people living in the early part of the nineteenth century, local time correct to a quarter of an hour satisfied their needs. Their lives were comparatively simple and unhurried, and the mode of travel was slow. There was hardly a reason for knowing what time it was in a town even 100 miles distant. Due to a difference of one minute in sun time for every 13 miles, east and west, each town, village, farm and city had its own suntime, even if they were located not too far apart.

The quickest way to travel from one place to another was by horseback or stage coach. A trip from New York to Philadelphia--a mere 90 miles--took two days to travel. But this did not hold true for the whole century for railroads were soon to follow the trails of the stage coach.

Railroads began developing rapidly just prior to and following the Civil War. Now that people could travel with more speed and ease, they began exploring this wide country of ours. But progress always presents unexpected problems. In this case the travelers were required to set their watch at every stop due to the centuries-old sun time reckoning.

The first route from Maine to California kept the passenger busy. If he was to make his connections on time, he had to set his watch back and forth some 20 times en route. If he boarded at Pittsburgh, he was faced with six clocks in the station, each one showing a different time standard governing train arrivals and departures.

We moderns feel that we have been terribly set upon trying to cope with the Daylight Saving Time issue, but obviously our ancestors had it even worse than we do. By 1880 there were 100 poorly defined time standards from coast to coast. In Michigan trains were scheduled by about 27 local times; in Wisconsin, by 38 times; in Illinois, by 27 times; and in Indiana, by 23 times.

This maddening situation spurred educators, railroad men, metrologists and engineers to try to solve the problem and establish a more uniform time pattern. Now that America was on the move, the speeded up social and economical conditions would not hold together unless more precision was brought into the time picture.

Sir Sanford Fleming, a Canadian civil engineer and scientist, had the background to help solve this problem. From 1845 into the 1870's, he had surveyed and located the first nationwide railway system in Canada. In 1878 he proposed a 24 meridian plan for the world.

Meridian concepts were not new. Maps of the known world drawn by ancient Greek thinkers were marked off by north-south lines like those drawn by the Babylonians. Thinking even then that the world was round, their talk was laced with such expressions as the "meridian of Athens" or the "meridian of Rome."

Naturally the whole globe is marked off in 360 meridians, each representing one degree (Babylonian fashion). Each degree can be divided into 60 minutes, and then each minute into 60 seconds. These meridians converge at the North Pole and the South Pole. As a rule, not every one of the 360 degree meridians is drawn. Usually they are drawn at spaced intervals, but the lines always slice up the earth like segments of an orange. The following diagram pictures this concept.

<u>THE MERIDIANS</u>

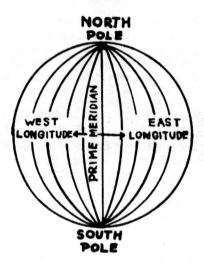

What Fleming suggested was 15° strips spreading across the United States and Canada, running from the Atlantic to the Pacific Ocean. Then each strip could legalize a single time of day, each differing from the preceding one by an hour, i.e., all clocks in any strip would show the same time.

Other men were working on the same problem. But it was William Frederick Allen in America who was able to assist Fleming in merging all previous plans into a practical pattern. Their time system, called standard time, was put into effect by the railroads in Canada and the United States at noon, November 18, 1883. Since fewer trains were running on that day, a Sunday was selected on which to initiate the plan.

When the railroads adopted standard time, the United States government did nothing about legalizing it across the country. Diehards, both in and out of government, resisted the change. Due to this strong opposition it was not until 1895 that most states had adopted standard time on their own, with one exception. See Minnesota in the <u>TIME REFERENCE TABLES</u>. Congress did not take action until March 19, 1918 when the Standard Time Act was passed. The 1918 time zone boundaries are designated by a broken line on the map of STANDARD TIME ZONES OF U.S.A.

From time to time over the years these zones have been revised. Some communities located either side of a time zone boundary found the constant changing of time presented difficulties in their mutual business transactions. Soon after the passage of the Standard Time Act they petitioned the Interstate Commerce Commission for a shift of boundaries.

In addition, the westward migration of people, the population explosion, and the development of new industrial areas brought about more time zone shifts. The dark continuous line on the map of STANDARD TIME ZONES OF U.S.A. shows this westward movement. The entire States of Michigan, Ohio and Georgia were moved from Central to Eastern Time. Although not as large, some areas were shifted in the Pacific and Mountain Time boundaries.

The United States and Canada were not the only countries concerned with time uniformity. During the nineteenth century ocean travel had also progressed rapidly, and the need for standardizing time around the world became obvious. At the Washington Meridian Conference held in 1884, the countries of the world agreed to our present standard time zone system. However, not all countries put them into effect immediately.

Because this world conference was held there, one would assume that Washington, D.C. would be selected as the first, or prime, meridian. But Great Britain was the most powerful nation in the world and had the largest navy and merchant marine. Naturally her interest for timing sea travel was of greater concern to her than to others. The conference set the Prime Meridian at Britain's Astronomical Observatory in Greenwich, an area of London. There the Prime Meridian marks 0° of longitude. England, Scotland and Wales had used this standard since 1848, and the United States had officially adopted it in 1850.

***

III   WORLD STANDARD TIME ZONES

The world system of standard time zones in use today is based on the theoretical division of the surface of the globe into 24 zones. The standard time of each zone is the mean astronomical time of one of the 24 meridians, 15° apart, beginning at Greenwich, England, meridian, and extending east and west around the globe to the International Date Line.

WORLD STANDARD TIME ZONES

MINUS ZONES			PLUS ZONES		
Faster than Greenwich			Slower than Greenwich		
Standard Meridian East Long. Degree	Zone Number	Zone Letter	Standard Meridian West Long. Degree	Zone Number	Zone Letter
0	0	Z	0	0	Z
15	-1	A	15	+1	N
30	-2	B	30	+2	O
45	-3	C	45	+3	P
60	-4	D	60	+4	Q
75	-5	E	75	+5	R
90	-6	F	90	+6	S
105	-7	G	105	+7	T
120	-8	H	120	+8	U
135	-9	I	135	+9	V
150	-10	K	150	+10	W
165	-11	L	165	+11	X
180	-12	M	180	+12	Y

The corresponding 24 standards of time have been designated by numbers running east and west of Greenwich. Those east of Greenwich are referred to as Minus Zones, and their local time may be converted into Greenwich time by subtracting the zone number. For instance, Rome, Italy, is located in the 15° East Longitude zone. By consulting the table above, we note that the 15° east (1st column) indicates the necessity of subtracting one hour from the Rome clock to convert it to Greenwich time. The zones west of Greenwich are designated Plus Zones, and their local time may be converted into Greenwich Time by adding the zone number (column 2).

These 24 standards of time are also designated by letters, with Greenwich as the Z zone and running east from A to M (J is omitted) to the International Date Line, and west of Greenwich from N to Y. The system of numbers and letters is shown in the Table above, and the U.S.A. letters and numbers may be seen on the map of STANDARD TIME ZONES OF THE U.S.

STANDARD TIME ZONES OF THE UNITED STATES

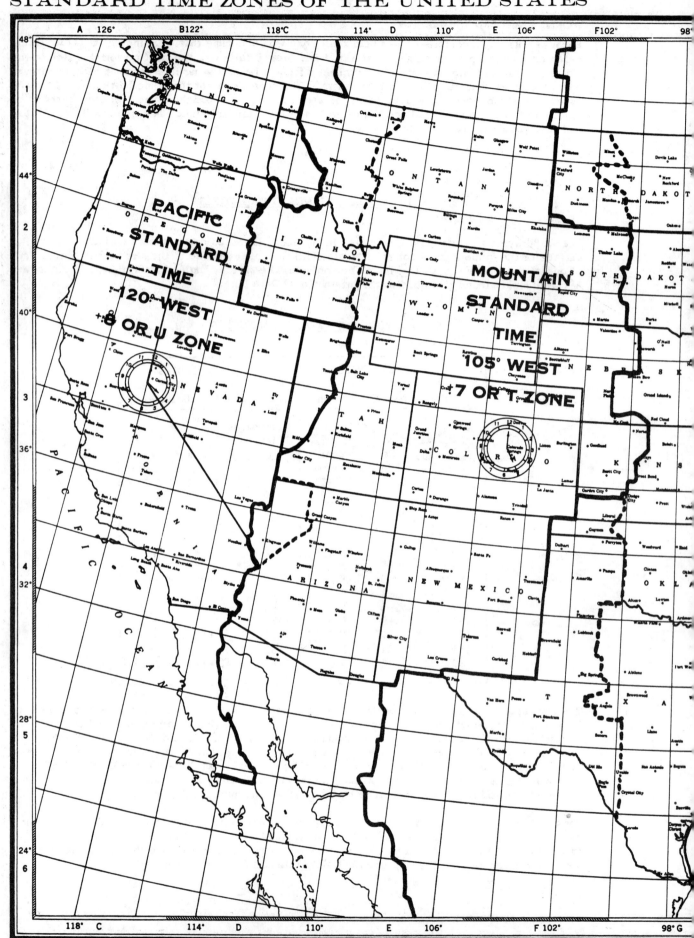

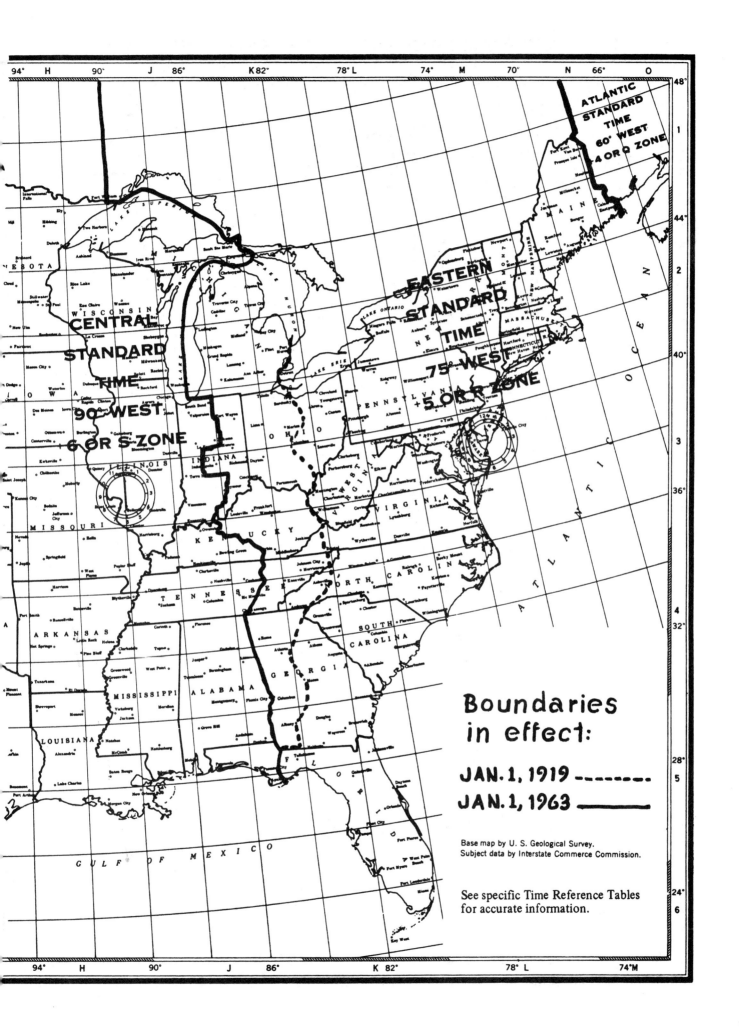

CENTRAL STANDARD TIME 90° WEST 6 OR S ZONE

EASTERN STANDARD TIME 75° WEST +5 OR R ZONE

ATLANTIC STANDARD TIME 60° WEST 4 OR Q ZONE

Boundaries in effect:

JAN. 1, 1919 -------

JAN. 1, 1963 ———

Base map by U. S. Geological Survey.
Subject data by Interstate Commerce Commission.

See specific Time Reference Tables
for accurate information.

In addition to the regular 24 standards of time based on hourly differences, some countries or sections have adopted standard time based on half-hour differences. For example, Newfoundland has a time midway between plus zones 3 and 4 (3-1/2 hours slower than Greenwich); Venezuela, midway between zones plus 4 and 5 (4-1/2 hours slower than Greenwich); India, midway between minus zones 5 and 6 (5-1/2 hours faster than Greenwich); and Iran, between minus zones 3 and 4 (3-1/2 hours faster than Greenwich).

Furthermore, not all countries base their standard time on an even hour or a half-hour of longitude. Among these are Afghanistan (4 hours and 26 minutes east of Greenwich), and British Guiana (3 hours and 45 minutes west of Greenwich). A few countries still ignore the World Time Zones. One of these is Saudi Arabia, where "Arabic Time" is observed. Every day all watches and clocks are set to midnight at sundown.

U.S.A. STANDARD TIME ZONES

West Long. Degree	Zone Number	Zone Letter	Designation of Time
60	+4	Q	U.S. Standard Atlantic Time
75	+5	R	U.S. Standard Eastern Time
90	+6	S	U.S. Standard Central Time
105	+7	T	U.S. Standard Mountain Time
120	+8	U	U.S. Standard Pacific Time
135	+9	V	U.S. Standard Yukon Time
150	+10	W	U.S. Standard Hawaii Time
165	+11	X	U.S. Standard Bering Time

Formerly the Hawaiian Standard Meridian was $157^{\circ}W30'$. In 1947 Hawaiian Standard Time was discontinued and Central Alaska Standard Time ($150^{\circ}W$) was adopted. Since then, Hawaiian Standard Time has been considered the same as Alaska Time (10 hours west of Greenwich). The zone west of the Pacific Zone, including a small portion of Southeastern Alaska and the Canadian Province of Yukon, observes Yukon Time (9 hours west of Greenwich). Along the west coast of Alaska and in the Aleutian Islands, Bering Time (11 hours west) is used. See maps of Alaska and Hawaii in the TIME REFERENCE TABLES. The time of the zone immediately to the east of the United States (4 hours west) is commonly referred to as Atlantic Time (formerly called Inter-Colonial Time).

On April 13, 1966, President Lyndon B. Johnson signed a new time bill which provided for three new time zones to be added to the five existing zones, primarily to provide a standard for Puerto Rico, Hawaii and certain U.S. Possessions. See U.S. POSSESSIONS, TERRITORIES AND TRUSTEE-SHIPS and UNIFORM TIME ACT OF 1966.

Before leaving the subject of World Standard Time Zones, let's look at the International Date Line, a hypothetical line following the meridian of 180° from the North Pole to the South Pole.

As there are 12 zones west and 12 zones east of the Prime Meridian, if two men left Greenwich at noon--one traveling east and one traveling west at the same rate of speed--they would both arrive at the International Date Line at midnight, but on different dates. The One traveling east would pass over areas where it is later and later in the day; the other traveling west would pass over areas where it is earlier and earlier in the day. The man going east would arrive at the Date Line a day later than Greenwich, and the man going west would arrive a day earlier. To solve this problem, a 24-hour correction must be made at the Date Line. But instead of adjusting the clock, as when crossing time zone boundaries, the calendar is adjusted. The adjustment is one day backward if the traveler is going from Asia to America (east) and one day forward if he is going from America to Asia (west). A day is not really lost. For by the time the travelers meet again at Greenwich they will not have lost a single second.

This date changeover line does not follow exactly the 180th meridian. Russia prefers to keep all of Siberia on the western side of the line; the United States prefers to keep the Aleutian Islands on the eastern side of the line; and some of the South Sea Islands are kept with Australia. All of the mentioned areas lie across the 180th meridian.

As a result, the International Date Line is not a straight line.   It zigzags about one-half of its length so that it will not cross any land area.   After all, a single nation would dislike the idea of observing two calendar dates at the same time within its own boundaries.

INTERNATIONAL DATE LINE

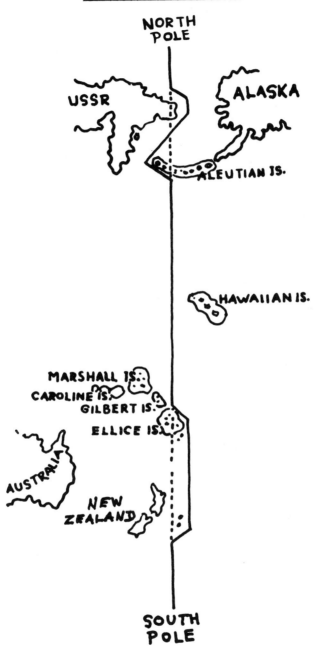

A study of the illustration of the International Date Line will show why it was wise to choose Greenwich, England, for the location of the Prime Meridian.   Because the 180th meridian must fall half-way around the globe from the Prime Meridian, if it had been placed at another starting point, the International Date Line would have run through several countries.

***

IV   DAYLIGHT AND WAR TIME

When Benjamin Franklin was ambassador to France in 1784, he suggested that people set their clocks ahead in the summer to make good use of the extra hours of daylight, because the sun "gives light as soon as he rises." His selling point was that by retiring early, they would have to buy less candles. Further they could enjoy the summer weather longer and avoid the unhealthy candle smoke. Franklin's idea was ignored. Living up to their reputation, Frenchmen continued **to burn the candle at both ends.**

Daylight Saving Time was first proposed in modern times by William Willet, an Englishman, in a pamphlet entitled "Waste of Daylight," published in 1907. But the first systematic use of Daylight Saving Time came about during World War I. In 1916, Germany observed it to conserve fuel used to produce electricity. Not long after this, Britain and most of the Western European countries adopted "Summer Time," a term synonymous with Daylight Saving Time.

The United States and Canada observed Daylight Saving Time' in 1918 and 1919, as a wartime measure. Then from February 9, 1942 until September 30, 1945, Daylight Saving Time was again observed nationwide. It was called War Time by President Franklin D. Roosevelt. These war periods have been the only times when Daylight Saving Time was observed uniformly across the nation. In 1920, a congressional act discontinued Daylight Saving Time; however, local communities began to pass ordinances to observe it anyway. That is where the confusion began.

The Local Ordinance Listing in the TIME REFERENCE TABLES under the States shows, in a graphic manner, the multiple variances which occurred. In some instances these listings are incomplete. As some cities and towns failed to keep records of these changes, or records were lost or destroyed, it would be difficult indeed to complete a work of this scope.

In spring and summer the sun rises earlier and sets later, thus making daylight hours longer. Therefore, the six months covered by Daylight Time have usually started in April and ended in September or October. But don't let that fact stick in your mind, for many communities did not conform to these dates. Starting dates vary anywhere from the middle of March to the middle of June. Ending dates occurred anywhere from late August to the first of November. In certain areas when there was a power shortage, Daylight Time was observed all year. So each and every community and date needs to be checked thoroughly.

When Daylight Saving is in effect, the clock is set one hour ahead. Then when standard time comes in again, the clock is set back the hour. A good way to remember what to do is to recall the old saying: "Spring ahead, fall back. "

Daylight Saving Time is the use of the time used as standard time in the next time zone to the east. Thus, D.S.T. is really one result of an international time standard. Even though these observance DST dates are confusing nationwide, and some railroads still run on standard time during the months that daylight time is observed, we still have it better than our ancestors. Instead of clocks displaying five or six times at the railway station, at the most there are only two; one for standard, and one for daylight.

***

V   TIME REFERENCE TABLES

Understanding the following points will allow you
to use the tables with more speed and accuracy.

(1)   REVIEW
A review of the other sections in this book, especially abbreviations, the calendar and
world standard time zones, will facilitate the use of the Time Tables.

(2)   LONGITUDE
The longitude of a specific standard meridian is indicated in parenthesis, i.e., EST $(75^{\circ}W)$.

(3)   HOURS
When an hour for the time switchover is given, it <u>always</u> indicates the kind of time which
has been in effect.
(a) 2:00 A.M. is the usual hour
(b) 0:01 A.M. is indicated by an *
(c) 1:00 A.M. is written out
(d) Noon is designated as such

(4)   YEARS, MONTHS AND DAYS
Years given are always inclusive. 1920-30 indicates 1920 through 1930. When months
and days are given numerically, the first figure represents months, i.e., May 27 is
written 5/27.

(5)   WAR TIME
Note carefully that War Time dates are not given in the Local Ordinance Listings, and the
beginning and ending dates are not given in the Table. Always check the references under
<u>DAYLIGHT (OR WAR) TIME OBSERVED</u>.

(6)   COMMUNITIES
A community is defined as a village, town or city.

(7)   COUNTIES
Note that Counties usually appear before communities in the Local Ordinance Listings. In
cases where a county observes DST, all of its communities are not listed. Consult an
atlas or a postal book to learn in which county the city you are looking for is located.

(8)   ARMY INSTALLATIONS
U.S. Army Installations usually observe DST of their specific local standard time zones,
even though the surrounding area may not.

(9)   PRACTICALLY STATE-WIDE
This reference means that rural communities may not observe DST even though most of the
State does. In these cases, local authorities of specific locations in the mentioned State
should be queried.

(10)   GENERAL INFORMATION
The variance of an Interstate Commerce Commission regulation and the actual observance
of a Standard Time Zone boundary is often wide. And the date of legislative action in the
observance of DST is not always the date when the law becomes effective. This is often
seen in dates given for the States of Michigan and Ohio. Road maps give a mixture of
I.C.C. and informal standard zone boundaries and cannot be relied upon.

(11)   LISTINGS
If a place <u>is</u> listed under "Observation by Local Ordinance", Daylight Time was observed. If it <u>is not</u>
listed, the place continued on Standard Time.

TABLE

1918	War Time
1919	War Time
*1935	5/18-9/2
1941	7/21-9/2
1942-45	War Time
1958	4/27-10/25
1959	4/26-9/27
1960	4/24-9/25

* Change at 0:01 A.M.

ALABAMA

1702		Area settled
1752	9/14	Gregorian (NS) Calendar adopted in U.S.A.
1819	12/14	State entered the Union
1883	11/18	Noon, Central Standard Time (90°W) adopted.
1889	5/30	Phenix City adopted Central Standard Time (90°W)

DAYLIGHT (OR WAR) TIME OBSERVED:
(Time changes at 2 A.M., unless otherwise indicated by asterisk)

1918	3/31 - 10/27	World War I
1919	3/30 -10/26	World War I
1920	To 1940	Not observed statewide. See Local Ordinance Listing.
1941	3/23 Noon	Phenix City adopted Eastern Standard Time (75°W) (Same as Columbus, GA)
1941	7/21 -10/1	* Observed statewide
1942	2/9 - 9/30/45	World War II
1946	To 1960	Not observed state-wide. See Local Ordinance Listing.
1961	To 1965	Not observed
1966		See Chapter VII
1967	To 1979	For dates, see Table, page 181.

OBSERVATION BY LOCAL ORDINANCE:
(Refer to Table for Month and Day)

COMMUNITIES

COUNTY

Madison County
(Huntsville, Co.Seat)
1958
1959
1960

Decatur
* 1958
Montgomery
* 1935

ALASKA

1799		Russian territory operated under Julian (OS) Calendar
1856		Russia first offered to sell it to the U.S.
1857	3/30	Treaty signed for its purchase
	4/9	Treaty ratified by the Senate
	10/16	Transferred to U.S. before payment. Calendar converted to Gregorian (NS). Instead of the usual 12 days (for 19th century), 11 days were dropped from the calendar as the extra day was supplied by the International Dateline.
1868	7/14	The House appropriated the money for its purchase.
1883	11/18	Noon. Theoretical adoption of Central Alaska Standard Time (CAT, 150°W). However, it was not observed until 1900.
1900	8/20	Four Alaska Time Zones established:

(1)	PST	(Pacific Standard Time)	120°W
(2)	YST	(Yukon Standard Time)	135°W
(3)	CAT	(Central Alaska Standard Time)	150°W
(4)	NT	(Nome Standard Time)	165°W

1912	8/24	Area organized as a territory
1959	1/3	State entered the Union
1967	11/25	New Standard Time Zone Boundary-Lines established:

(1)	YST	(Yukon Standard Time)	135°W
		Extends from 127W30 to 141W00	
(2)	AHST	(Alaska-Hawaii Standard Time)	150°W
		Extends from 141W00 to 157W30	
(3)	BST	(Bering Standard Time)	165°W
		Extends from 157W30 to 172W30	

1983	10/30 2:AM	New Standard Time Zone Lines established: Yukon Time Zone: Southeastern Alaska, including Juneau; Central part of the state, including Anchorage and Fairbanks; Nome and Western Alaska. Alaska-Hawaii Time Zone: Western end of Aleutian Chain, including islands of Atka. Adak, Shemya and Attu.

NOTE: CAT (Central Alaska Time) is replaced by AHST above; NT (Nome Standard Time) is replaced by BST above.

DAYLIGHT (OR WAR) TIME OBSERVED:
(Changes at 2 A.M.)

1942	2/9 - 9/30/45	World War II

No Daylight Time observed. This was due in part to the widely spread and sparsely populated communities, and to the fact that its location is so far north.

NOTE: When the North Pole is tilted away from the sun as much as possible, the farthest points in the North which can still be reached by the sun's rays are 23° and 17' from the pole. This is the Arctic Circle. The midnight sun is a phenomena of the Northern part of the State. The sun does not set from the middle of May until the end of July, nor does it rise above the horizon from approximately November 20 to January 24.

1969	To 1973	For dates, see Table, page 181.	1973, 1/1-12/31

Anchorage
1974	1/6 -10/27		Juneau 1980 4/27-10/26
1975-76		For dates, see Table, page 181.	

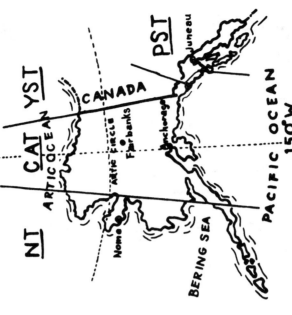

TABLE	
1918	War Time
1919	War Time
1942-45	War Time
1967	4/30-10/29

NOTE: Navajo Reservation, a large part of Arizona, observes DST, while the Hopi Reservation stays on standard time. Winslow, just south of the Navajo Reservation, observes standard time.

ARIZONA

	Area Settled	
1580		
1752	9/14	Gregorian (NS) Calendar adopted in U.S.A.
1883	11/18	Noon, Mountain Standard Time (105°W) adopted east of and including Seligman (112W53): Pacific Standard Time (120°W) adopted west of Seligman.
1912	2/14	State entered the Union
1945	3/7	Mountain Standard Time state-wide. (Portions of state which had been on PST switched to MST.)

Note: Although the state had adopted MST in 1945, the I.C.C. regulation was not effective until 4/30/50.

DAYLIGHT (OR WAR) TIME OBSERVED

(Changes at 2 A.M.)

1918	3/31-10/27	World War I
1919	3/30-10/26	World War I
1920	To 1941	Not observed
1942	2/9-9/30/45	World War II
1946	To 1956	Not observed
1950	4/30	2 A.M. Yuma County changed from Pacific Time to Mountain Time.
1957		Observed. Refer to Table for dates.
1958	To 1966	Not observed
1967		Observed. Refer to Table for dates.
1968	To 1980	Not observed

ARKANSAS

1685		Area settled
1752	9/14	Gregorian (NS) Calendar adopted in U.S.A.
1836	6/15	State entered the Union
1883	11/18	Noon, Central Standard Time (90°W) adopted.

DAYLIGHT (OR WAR) TIME OBSERVED:
(Changes at 2 A.M.)

1918	3/31 – 10/27	World War I
1919	3/30 – 10/26	World War I
1920	To 1941	Not observed
1942	2/9 – 9/30/45	World War II
1946	To 1965	Not observed
1946	To 1966	Not observed
1967	To 1979	For dates, see Table, page 181.

TABLE

1918	War Time
1919	War Time
1942-45	War Time

TABLE

1918	War Time
1919	War Time
1942-45	War Time
1948-49	Power Shortage
1950	4/30-9/24
1951	4/29-9/30
1952	4/27-9/28
1953	4/26-9/27
1954	4/25-9/26
1955	4/24-9/25
1956	4/29-9/30
1957	4/28-9/29
1958	4/27-9/28
1959	4/26-9/27
1960	4/24-9/25
1961	4/30-9/24
1962	4/29-10/28
1963	4/28-10/27
1964	4/26-10/25
1965	4/25-10/31

CALIFORNIA

1752	9/14	Gregorian (NS) Calendar adopted in U.S.A.
1769		Area settled
1850	9/9	State entered the Union
1883	11/18	Noon, Pacific Standard Time (120°W) adopted.

DAYLIGHT (OR WAR) TIME OBSERVED:
(Time changes at 2 A.M., unless otherwise indicated.)

1918	3/31 - 10/27	World War I
1919	3/30 - 10/26	World War I
1920	To 1941	Not observed
1942	2/9 - 9/30/45	World War II
1946	To 1947	Not observed
1948	3/14 - 1/1/49	Observed state-wide due to a power shortage
1949		Not observed
1950	To 1965	Observed state-wide. Refer to Table for dates.
1966	To 1979	For dates, see Table, page 181.

TABLE

1918	War Time
1919	War Time
1920	3/28-10/31
1921	3/27-5/22
1942-45	War Time
1964	5/2-9/27
1965	4/25-10/31

COLORADO

1752	9/14	Gregorian (NS) Calendar adopted in U.S.A.
1858		Area settled
1876	8/1	State entered the Union
1883	11/18	Noon, Mountain Standard Time (105°W) adopted

DAYLIGHT (OR WAR) TIME OBSERVED:
(Changes at 2 A.M.)

1918	3/31 - 10/27	World War I
1919	3/30 - 10/26	World War I
1920	To 1941	Not observed state-wide. See Local Ordinance Listing.
1942	2/9 - 9/30/45	World War II
1946	To 1964	Not observed state-wide. See Local Ordinance Listing.
1965		Observed state-wide. Refer to Table for dates.
1966	To 1979	For dates, see Table, page 181.

OBSERVATION BY LOCAL ORDINANCE:

Aspen
  1964, 5/2-9/27
Denver
  1920, 3/28-10/31
  1921, 3/27-5/22

CONNECTICUT

1635		Area settled
1752	9/14	Gregorian (NS) Calendar adopted in U.S.A.
1788	1/9	State entered the Union
1883	11/18	Noon, Eastern Standard Time (75°W) adopted.

DAYLIGHT (OR WAR) TIME OBSERVED:
(Changes at 2 A.M.)

1918	3/31 – 10/27	World War I
1919	3/30 – 10/26	World War I
1920	To 1937	Not observed state-wide. See Local Ordinance Listing.
1942	2/9 – 9/30/45	World War II
1942	2/9 – 12/31/45	World War II (Terminated at 2400 hours)
1938	To 1965	Observed state-wide. Refer to Table for dates.
1966	To 1979	For dates, see Table, page 181.

OBSERVATION BY LOCAL ORDINANCE:
(Refer to Table for Month and Day)

Hartford
  1920
  1921
New Britain
  1920
New London
  1920
  1921
Putnam
  1920
  1921

TABLE

1918	War Time
1919	War Time
1920	3/28-4/4
1921	4/24-5/5
1938	4/24-10/2
1939	4/30-9/24
1940	4/28-9/29
1941	4/27-9/28
1942-45	War Time
1946	4/28-9/29
1947	4/27-9/28
1948	4/25-9/26
1949	4/24-9/25
1950	4/30-9/24
1951	4/29-9/30
1952	4/27-9/28
1953	4/26-9/27
1954	4/25-9/26
1955	4/24-10/30
1956	4/29-10/28
1957	4/28-10/27
1958	4/27-10/26
1959	4/26-10/25
1960	4/24-10/30
1961	4/30-10/29
1962	4/29-10/28
1963	4/28-10/27
1964	4/26-10/25
1965	4/25-10/31

DELAWARE

1726		Area settled
1752	9/14	Gregorian (NS) Calendar adopted in U.S.A.
1787	12/7	State entered the Union
1883	11/18	Noon, Eastern Standard Time (75°W) adopted

DAYLIGHT (OR WAR) TIME OBSERVED:
(Changes at 2 A.M.)

1918	3/31 - 10/27	World War I
1919	3/30 - 10/26	World War I
1920	To 1941	Not observed state-wide. See Local Ordinance Listing
1942	2/9 - 9/30/45	World War II
1946	To 1954	Not observed state-wide. See Local Ordinance Listing
1955	To 1959	** Generally observed throughout the state. Refer to Table for dates.
1960	To 1965	Observed state-wide. Refer to Table for dates.
1966	To 1979	For dates, See Table, page 181.

OBSERVATION BY LOCAL ORDINANCE:
(Refer to Table for Month & Day)

COUNTIES:

New Castle
See list below

COMMUNITIES:

TABLE

Year	Dates	Year	Dates
1918	War Time	1940	4/28-9/29
1919	War Time	1941	4/27-9/28
1920	3/28-10/31	1942-45	War Time
1921	4/24-9/25	1946	4/28-9/29
1922	4/30-9/24	1947	4/27-9/28
1923	4/29-9/30	1948	4/25-9/26
1924	4/27-9/28	1949	4/24-9/25
1925	4/26-9/27	1950	4/30-9/24
1926	4/25-9/26	1951	4/29-9/30
1927	4/24-9/25	1952	4/27-9/28
1928	4/29-9/30	1953	4/26-9/27
1929	4/28-9/29	1954	4/25-9/26
1930	4/27-9/28	1955	4/24-9/25
1931	4/26-9/27	1956	4/29-10/28
1932	4/24-9/25	1957	4/28-10/27
1933	4/30-9/24	1958	4/27-10/26
1934	4/29-9/30	1959	4/26-10/25
1935	4/28-9/29	1960	4/24-10/30
1936	4/26-9/27	1961	4/30-10/29
1937	4/25-9/26	1962	4/29-10/28
1938	4/24-9/25	1963	4/28-10/27
1939	4/30-9/24	1964	4/26-10/25
		1965	4/25-10/31

** Check with local authorities

DELAWARE (cont.)

Place	Years	Place	Years	Place	Years	Place	Years	Place	Years
Armstrong	1953 - 54	Delaware City	1953 - 54	Kenton	1953 - 54	Redden	1953 - 54	Woods Branch	1953 - 54
Audeureid	1953 - 54	Delmar	1948 - 54	Kirkwood	1947 - 54	Redlion	1953 - 54	Wyoming	1948 - 54
Bacons	1953 - 54	Dover	1920 - 54	Laurel	1946 - 54	Rehoboth	1951 - 52		
Bear	1953 - 54	Edge Moor	1946 - 54	Lewes	1951 - 54	Reybold	1953 - 54		
Bellefonte	1953 - 54	Ellendale	1948 - 54	Lincoln	1953 - 54	Richardson Park	1953 - 54		
Bellevue	1946 - 54	Farmington	1953 - 54	Marydel	1947 - 52	Robbins	1953 - 54		
Bennum	1953 - 54	Farnhurst	1953 - 54	Messick	1953 - 54	Ross	1953 - 54		
Binstead	1953 - 54	Felton	1947 - 54	Middletown	1946 - 54	Ruthby	1953 - 54		
Blackbird	1953 - 54	Forest	1953 - 54	Milford	1946	Seaford	1946 - 54		
Brentford	1953 - 54	Frankford	1948 - 54	Millsboro	1948 - 54	Selbyville	1947 - 54		
Bridgeville	1947 - 54	Georgetown	1948 - 54	Mt. Pleasant	1947 - 54	Slaughter	1953 - 54		
Broad Creek	1953 - 54	Glasgow	1953 - 54	Naaman	1953 - 54	Smyrna	1946		
Cannon	1953 - 54	Green Spring	1953 - 54	Nassau	1946 - 52	State Road	1953 - 54		
Cheswold	1953 - 54	Greenwood	1946 - 52	New Castle	1953 - 54	Stockley	1953 - 54		
Claymont	1953 - 54	Harbeson	1953 - 54	New Castle County (In general) **	1920 - 54	Thompson	1948 - 54		
Clayton	1946 - 54	Harrington	1953 - 54	Newark	1938 - 41	Townsend	1953 - 54		
Coohs Bridge	1946 - 54	Hartly	1948 - 54	Newport	1946 - 54	Vandyke	1948 - 54		
Cool Spring	1953 - 54	Hollyoak	1953 - 54	Oak Grove	1946 - 54	Viola	1953 - 54		
Corbit	1953 - 54	Houston	1946 - 54	Porters	1953 - 54	Wilmington	1953 - 54		
Dagsboro	1953 - 54	Keeney	1948 - 54		1953 - 54	Wilson	1920 - 54		
	1948 - 54		1953 - 54				1953 - 54		

** Check with local authorities

DISTRICT OF COLUMBIA, WASHINGTON

1752	9/14	Gregorian (NS) Calendar adopted in U.S.A.
1790		Congress directed the selection of a new site for the Capitol of the Union, 10 miles square, on the Virginia side of the Potomac River.
1800	12/1	Seat of U.S. Government transferred to D.C.
1871	2/21	Legislated as an independent municipal corporation
1884	3/13	Noon, Eastern Standard Time (75°W) adopted

DAYLIGHT (OR WAR) TIME OBSERVED:
(Changes at 2 A.M.)

1918	3/31 – 10/27	World War I
1919	3/30 – 10/26	World War I
1920	To 1921	Not observed
1922		Observed. Refer to Table for dates.
1923	To 1941	Not observed
1942	2/9 – 9/30/45	World War II
1946		Not observed
1947	To 1965	Observed. Refer to Table for dates.
1966	To 1979	For dates, see Table, page 181.

TABLE

1918	War Time	1954	4/25-9/26
1919	War Time	1955	4/24-9/25
1922	5/2-9/4	1956	4/29-10/28
1942-45	War Time	1957	4/28-10/27
1947	5/11-9/21	1958	4/27-10/26
1948	5/2-9/26	1959	4/26-10/25
1949	4/24-9/25	1960	4/24-10/30
1950	4/4-9/24	1961	4/30-10/29
1951	4/29-9/30	1962	4/29-10/28
1952	4/27-9/28	1963	4/28-10/27
1953	4/11-9/27	1964	4/26-10/25
		1965	4/25-10/31

Map labels: MD., D.C., MD., Prince Georges Co., U.S. CAPITOL, POTOMAC RIVER, Montgomery Co., Fairfax Co., Arlington Co., VIRGINIA, Fairfax Co., Alexandria City, 77°W 00'35.7"

30

FLORIDA

1918	War Time	1954	4/25-9/26
1919	War Time	1955	4/24-9/25
1942-45	War Time	1956	4/29-10/28
1946	4/28-9/29	1957	4/28-10/27
1947	4/27-9/28	1958	4/27-10/26
1948	4/25-9/26	1959	4/26-10/25
1949	4/24-9/25	1960	4/24-10/30
1950	4/30-9/24	1961	4/30-10/29
1951	4/29-9/30	1962	4/29-10/28
1952	4/27-9/28	1963	4/28-10/27
1953	4/26-9/27	1964	4/26-10/25
		1965	4/25-10/31

TABLE

1559		Area settled
1752	9/14	Gregorian (NS) Calendar adopted in U.S.A.
1845	3/3	State entered the Union
1889	5/30	Noon, Eastern Standard Time (75°W) adopted east of and including River Junction (84W50). Central Standard Time (90°W) adopted west of River Junction, with exception of Apalachicola (85W00) on EST
1918	1/1	Entire state adopted Eastern Standard Time (75° W)

DAYLIGHT (OR WAR) TIME OBSERVED
(Changes at 2 A.M.)

1918	3/31 - 10/27	World War I
1919	3/30 - 10/26	World War I
1920	To 1941	Not observed
1942	2/9 - 9/30/45	World War II
1946	To 1966	Not observed state-wide. See Local Ordinance Listing.
1967	To 1979	For dates, see Table, page 181.

OBSERVATION BY LOCAL ORDINANCE:
(Refer to Table for Month & Day if not shown)

Elgin Air Force Base
  1946-65
Pensacola
  1946
  1947, 5/4-9/28
  1948-54
  1955, 4/24-10/30
  1956-65

ATLANTIC OCEAN
GULF OF MEXICO
GA.
ALA.
River JC.
84W50'

31

GEORGIA

1733		Area settled
1752	9/14	Gregorian (NS) Calendar adopted in U.S.A.
1788	1/2	State entered the Union
1888		Athens adopted Eastern Standard Time (75°W)
1888	3/25	Savannah adopted Eastern Standard Time (75°W)
1888	5/1	Brunswick adopted Eastern Standard Time (75°W)
1903		Eastern Standard Time (75°W) adopted east of 84W00, Central Standard Time (90°W) adopted west of 84W00.
1918	1/1	Atlanta adopted Central Standard Time (90°W)
1931	12/3	Atlanta voted to retain Central Standard Time (90°W)
1941	1/4	Moultrie adopted Eastern Standard Time (75°W)
1941	3/21	State law put the whole state on Eastern Standard Time (75°W) at 11:35 A.M. (CST). Some communities did not comply immediately. Rossville and West Point remained on Central Standard Time (90°W).
1941	3/22	Atlanta, Griffin, Newnan, Rome and Thomaston adopted Eastern Standard Time (75°W) at 0 hour.
	3/23	Columbus and adjacent towns adopted Eastern Standard Time (75°W) at noon.
	3/24	Americus adopted Eastern Standard Time (75°W)

DAYLIGHT (OR WAR) TIME OBSERVED: ____

(Changes at 2 A.M.)

1918	3/31-10/27	World War I
1919	3/30-10/26	World War I

TABLE

1918	War Time	Start: 1 A.M.	End: 2 A.M.
1919	War Time	Start: 0 hr.	End: 2 A.M.
1935	4/28-9/29	Changes at 0 hrs.	
1936	4/26-9/27	Changes at 0 hrs.	
1937	4/25-9/26	Changes at 0 hrs.	
1938	4/24-9/25	Changes at 0 hrs.	
1939	4/30-9/24	Changes at 0 hrs.	
1940	4/28-9/29	Changes at 0 hrs.	
1942 – 1945	War Time		

** Check with local authorities

ATLANTIC OCEAN — S.C. — N.C. — TENN. — ALA. — FLA. — ●Atlanta — CST — EST — 84°W

GEORGIA (cont.)

1920	to 1934	Not observed
1935	to 1940	Not observed statewide. See local Ordinance Listing.
1941	7/20	West Point on Central Daylight Time and Rossville.
	8/4	Harlem and Augusta on Eastern Daylight Time
1942	2/9-9/30/45	World War II
	9/27	Dalton on Central War Time
1943	1/28	State adopted Central War Time at 12:30 P.M. (EWT), but not all communities complied. Athens, Augusta, Gainesville, Savannah, Waycross, and Hall County remained on Eastern War Time.
	1/28	Valdosta went to Central War Time at noon for a week; then back to Eastern War Time on Feb. 5, 1943.
	1/29	Atlanta and Fulton County went to Central War Time at 0:01 A.M. Rome went to Central War Time.
	2/5	Macon went to Central War Time
	2/14	Columbus went to Central War Time
1945	9/30	Entire state returned to Eastern Standard Time (75°W)
1946	. to 1966	Not observed
1967	To 1979	For dates, see Table, page 181.

OBSERVATION BY LOCAL ORDINANCE:
(Refer to Table for Month and Day if not shown)

Albany 1937-40	College Park 1935-40	East Point 1935-40	Hapeville 1935-40	McDonough 1937-40
Atlanta 1935-40	Decatur 1935-40	Griffin 1937-40	Jonesboro 1937-40	Marietta 1935-40

HAWAII

1778	Discovered by Capt. James Cook, who named it the Sandwich Islands. Ruled by native monarchs until 1893.
1843	Seized by a British naval officer, but was disavowed. Britain and France recognized the independent status of the Kingdom of Hawaii.
1849	France seized it but restored it at once.
1851	The King offered it to the U.S. who refused it.
1875	Reciprocity treaty with U.S. Increased trade.
1884	Treaty renewed to include lease of Pearl Harbor for a U.S. Naval Base.
1893	Revolution; became a Republic, operating under the Gregorian (NS) Calendar.
1894	Asked U.S. for annexation.
1898 7/7 8/12	U.S. voted on its annexation. Annexation effective.
1900 **	Organized as a territory. Hawaiian Standard Time (HST, 157°W30') observed in various parts.
1947 6/8	Central Alaska Standard Time (CAT, 150°W) adopted at 2 A.M. (This, in effect, added 30 minutes.) Hawaiian Standard Time was discontinued.
1959 8/21	State entered the Union.
1967 11/25	New Time Zone Name: AHST (Alaska-Hawaii Standard Time) 150°W Extends to entire State.

NOTE: Formerly used CAT (Central Alaska Time) or HST (Hawaii Standard Time), now called AHST as above.

** Check with local authorities

CAT

HST

Honolulu

NORTH PACIFIC OCEAN

157°W30'

150°W

HAWAII (cont.)

<u>DAYLIGHT (OR WAR) TIME OBSERVED:</u>
(Changes at 2 A.M.)

1918	3/31–10/27	World War I, U.S. officials only
1919	3/30 – 10/26	World War I, U.S. officials only
1920	To 1932	Not observed
1933	4/30 – 5/1	Observed 24 hours only
1934	To 1941	Not observed
1942	2/9 – 9/30/45	World War II
1946	To 1979	Not observed

IDAHO

Year	Date	Event
1752	9/14	Gregorian (NS) Calendar adopted in U.S.A.
1824		Area settled
1883	11/18	Noon, Pacific Standard Time (120°W) adopted by the railroads. However, local time was used in most communities.**
1890	7/3	State entered the Union
1919	6/1	Mountain Standard Time boundary extended west to include a small portion of Idaho. (See map on page 14.)
1923	5/13	Southern portion of State adopted MST (105°W), except places north of Lewiston (46N24, 117W01) and Grangeville (45N56, 116W07). Line drawn at Avery (47N15, 115W48); however, Saint Maries (47N18, 116W35) remained on PST.

DAYLIGHT (OR WAR) TIME OBSERVED:
(Changes at 2 A.M.)

Year	Period	Note
1918	3/31 - 10/27	World War I
1919	3/30 - 10/26	World War I
1920	To 1941	Not observed state-wide. See Local Ordinance Listing.
1942	2/9 - 9/30/45	World War II
1946	To 1965	Not observed state-wide. See Local Ordinance Listing.
1964:		Communities north of Salmon River observed varying beginning and termination dates, and are not listed under Local Ordinance Listing.**
1966		See Chapter VII
1967	To 1979	For dates, see Table, page 181.

OBSERVATION BY LOCAL ORDINANCE:
(Refer to Table for month & day)

TABLE

Year	War Time	1942-45	War Time
1918	War Time		4/27-9/1
1919	War Time	1952	4/30-10/29
1938	5/1-10/1	1961	4/29-10/28
1939	5/7-10/1	1962	4/28-10/27
1940	5/5-9/29	1963	4/26-10/25
1941	5/4-9/28	1964	4/25-10/31
		1965	

CANADA

WASH. MONT.

PST MST

SALMON RIVER AREA

OREG. ⊙Boise WYO.

NEV. UTAH

115°W

** Check with local authorities

IDAHO (cont.)

Ashton
1961-63
Athol
1961-63
Beaver
1938-41
Blackfoot
1961-63
Bonners Ferry
1961-63
1965
Bovard
1964-65
Bradley
1938-41
1961-63
Burke
1938-41
1961-63
Camas
1938-41
Gibbs
1964-65
Carbonite
1938-41
Clyde
1964-65
Coeur d'Alene
1961-63
1964-65
Cottonwood
1961-63

Dalton
1964-65
Declo
1961-63
Delta
1938-41
Dorsey
1938-41
Eastport
1961-63
Emmett
1961-63
Eraville
1938-41
Estes
1964-65
Ferris
1964-65
Gem
1938-41
1961-63
Grangeville
1691-63
Hagen
1964-65
Haight
1938-41
Hayden Lake
1964-65
Headlund
1938-41
Headquarters
1961-63
Howell
1964-65

Idaho Falls
1961-63
Jarvey
1938-41
Jefferson
1938-41
Joel
1964-65
Joki
1938-41
Kellogg-Wardner
1938-41
Kingston
1938-41
Larson
1938-41
Lava Hot Springs
1961-63
Lewiston
1961-63
Linfor
1938-41
Malad
1961-63
McCall
1961-63
McCammon
1961-63
McClellan
1964-65
Minidoka
1961-63
Montpelier
1961-63
Moscow
1961-63
1964-65

Mullan
1938-41
Murray
1938-41
New Meadows
1961-63
Nezperce
1961-63
Oakley
1961-63
Orchard
1961-63
Orofino
1961-63
Osburn
1938-41
Page
1938-41
Paragon
1964-65
Payette
1938-41
Pine Creek
1961-63
Plummer
1938-41
Pocatello
1961-63
Post Falls
1964-65
Preston
1961-63
Prichard
1938-41
Saint Anthony
1961-63

Sand Point
1952
1961-63
1965
Shont
1938-41
Silver King
1961-63
Soda Springs
1961-63
Steamboat
1931-48
Stites
1961-63
Stoddard
1961-63
Sunset
1938-41
Troy
1964-65
University
1964-65
Victor
1961-63
Viola
1964-65
Wallace
1938-41
Weiser
1961-63
Wilder
1961-63
Winchester
1961-63

ILLINOIS

1720	Area settled
1752	9/14	Gregorian (NS) Calendar adopted in U.S.A.
1818	12/3	State entered the Union
1883	11/18	Noon, Central Standard Time (90°W) adopted
1936		See this year under daylight time listing.

DAYLIGHT (OR WAR) TIME OBSERVED:
(Changes at 2 A.M.)

1918	3/31 - 10/27	World War I
1919	3/30 - 10/26	World War I
1920	To 1936	Not observed state-wide. See Local Ordinance Listing.
1936	3/1 - 11/1	Some communities (as in Local Ordinance Listing) switched to Eastern Standard Time (75°W), then returned to CST. For convenience and because CDST coincides with EST, this information appears in Table I, even though it is a standard time reference.
1937	To 1941	Not observed state-wide. See Local Ordinance Listing
1942	2/9 - 9/30/45	World War II (Exception: Chicago until 10/28)
1946	To 1958	Not observed state-wide. See Local Ordinance Listing.

1955: By this time 628 communities were observing DST
1957: 385 communities ended DST on 9/29; and 365 on 10/27
1958: By now DST generally observed from April to October by Chicago, Peoria and 500 communities. In a number of other places, DST observed until 9/28.

1959	7/1	Entire State adopted DST, which terminated 10/25. However, the places which had been observing DST in previous years turned the clocks ahead one hour on 4/26

TABLE I

1918	War Time
1919	War Time
1920	6/13-10/31
1921	3/27-10/30
1922	4/30-9/24
1923	4/29-9/30
1924	4/27-9/28
1925	4/26-9/27
1926	4/25-9/26
1927	4/24-9/25
1928	4/29-9/30
1929	4/28-9/29
1930	4/27-9/28
1931	4/26-9/27
1932	4/24-9/25
1933	4/30-9/24
1934	4/29-9/30
1935	4/28-9/29
1936	3/1-11/1
1937	5/8-9/26
1938	5/1-9/25
1939	5/7-9/24
1940	5/5-9/29
1941	5/4-9/28
1942-45	War Time
1946	4/28-9/29

1947	4/27-9/28
1948	4/25-9/26
1949	4/24-9/24
1950	4/30-9/24
1951	4/29-9/30
1952	4/27-9/28
1953	4/26-9/27
1954	4/25-9/26
1955	4/24-10/30
1956	4/29-10/28
1957	4/28-10/27
1958	4/27-10/26
1959	4/26-10/25

TABLE II

1936	4/26-9/27
1937	4/25-9/26
1938	4/24-9/25
1939	4/30-9/24
1940	4/28-9/29
1941	4/27-9/28
1955	4/24-9/25
1956	4/29-9/30
1957	4/28-9/29
1958	4/27-9/28

See Illinois Supplement, page 193, recording of birth hours.

ILLINOIS (cont.)

1959 To 1980

For dates, see Table, page 181.

OBSERVATION BY LOCAL ORDINANCE:
(Refer to Tables for Month & Day if not shown)

Place	Years	Class
Abingdon	1946-57	I
Addison	1955-58	II
	1941	I
	1946-54	II
	1955	I
	1956-58	II
Adeline	1957-58	I
Adenmoor	1955-56	II
	1957-58	I
Albers	1953-54	I
	1955-57	II
Algonquin	1941	II
	1946-54	I
	1955	II
	1956-59	I
Alhambra	1951-54	I
	1955-58	II
Allenville	1955-58	II
Allerton	1955-58	II
Alorton	1957-58	II
Alsey	1958	II
Alsip	1955-58	I
Altamont	1955-56	II
	1957-58	I
Alton	1946-54	I
	1955-58	II
Alvin	1949-54	I
	1955-58	II
Amboy	1947-54	I
	1955-58	II
Antioch	1941	II
	1946-58	I
Apple River	1958	II
Arcola	1957-58	II
Arenzville	1958	II
Argenta	1955	II
	1956-58	I
Argo	1941	II
	1946-58	I
Arlington	1955-58	I
Arlington Heights	1920-30	I
	1931, 4/26-10/25	II
	1932-41	II
	1946-58	II
Arlington Park	1955-58	II
Armington	1955-58	II
Aroma Park	1947-58	I
Arrowsmith	1947-54	II
	1955	I
	1956-58	I
Arthur	1953-54	I
	1955-58	II
Asbestos	1955-58	II
Ashburn	1938	II
	1946-54	I
	1955-58	II
Ashkum	1947-54	I
Ashland	1955	II
	1956-57	I
	1958	II
	1957-58	II
Ashmore	1957-58	I
Ashton	1947-54	I
Assumption	1955-58	II
Astoria	1958	II
Athens	1955-58	II
Athol	1955-58	II
Atlanta	1952-54	I
	1955-58	II
Atwood	1955-58	II
Auburn	*1920-41	I
	1946-54	I
	1955-58	II
Aurora	*1933-35	I
	*1936	II
	*1937-41	I
	1946-54	II
	1955	I
Avena	1956-58	II
	1955-56	II
	1957-58	I
Aviston	1955-58	II
Avondale	1955-56	II
	1957-58	I
Baldwin	1947-54	I
	1955-58	II
Ballard	1956-57	I
	1954-58	II
Bannockburn	1955-58	II
Barclay	1951	I
Barrington	1920-41	I
	1946-58	I
Bartelso	1955-58	II
Bartlett	1941	II
	1946-54	I
Bartonville	1955	II
	1956-58	I
Batavia	1928	I
	1932-35	II
	1936	I
	1937-40	II
	1941	II
	1946-54	I
Batchtown	1955	II
	1956-58	I
Bath	1957-58	II
Beach	1957-58	II
	1946	I
Beardstown	1946-54	I
	1955-58	II
Beaverville	1955-58	II
Beckemeyer	1938-40	I
	1941	II
Bedford Park	1946-54	I
	1955	II
Beecher	1956-58	I
	1946-58	I
Belden	1955-58	II
Belgium	1955-58	II
Belleville	1946-54	I
	1955-56	II
	1957-58	I
Bellevue	1955	II
	1956-58	I
Bellflower	1955-56	II
	1957-58	I
Bellmont	1938	II
Bellwood	1946-54	I
	1955	II
	1956-58	I
Belvidere	1946-54	I
	1955	II
	1956-58	I
Bement	1955-58	II
Benld	1955-58	II
Bensenville	1938-40	I
	1941	II
	1946-54	I
	1955	II
	1956-58	I

*Changes at 0:01 A.M.

ILLINOIS (cont.)

Location	Period	Zone
Benson	1955-56	II
	1957-58	I
Berkeley	1946-58	I
Berwyn	1920-41	I
	1946-58	I
Bethalto	1955	II
	1956-58	I
Braceville	1955-58	II
Bethany	1955-56	II
	1957-58	I
Bierd	1954-58	I
Bismarck	1951-54	I
	1946-54	I
Bissell	1954	I
Bloomingdale	1955	I
Bloomington (1) 1940, 5/17-9/29	1941	II
	1946-54	I
	1955	II
	1956-58	I
Blue Island	1920-41	I
	1946-54	I
	1955	II
	1956-58	I
Blue Mound	1955	II
	1956-57	I
	1958	II
Bluff City	1955-58	II
Bluffs	1957-58	II
Bondville	1952	I
Bonfield	1955-58	II
Bourbonnais	1955	I
	1956-58	II
Bradley	1946-54	I
	1955-58	II
Braeside	1951-54	I
	1955-58	II
Braidwood	1948-54	I
	1955	II
	1956-58	I
Breese	1946-54	I
	1955-58	II
Bridgeview	1955-58	I
Briergate	1946-54	I
	1955	II
	1956-58	I
Brighton	1948-54	I
	1955-58	II
Brighton Park	1953	I
Brimfield	1955	II
	1956-57	I
	1958	II
Brisbane	1946-54	I
	1955-58	II
Bristol	1946-54	I
	1955-58	II
Broadlands	1955-58	II
Broadview	1938-39	I
	1950-54	I
	1955	II
	1956-58	I
Broadwell	1955-58	I
Brookfield	1936-41	II
	1946-58	I
Brooklyn	1955-58	II
Brookport	1955-58	II
Brownstown	1956-58	I
Bryant	1957-58	II
Buckingham	1955	II
	1956-58	I
Buckley	1951-54	II
	1955	I
Buda	1956-58	I
Buffalo	1952-54	II
	1955-58	I
Bulpitt	1957-58	II
Bunker Hill	1955-58	II
Bureau	1955-58	II
Burlington	1951-54	I
	1955-58	II
Burnham	1946-58	I
Butler	1955-58	II
Byron	1955	II
	1956-58	I
Cabery	1950-54	I
	1955-56	II
	1957-58	I
Cahokia	1955-58	II
Caledonia	1952-54	I
Calumet City	1941	II
	1946-54	I
	1955	II
	1956-58	I
Calumet Park	1955-58	II
Calvary	1955	I
Calzell	1955-58	II
Camargo	1957-58	II
Camp Point	1958	II
Campus	1948-54	I
	1955-58	II
Cantine	1955-56	II
	1957-58	I
Canton	1946-54	I
	1955-58	II
Cantrall	1955-58	II
Capron	1952-54	I
	1955-58	II
Carbon Hill	1955	II
	1956-58	I
Carlinville	1952-54	I
	1955-58	II
Carlock	1947	I
Carlyle	1955-58	II
Carpentersville	1920, 6/13-10/31	I
	*1933-35	II
	*1936	I
	*1937-40	II
	*1941	I
Carrollton	1955-58	I
Carthage	1946	I
Cary	1920-41	I
	1946-58	I
Casey	1955-56	II
	1957-58	I
Caseyville	1955-58	I
Catlin	1955-58	II
Cayuga	1953-54	II
	1955-58	I
Cedar Point	1955	II
	1956-58	I
Cedarville	1955-58	II
Central City (Gundy County)	1955-58	II
Cerro Gordo	1955-58	I
Champaign	1946-54	I
	1955	II
	1956-58	I
Chandleville	1947-54	I
	1955-58	II
Chapin	1957-58	II
Carleston	1946, 5/5-9/29	II
	1947-54	I
	1955-58	II
Chatham	1947-54	I
	1955-58	II
Chatsworth	1955	II
	1956-57	I
	1958	II
Chebanse	1955-56	II
	1957-58	I
Chenoa	1947-54	I
	1955-58	II
Cherry	1955	II
	1956-57	I
	1958	II

* Change at 0:01 A.M.
(1) Not observed by Farm Bureau

ILLINOIS (cont.)

Place	Year	Class
Cherry Valley	1947-54	I
	1955	II
	1956-58	I
Chester	1958	II
Chesterfield	1954	I
	1957-58	II
Chestnut	1947-48	I
Chicago	1920-41	I
	1946-58	I
Chicago Heights	1920-41	I
	1946-58	I
Chicago Lawn	1938-39	I
Chicago Ridge	1956-58	II
Coalton	1920-41	I
	1946-58	I
Chillicothe	1954-58	I
Chrisman	1946-54	I
	1955-58	II
Cicero	1920-41	I
	1946-58	I
Cisco	1955	II
	1956-58	I
Cissna Park	1955	II
	1956-58	I
Clarence	1949-54	II
Clarendon Hills	1920-41	I
	1946-58	I
Clark City	1955-58	II
	1956-57	I
Clayton	1957-58	II
Clifton	1954	I
	1955-58	II
Clinton	1954	I
	1955-58	II
Cloverdale	1920-41	I
	1946-58	I
Clybourn	1955	II
Clyde	1950-54	I
	1955-58	II
Coal City	1947-54	I
Coffeen	1957-58	II
Coleman	1949-54	I
Colfax	1955	I
Collinsville	1920-41	I
	1946-58	I
Colona	1946-54	I
	1955-58	II
Columbia	1952-54	I
	1955-56	I
	1957-58	II
Columbus	1957-58	I
Compton	1955	II
	1956-57	I
Concord	1958	II
Congerville	1947-49	I
Congress Park	1920-41	I
	1946-58	II
Cooksville	1955	II
	1956-58	I
Cornell	1951-54	I
	1955-58	II
Cortland	1955	I
Cowden	1955	II
	1956-58	I
Cragin	1956-58	II
Crescent City	1955	I
Creston	1950-54	I
	1955	II
Crestwood	1955	I
Crete	1938-39	I
	1946-54	I
Creve Coer	1956-58	II
Crotty	1955	II
	1956-58	I
Crystal Lake	1920-35	I
	1936	II
	1937-41	I
	1946-54	I
	1955	II
Cuba	1956-58	I
Cullom	1956-58	I
Cumberland	1951-54	I
	1955-56	II
	1957-58	I
Cutler	1956-58	I
Custer Park	1958	I
Dakota	1948	II
Dalton City	1958	II
Dalzell	1955-58	II
Dana	1957-58	II
Danforth	1955	I
Danvers	1955-58	II
Danville	1955-56	II
	1957-58	I
Davis	1952-54	I
	1955	II
	1956-58	I
Dawson	1955-58	II
Decatur	1946-54	I
	1955	II
Deer Creek	1951-54	I
	1955	II
	1956-58	I
Deerfield	1956-58	II
Deering	1955	I
Deerpath	1946-54	I
	1955-56	II
	1957-58	I
DeKalb	1946-54	I
	1955	II
	1956-58	I
De Land	1955-58	II
Delavan	1947-54	I
	1955-56	II
	1957-58	I
Dennison	1955-56	II
	1957-58	I
De Pue	1952-54	I
	1955	II
	1956-58	I
Deval	1920-41	I
	1946-58	I
Dewitt	1955	II
	1957-58	I
Dexter	1955-56	II
	1957-58	I
Diamond	1955-58	II
Dickson	1956	I
Divernon	1955-58	II
Dixmoor	1955-56	II
	1957-58	I
Dixon	1946-54	I
	1955-56	II
	1957-58	I
Dolton	1920-41	I
	1946-58	I
Dongola	1946	I
Donovan	1955	II
	1956-58	I
Dorchester	1957	II
Dover	1957-58	II
Downer's Grove	1956-58	I
Downeys	1955	II
	1956-58	I
Downs	1955	II
	1956	I
	1957-58	II
Dundee	1920	I
	1933-41	I
	1946-58	I

ILLINOIS (cont.)

Location	Year	Zone
Dunes Park	1955	II
Dunfermline	1955-58	II
Dunlap	1955	II
	1956-58	I
Dupo	1941	II
	1955-58	II
Durand	1955-58	II
Dwight	1946-54	I
	1955	II
	1956-58	I
Eagerville	1957	II
Earlsville	1946-54	I
	1955	II
	1956-57	I
	1958	II
East Alton	1955-58	II
East Brooklyn	1955-56	II
	1957-58	I
East Carondelet	1955-58	II
East Chicago	1946-58	I
East Chicago Heights	1955-58	I
East Dundee	1920	I
	1933-41	I
	1946-58	I
East Elgin	1947-58	I
East Gillespie	1957	II
East Hazelcrest	1955-58	I
East Lynn	1948	I
Easton	1950-54	I
	1955-58	II
East Peoria	1941	II
	1946-58	I
East St. Louis	1946-54	I
	1955-58	II
Edinburg	1946-54	I
	1955	II
	1956-58	I
Edgebrook	1955	II
Edison Park	1955	II
	1956-58	I
Edwardsville	1946-54	I
	1955-56	II
	1957-58	I
Effingham	1955	I
Eileen	1955-56	II
	1957-58	I
Elburn	1950-54	I
	1955	II
	1956-58	I
Eldred	1958	II
Elgin	1920	I
	*1933-35	I
	*1936-41	II
	1946-54	I
	1955	II
	1956-58	I
Elkhart	1947-54	I
	1955-58	II
Elliott	1950-54	I
	1955-58	II
Ellis Grove	1958	II
Ellsworth	1947-54	I
	1955-58	II
Elmhurst	1920-41	I
	1946-54	I
	1955	II
	1956-58	I
Elmwood	1950-54	I
	1955	II
	1956-58	I
Elmwood Park	1955-56	II
	1957-58	I
El Paso	1941	I
	1955	II
	1956-58	I
Emden	1957-58	II
Emington	1948-54	I
	1955	II
	1956-58	I
Energy	1957-58	II
Englewood	1946-54	I
	1955-56	II
	1957-58	I
Eola	1938-40	I
	1941	II
	1955	II
	1956-57	I
Essex	1947-54	I
	1955-58	II
Eureka	1951-54	I
	1955	I
	1956-58	II
Evanston	1920-41	I
	1946-58	I
Evansville	1957-58	II
Evergreen Park	1920-41	II
	1946-58	I
Fairbury	1955	I
	1956-58	II
Fairmont City	1955-58	II
Fairmount	1955-58	I
Fairview	1941	II
	1948-54	I
	1955	II
	1956-58	I
Farmer City	1955	II
	1956-58	I
Farmersville	1957-58	II
Farmington	1955	II
	1956	I
	1957-58	II
Fayetteville	1955-58	II
Fieldon	1955-58	II
Fillmore	1958	II
Findlay	1956-58	II
Fisher	1955	II
	1956-58	I
Flagg	1956-58	I
Flanagan	1955-58	II
Flossmoor	1920-41	I
	1946-58	I
Ford City	1946-48	I
Forest City	1946-54	I
	1955-58	II
Forest Glenn	1955-58	II
Forest Park	1920-41	I
	1946-58	II
Forest View	1955-58	II
Formosa	1955-56	I
	1957-58	II
Forrest	1949-54	I
	1955	II
	1956-58	I
Forreston	1955	II
	1956-57	I
	1958	II
Fort Sheridan	1946-54	I
	1955	II
	1956-58	I
Fox Lake	1920-41	I
	1946-58	I
Fox River Grove	1920-41	I
	1946-58	I
Frankfort	1955-58	II
Franklin	1957-58	II
Franklin Grove	1950-54	I
	1955	II
	1956	I
	1957-58	II
Franklin Park	1920-41	I
	1946-58	I
Freeburg	1947-54	I
	1955-58	II
Freeport	1946	I
	1947, 4/27-10/25	I
	1948-54	I
	1955	II
	1956-58	I
Fults	1955-56	II
	1957-58	II
Funkhouser	1955-56	II
	1957-58	I

*Change at 0:01 A.M.

ILLINOIS (cont.)

Funk's Grove
- 1954 — I
- 1955 — II

Galesburg
- 1946-49 — I

Galewood
- 1955-58 — II

Garden Prairie
- 1947-54 — I

Gardner
- 1949-54 — I
- 1955 — II
- 1956-58 — I

Garrett
- 1957-58 — II

Gays
- 1957-58 — II

Geneva
- 1920-40 — I
- 1941 — I
- 1946 — I
- 1947, 4/27-10/29 — I
- 1948-54 — I
- 1955 — II
- 1956-58 — I

Genoa
- 1947, 4/27-10/29 — I
- 1948-54 — I
- 1955-58 — II

Georgetown
- 1955-56 — II
- 1957 — I

Germantown
- 1953-54 — I
- 1955-58 — II

German Valley
- 1958 — II

Gibson City
- 1946-48 — I
- 1949, 5/29-9/3 — I
- 1950-54 — I
- 1955-58 — II

Gifford
- 1957-58 — II

Gilberts
- 1952-54 — I
- 1955-58 — II

Gillespie
- 1955-58 — II

Gilman
- 1947-54 — I
- 1955-58 — II

Girard
- 1947-54 — I
- 1949-54 — II
- 1955 — I

Gladstone Park
- 1955 — II

Glasford
- 1955-58 — II

Glenarm
- 1947-48 — I

Glenayre
- 1951-54 — I
- 1955 — II
- 1956-58 — I

Glen Carbon
- 1951-54 — I
- 1955-58 — II

Glencoe
- 1920-41 — I
- 1946-58 — I

Glen Ellyn
- 1946-54 — I
- 1955 — II
- 1956-58 — I

Glenn
- 1953-54 — I
- 1955-56 — II

Glenview
- 1920-41 — I
- 1946-58 — I

Glenwood
- 1938-40 — I
- 1941 — II
- 1946-58 — I

Glover
- 1949 — I

Godfrey
- 1951-54 — I
- 1955-58 — II

Golden
- 1958 — II

Goldsmith
- 1950 — I

Golf
- 1938-41 — I
- 1946-58 — I

Goodenow
- 1955 — I

Goodfield
- 1956-58 — II

Goodwine
- 1947 — I
- 1948, 4/25-10/30 — I
- 1949-54 — I
- 1955-58 — II

Grafton
- 1938-41 — I
- 1946-54 — I
- 1955-58 — II

Grand Ridge
- 1951-54 — I
- 1955-58 — II

Grandview
- 1955-58 — II

Granite City
- 1946-54 — I
- 1955-58 — II

Grantfork
- 1955-58 — II

Grant Park
- 1946-54 — I
- 1955 — II
- 1956-58 — I

Granville
- 1955 — II
- 1956-58 — I

Grassland
- 1955 — II

Grayslake
- 1938-41 — I
- 1946-54 — I
- 1955 — II
- 1956-58 — I

Great Lakes
- 1946-54 — I
- 1955 — II
- 1956-58 — I

Greenfield
- 1955-58 — II

Greenridge
- 1954 — I
- 1955 — I
- 1956-58 — II

Greenup
- 1955-58 — II

Green Valley
- 1955-56 — II
- 1957-58 — I

Greenview
- 1947-54 — I
- 1955-58 — II

Greenville
- 1951-54 — I
- 1955-58 — II

Gridley
- 1955 — I
- 1956-58 — II

Griggsville
- 1954 — I
- 1955-58 — II

Gurnee
- 1946-58 — I

Hagarstown
- 1955-56 — I
- 1957-58 — II

Hainesville
- 1955 — I

Hamburg
- 1957-58 — II

Hamel
- 1947-54 — I
- 1955-58 — II

Hammond
- 1955-58 — II

Hampshire
- 1955-58 — II

Hanna City
- 1955 — II
- 1956-58 — I

Hanson Park
- 1955 — II

Hardin
- 1955-58 — II

Harmon
- 1955-58 — II

Harmswood
- 1946-54 — I
- 1955 — II
- 1956-58 — I

Hartford
- 1955-58 — II

Hartsburg
- 1951-54 — I
- 1955-58 — II

Hartland
- 1955-58 — I

Harvard
- 1946-54 — I
- 1955-58 — II

Harvel
- 1957-58 — II

Harvey
- 1920-41 — I
- 1946-54 — I
- 1955-58 — II

Harwood Heights
- 1955 — I

Havana
- 1955-58 — II

Hazel Crest
- 1950-54 — I
- 1955 — II
- 1956-58 — I

Healy
- 1955 — I

Hebron
- 1955-58 — I

Hecker
- 1952-54 — I
- 1955 — II
- 1956-58 — I

Hegewisch
- 1946-54 — I
- 1955 — II

Hennepin
- 1955-58 — II

Henning
- 1955 — I
- 1956-58 — II

Henry
- 1952-54 — I
- 1955-58 — II

Hermosa
- 1955 — I

Herrick
- 1957-58 — II

Herscher
- 1950-54 — I
- 1955-58 — II

Hettick
- 1957-58 — II

Heyworth
- 1947-54 — I
- 1955-56 — II
- 1957-58 — I

Hickory Hills
- 1955-58 — I

Highland
- 1955-56 — II
- 1957-58 — I

ILLINOIS (cont.)

Location	Period	Type
Highland Park	1920-41	I
	1946-58	I
Highmoor	1951-58	I
Highwood	1920-41	I
	1946-54	I
Hillsboro	1946-58	I
	1955-58	II
Hillside	1938-40	I
	1941	II
	1946-58	I
Hillview	1957-58	II
Hinckley	1951-54	I
	1955	II
	1956-58	I
Hindsboro	1957-58	II
Hines	1938-40	I
	1941	II
	1946-54	I
	1955	II
	1956-57	I
Hinsdale	1920-41	I
	1946-54	I
	1955	II
	1956-58	I
Hodgkins	1955-58	I
Holder	1949-51	I
Hollowayville	1955-58	II
Homer	1955	II
	1956-58	I

Location	Period	Type
Hometown	1955	II
	1956-58	I
Homewood	1920-41	I
	1946-54	I
	1955	II
	1956-58	I
Homewood Park	1955	II
	1956-58	I
Hoopeston	1946-51	I
	1955	II
	1957-58	I
Hopedale	1949-54	I
	1955	II
	1956-58	I
Hubbard Woods	1920-41	I
	1946-58	I
Hudson	1951-54	I
	1955-58	II
Humboldt	1955	II
	1956-57	I
Hume	1957-58	II
Humphrey	1955	I
	1957-58	II
Huntley	1941	II
	1946-54	I
	1955-58	I
Iles	1955	II
Illipolis	1947-54	I
	1955-58	II

Location	Period	Type
Indian Hill	1949-54	I
	1955	I
	1956-58	I
Ingleside	1938-40	I
	1941	II
	1955	II
	1956-58	I
Irene	1950-54	I
	1955	II
Iroquois	1955-56	II
	1957-58	I
Irving	1956	I
	1957	II
Irving Park	1955	II
Irwin	1950-54	I
	1955	II
	1956-58	I
Island Lake	1955-58	I
Itasca	1938-40	I
	1941	II
	1955	II
Ivesdale	1955	I
Jacksonville	1946-48	I
	1949, 4/24-9/26	I
	1950-54	I
	1955-58	II
Jefferson Park	1955	II
Jeisyville	1957-58	II

Location	Period	Type
Jerome	1955-58	I
Jerseyville	1946-54	I
	1955-56	II
	1957-58	I
Jewett	1955-58	I
Joliet	1935	I
	1936-40	II
	1941, 4/27-10/26	I
	1946-54	II
	1955	I
	1956-58	I
Joppa	1957-58	II
Justice	1955-58	II
Kampsville	1957-58	I
Kane	1955-58	II
Kangley	1955-56	II
	1957-58	I
Kankakee	1941, 4/27-10/26	I
	1946-54	II
	1955	I
	1956-58	I
Kansas	1958	II
Kappa	1951-54	I
	1955-58	II
Kaskaskia	1957-58	I
Kedzie	1950-54	I
	1955	II

Location	Period	Type
Keithsburg	1958	II
Kempton	1951-54	I
	1955-56	II
	1957-58	I
Kenilworth	1920-41	I
	1946-54	I
	1955	II
	1956-58	I
Kenmore	1955-58	II
Kenney	1955-58	II
Kensington	1946-58	I
Kilbourne	1958	II
Kincaid	1946-54	I
	1955	II
	1956-58	I
Kingston	1957-58	I
Kingston Mines	1955	II
	1956-58	I
Kinsman	1955-58	II
Kirkland	1955-56	II
	1957-58	I
Knollwood	1946-54	I
	1955	II
	1956-58	I
Knoxville	1946-49	II
Lacon	1947-54	I
	1955	II
	1956-58	I

Location	Period	Type
Ladd	1955	II
	1956-58	I
La Fox	1950-54	I
	1955	II
	1956-58	I
La Grange	1920-41	I
	1946-58	I
La Grange Park	1955-58	I
Lake Bluff	1920-41	I
	1946-54	I
	1955	II
	1956-58	I
Lake Forest	1920-35	I
	1936, 3/1-10/4	II
	1937-41	I
	1946-54	II
	1955	I
	1956-58	II
Lake 'n The Hills	1955	I
	1956-58	II
Lakemoor	1955	II
	1956-58	I
Lake Villa	1946-54	I
	1955-58	II
Lakeville	1948	I
Lakewood	1955-56	II
	1957-58	I
Lake Zurich	1946-58	I
Lambert	1955	II

ILLINOIS (cont.)

Place	Years	Vol.
La Moille	1955–58	II
Lansing	1938–40	I
	1941	II
	1946–58	I
La Rose	1955–56	II
	1957–58	I
La Salle	1941, 5/25–9/28	II
	1946–56	I
	1957–58	II
Latham	1955–56	II
	1957–58	I
La Vergne	1938–41	I
Lawndale	1948–54	I
	1955	II
	1956–58	I
Leaf River	1955–58	II
Lebanon	1946–54	I
	1955–58	II
Lee	1951–54	I
	1955	II
	1956–58	I
Lefton	1954	I
	1955	II
	1955–58	I
Leland	1946–54	I
	1955	II
	1956–57	I
Leland Grove	1955–58	II
Lemont	1920–41	II
	1946–58	I
Le Moyne	1955	II
Lena	1957–58	II
Lenzburg	1950–54	II
	1955–58	I
Leonore	1955	II
	1956–58	I
Lerna	1957–58	II
Le Roy	1951–54	I
	1955	II
	1956	I
	1957–58	II
Lewistown	1946–54	I
	1955–58	II
Lexington	1946–54	I
	1955–58	II
Libertyville	1938–41	I
	1946–58	I
Lima	1957–58	II
Lincoln	1947–54	I
	1955–58	II
Lincolnwood	1955–58	I
Lisbon	1955–58	II
Lisle	1938–40	I
	1941	II
Litchfield	1948–54	I
	1955–58	II
Liverpool	1958	II
Livingston	1955–58	II
Loami	1951–54	I
Lockport	1955–58	II
Loda	1955–58	II
Lodge	1958	II
Lombard	1941	II
	1946–54	I
	1955	II
	1956–58	I
Long Lake	1938–39	I
	1955	II
Long Point	1955–58	II
Longview	1957–58	II
Loraine	1954	I
	1955–58	II
Lostant	1951–54	I
	1955	II
Lovejoy	1955–58	II
Loves Park	1955–58	II
Lovington	1955	II
	1956	I
	1957–58	II
Low Point	1947	II
Ludlow	1951–54	I
	1955	II
	1956–58	I
Lyons	1941	II
	1946–54	I
	1955	II
	1956–58	I
Mackinaw	1940, 5/13–9/29	II
Macomb	1941	II
	1946–54	I
	1955	II
	1956–58	I
Macon	1958	II
Macoupin	1954–58	II
Madison	1947–54	I
	1955–56	II
	1957–58	I
Maeystown	1957–58	II
Magnolia	1955–56	II
	1957–58	I
Mahomet	1955	II
	1956–58	I
Malden	1955–58	II
Malta	1950–54	I
	1955	II
Manhattan	1957–58	II
Manito	1955–58	I
Manlius	1955–58	I
Mannheim	1955–58	II
Mansfield	1955–58	II
Manteno	1946–54	I
	1955	II
	1956–58	I
Maple Park	1947–54	I
	1955–57	II
	1958	I
Maplewood	1956–58	II
Marengo	1941, 5/12–10/26	II
	1954–58	I
Marietta	1957–58	II
Marine	1955–58	II
Marissa	1954	I
	1955–58	II
Mark	1955	II
	1956–58	I
Markham	1955–58	I
Maroa	1952–54	I
	1955–58	II
Mars	1955–58	II
Marseilles	1941, 5/25–9/25	II
	1946–54	II
	1955–58	II
Marshall	1955–58	II
Martinsville	1955–58	II
Martinton	1947–54	I
	1955	II
	1956–58	I
Maryville	1955–58	II
Mascoutah	1955–58	II
Mason City	1947–54	I
	1955	II
	1956, 6/1–9/1	I
Matteson	1946–54	I
	1955	II
	1956–58	I
Mattoon	1956–57	II
Mayfair	1955–58	I
Maywood	1920–41	II
	1946–58	I

ILLINOIS (cont.)

Mazon
1954 — I
1955-57 — II
1958, 5/1-10/1
McCook
1955-58 — I
McCullom Lake
1956-58 — I
McHenry
1947-54 — I
1955 — II
1956-58 — I
McLean
1949-54 — I
1955 — II
1956-58 — I
Mechanicsburg
1955-58 — II
Medinah
1955-58 — II
Medora
1955-58 — II
Melrose Park
1920-41 — I
1946-58 — I
Melvin
1955 — II
1956-58 — I
Mendota
1941, 6/4-9/28
1946-54 — I
1955-58 — II
Meredosia
1958 — II
Meriden
1946 — I
Merrionette Park
1955-58 — I
Metamora
1955 — II
1956-58 — I

Metcalf
1955-58 — II
Metropolis
1956-58 — I
Middlebury
1957-58 — II
Middletown
1957-58 — II
Midlothian
1920-41 — I
1946-58 — I
Miles
1954-58 — I
Milford
1955 — .
1946-54 — II
1955-58 — I
Milledgeville
1957-58 — II
Millington
1955 — II
Millstadt
1955-56 — II
1957-58 — I
Mindale
1947 — I
Mineral
1955 — II
1956-58 — I
Minier
1947-54 — I
1955 — II
1956 — I
1957-58 — II
Minonk
1941, 6/1-9/18
1946-54 — I
1955 — II
1956-58 — I
Minooka
1952-54 — I
1955 — II
1956-58 — I

Modesto
1957-58 — II
Mokena
1920-41 — I
1946-54 — II
1955-58 — I
Moline
1941 — II
Momence
1938-41 — I
1946-54 — I
1955-58 — II
Monee
1957-58 — II
Monmouth
1946 — I
Monsanto
1955-58 — II
Mont Clare
1955 — II
Montgomery
1946-54 — II
1955-58 — I
Monticello
1947-54 — I
1955 — II
1956-58 — I
Montrose
1955-56 — II
1957-58 — I
Morgantown
1951 — I
Morris
1941, 5/11-10/26 — II
1946-54 — I
1955 — II
1956-58 — I
Morrison
1946 — I

Morrisville
1955-58 — II
Morton
1947-54 — I
1955 — II
Morton Grove
1955-58 — I
Morton Park
1938-41 — I
1946-58 — I
Mount Auburn
1957-58 — II
Mount Carmel
1955 — II
Mount Morris
1946-54 — I
1955 — II
1956-57 — I
1958 — II
Mount Olive
1955-58 — II
Mount Prospect
1920-41 — I
1946-58 — I
Mount Pulaski
1947-54 — I
1955-58 — II
Mount Sterling
1958 — II
Mount Zion
1955-56 — II
1957-58 — I
Moweaqua
1955-58 — II
Mulberry Grove
1955-58 — I
Mundelein
1938-40 — II
1941, 4/27-10/26 — I
1946-58 — II

Munger
1949-54 — I
1955-58 — II
Murrayville
1957-58 — I
Nameoki
1952 — I
Naperville
1955-58 — I
Naplate
1955-56 — I
1957-58 — II
National City
1955-58 — II
Nelson
1947-54 — I
1955 — II
1956 — I
1957-58 — II
Neoga
1957-58 — II
Neponset
1958 — II
Newark
1955-58 — I
New Athens
1947-54 — I
1955-58 — II
New Baden
1951-54 — I
1955-58 — II
New Bedford
1946-54 — I
1955 — II
New Berlin
1956 — I
1955-58 — II
New Douglas
1946-54 — I
1955-58 — II
New Holland
1956-58 — II

New Lenox
1920-41 — I
1946-58 — I
Newman
1955-58 — II
Niantic
1955 — II
1956-58 — I
Niles
1955 — II
1956-58 — I
Niles Center
1955 — II
1956-58 — I
Nilwood
1954 — I
1955-58 — II
Nokomis
1946-54 — I
1955-58 — II
Normal
(1) 1940, 5/17-9/29 — II
1941, 4/27-9/28 — II
1946-54 — I
1955 — II
1956-58 — I
Norridge
1955-58 — II
North Aurora
*1933-35 — I
*1936 — II
*1937-41 — I
1946-54 — II
1955 — I
1956-58 — II
Northbrook
1920-41 — I
1946-58 — I

---

* Change at 0:01 A.M.
(1) Not observed by Farm Bureau

ILLINOIS (cont.)

Place	Years	Zone
North Chicago	1920-41	I
	1946-58	I
North Chicago Junction	1938-41	I
	1946-58	I
North Chillicothe	1953-58	I
	1955	II
	1956-58	I
Northfield	1955-56	II
	1946-58	I
Northlake	1957-58	I
	1955-56	I
	1957-58	II
North Liberty	1954-58	I
	1947, 4/27-9/1	I
North Pekin	1941	II
	1946-54	I
	1955-58	II
North Riverside	1955-58	I
North Utica	1955-58	I
	1955-57	I
	1958	II
Norwood Park	1920-41	I
	1946-58	I
Oakford	1958	II
Oak Forest	1958	II
	1920-41	I
	1946-58	I
Oak Glen	1941	I
	1946-54	II
	1955	II
	1956-58	I
Oak Grove Park (Woodford Co.)	1955-58	II

Place	Years	Zone
Oakland	1957-58	II
Oaklawn	1938-41	I
	1946-58	I
Oak Park	1920-41	II
	1946-58	I
Oakwood	1955-56	II
	1957-58	I
Oconee	1958	II
Ocoya	1955	I
	1954-58	I
Odell	1941, 6/8-9/28	I
	1946-54	I
	1955-58	II
O'Fallon	1955-58	II
Ogden	1955-58	II
Oglesby	1947-54	I
Ohio	1955	II
	1956-58	I
Ohlman	1958	II
Old Marissa	1958	II
	1920-41	I
	1946-58	I
Old Ripley	1955-58	II
Olympia Fields	1946-54	I
	1955	II
	1956-58	I
Onarga	1947-54	I
	1955	I
	1956-58	II

Place	Years	Zone
Ontarioville	1938-40	I
	1941	II
	1946-54	I
	1955	I
	1956-58	I
Orangeville	1920-41	I
	1946-58	II
	1957-58	II
Oreana	1955	II
	1956-58	I
Oregon	1946-54	I
	1955	II
	1956-57	I
	1958	II
Orland Park	1920-41	I
	1946-58	I
Oswego	1951-54	I
	1955	I
	1956-58	II
Ottawa	1946-58	I
Otterville	1955	I
	1957-58	II
Owaneco	1957-58	I
Palatine	1955-58	II
Palmer	1920-41	I
	1946-58	II
Palmyra	1957-58	II
Palos Park	1955-58	I
	1938-40	I
	1941	II
Pana	1946-58	I
	1956-58	II

Place	Years	Zone
Panama	1957-58	II
Panola	1955-58	II
Papineau	1946-54	I
	1955	II
	1956-58	I
Paris	1946-53	II
	1954, 5/1-10/2	I
	1955-58	II
Park Forest	1955-58	I
Park Ridge	1920-41	I
	1946-58	I
Parkview	1955	I
Pawnee	1955-58	II
Pawpaw	1955-56	II
	1957-58	I
Paxton	1946-48	I
	1949, 5/29-9/3	II
	1951-54	I
Payson	1955	I
	1956-58	II
Pearl City	1958	II
Pecatonica	1947-54	I
	1955	II
	1956-58	I
Pekin	1941	II
	1946-54	I
	1955	II
	1956-58	I

Place	Years	Zone
Peoria	1941	II
	1946-54	I
	1955	II
	1956-58	I
Peoria Heights	1955-58	I
Peotone	1947-54	I
	1955	II
	1956-58	I
Percy	1957-58	II
Perdueville	1946-49	I
	1950, 4/30-9/1	I
Peru	*1941, 6/1-9/28	I
	1946-58	I
Pesotum	1955-58	II
Petersburg	1947-54	I
	1955-58	II
Philo	1955	II
	1956-58	I
Phoenix	1955	II
	1956-58	I
Pierron	1955-57	II
	1958	I
Pingree Grove	1955-58	II
Piper City	1955	II
	1956-58	I
Pittsfield	1957-58	II
Pittwood	1950-53	I
Plainfield	1941	II
	1946-54	I
	1955-58	II

Place	Years	Zone
Plainview	1954	I
	1955-58	II
Plano	1946-54	I
	1955-58	II
Plato Center	1955-58	I
Peotone	1947-54	I
	1955-58	II
Pleasant Plains	1947-54	I
	1955	II
	1956-58	I
Percy	1955-58	II
Pocahontas	1957-58	I
	1955-58	II
Polo	1946-54	I
	1955-58	II
Pontiac	1941, 6/8-9/28	I
	1946-54	I
	1955-58	II
Popular Grove	1952-54	I
	1955	II
	1956-57	I
	1958	II
Posen	1955-58	I
Potomac	1956-58	I
Pierron	1950-54	I
	1955-56	II
	1957-58	I
Prairie du Rocher	1955-58	II
Princeton	1946-54	I
	1955-57	II
	1958, 4/27-9/7	I
Princeville	1955-58	II

*Change at 0:01 A.M.

ILLINOIS (cont.)

Place	Years	Class
Prophetstown	1946	I
Proviso	1955	II
Putnam	1952-54	I
	1955-58	II
Quincy	1941	II
	1946-54	I
	1955-56	II
	1957-58	I
Rainbow Gardens	1957-58	II
Rankin	1947-48	I
	1949, 4/24-9/3	I
	1950, 4/30-9/3	I
	1951-54	I
	1955	II
	1956-58	I
Ransom	1955-56	II
	1957-58	I
Rantoul	1947-54	I
	1955-58	II
Ravenswood	1920-41	I
	1946-54	I
	1955	II
	1956-58	I
Ravinia	1920-41	I
	1946-58	II
Raymond	1956-58	I
Red Bud	1953-54	I
	1955	II
	1956-58	I
Reddick	1948-54	I
	1955	II
	1956-58	I
Redmon	1958	I
Richmond	1952-54	I
	1955	II
	1956-58	I
Richton Park	1941	II
	1946-58	I
Ridge Farm	1955-58	II
Ridgefield	1955	II
	1956-58	I
Ridgely	1954	I
	1955	II
	1956-58	I
Ridott	1952-54	II
	1955-56	I
	1957-58	II
Rinaker	1955	I
Ringwood	1952-54	II
Ripley	1958	I
Ritchie	1950-54	I
	1955-58	II
Riverdale	1920-41	I
	1946-58	I
River Forest	1920-41	I
	1946-58	I
River Grove	1955-58	I
Riverside	1955-58	I
Riverton	1947-54	I
	1955-58	II
Roanoke	1941	II
	1955	II
	1956-58	I
Robbins	1941	II
Roberts	1947-54	II
	1956-58	I
Robinson	1947	I
	1956-58	I
Rochelle	1955	II
	1956-58	I
Rochester	1956-58	II
Rockbridge	1957-58	II
Rock City	1957-58	II
Rockdale	1956-58	II
Rock Falls	1955-58	I
Rockford	1946-54	I
	1955	II
	1956-57	I
	1958	II
Rock Island	1941	I
	1946-58	I
Rockton	1957-58	I
Rockwood	1957-58	I
Rogers Park	1920-41	I
	1946-54	II
	1955	I
Rolling Meadows	1956-58	I
Romeo	1954	II
	1955	I
	1956-58	II
Rondout	1938-41	II
	1946-54	I
Roodhouse	1955	II
	1956-58	I
Rose Hill	1957-58	I
Roselle	1938-41	II
	1946-54	I
	1955	II
	1956-58	I
Rossville	1956-58	II
Round Grove	1950-54	I
Round Lake	1938-40	II
	1941	I
	1946-54	II
	1955	I
	1956-57	II
	1958	I
Round Lake Beach	1955-58	I
Round Lake Park	1955-58	I
Roxana	1955-58	II
Royal	1955	II
Royalton	1956-58	I
Ruma	1955-56	II
Rushville	1955-58	II
Rutland	1957-58	II
Sadorus	1950-54	I
	1955-58	II
Saint Anne	1956-58	I
Saint Charles	1920-35	I
	1936	II
	1937-40	I
	1941	II
	1946-54	I
	1955-58	II
Saint David	1957-58	I
Saint Elmo	1957-58	I
Saint Jacob	1957-58	I
Saint Joseph	1952-54	II
	1955-58	I
Saint Libory	1955-58	II
Saint Louis	1956	II
Saint Mary of the Lake	1953-54	I
Sandwich	1946-54	I
	1955-58	II
San Jose	1957-58	II
Saunemin	1948-54	I
	1955	II
	1956-58	I
Savanna	1946	I
Savoy	1949-54	I
	1955-58	II
Sawyerville	1957-58	II
Saybrook	1948-54	I
	1955	II
	1956-58	I
Schillar Park	1955-58	I
Schram City	1957-58	II
Scott Air Force Base	1946-58	I
Scott Field	1946-53	I
Scottville	1957-58	II
Seatonville	1957-58	II
Secor	1955-58	II

ILLINOIS (cont.)

Place	Period	Zone
Seeger	1955	II
Seneca	1952–54	I
	1955–56	II
	1957–58	I
Serena	1951–52	I
Shabbona	1955–56	II
	1950–54	I
	1955	II
	1956–58	I
Shannon	1958	II
Sheffield	1957–58	II
Shelbyville	1946–54	I
	1955–58	II
Sheldon	1955–58	II
Sheridan	1955	II
	1956–58	I
Sheridan Elms	1951–54	I
	1955	II
	1956–58	I
Sherman	1954	I
	1955–58	II
Shiloh	1955–58	II
Shipman	1920	I
	*1933–35	I
	*1936–41	II
	1946–54	I
	1955–58	II
Shirley	1948–54	I
	1955	II
	1956–58	I
Sibley	1955–58	II

Place	Period	Zone
Sidell	1949–54	I
	1955–58	II
Sidney	1955–56	I
	1955–58	II
Skokie	1938–41	I
	1946–58	I
Smithboro	1955–56	II
	1957–58	I
Smithfield	1957–58	II
Smithton	1955–58	II
Sollitt	1946	I
Solon Mills	1955	I
Somonauk	1946–54	I
	1955–58	II
Sorento	1957–58	II
South Beloit	1957–58	I
South Chicago	1920–41	I
	1946–58	I
South Chicago Heights	1920–41	I
	1946–58	II
South Elgin	1955–58	II
Southern View	1955–58	II

Place	Period	Zone
South Holland	1938–40	I
	1941	II
	1946–54	I
	1955	II
	1956–58	I
South Jacksonville	1955–58	II
South Joliet	1935	I
	1936–40	II
	1941, 4/27–10/26	II
	1946–54	I
	1955	II
	1956–58	I
Southmoor	1947	I
South Pekin	1941	II
	1946–54	I
	1955	II
	1956–58	I
South Upton	1946	II
South Wilmington	1955	II
	1956–58	I
Sparland	1952–54	I
	1955	II
	1956–58	I
Sparta	1955–58	II
Spaulding	1938–39	I
Steward	1946–54	I
	1955–58	II
Spring Bay	1955–56	II
	1957–58	I

Place	Period	Zone
Springfield	1940, 5/24–9/29	II
	1946–54	I
	1955–58	II
Spring Grove	1955–58	II
Spring Valley	1941, 6/1–9/28	II
	1946–54	I
	1955	II
	1956–58	I
Standard	1955	II
	1956–58	I
Standard City	1957–58	II
Stanford	1949–54	I
	1955	II
	1956–58	I
Staunton	1946–54	I
	1955	II
	1956–58	I
Steele	1949–54	I
	1955–58	II
Steeleville	1958	I
Steger	1946–58	II
Sterling	1946–54	I
	1955	II
	1956–58	I
Steward	1951–54	I
	1955–58	II
Stewardson	1957–58	II
Stickney	1955–58	I

Place	Period	Zone
Stillman Valley	1955–56	II
	1957–58	I
Stockton	1958	II
Stone Park	1956–58	I
Stonington	1957–58	II
Strasburg	1955	II
	1957–58	I
Strawn	1955–58	II
Streator	1941, 5/25–9/28	II
	1946–54	I
	1955–56	II
	1957–58	I
Stubbefield	1955–56	II
	1957–58	I
Sublette	1955	II
	1956–58	I
Sugar Grove	1951–52	I
Sullivan	1946–54	I
	1955–58	II
Summerdale	1955	II
Summerfield	1955	II
	1956–58	I
Summit	1920–41	I
	1946–58	II
Swansea	1957–58	II
Sycamore	1946–58	I

Place	Period	Zone
Symerton	1946–54	I
	1955–58	II
Tallula	1955–58	II
Taylor Springs	1957–58	II
Taylorville	1946–54	I
	1955–58	II
Techny	1938–41	I
	1946–54	II
Teutopolis	1955	I
	1956–58	II
Thawville	1955–58	II
Thayer	1955–58	II
Thomasboro	1951–54	I
	1955–58	II
Thornton	1938–41	I
	1946–58	I
Tilden	1955–58	II
Tilton	1955–58	II
Tinley Park	1955	I
	1956–58	II
Tiskilwa	1920–41	I
	1946–58	I
Tolono	1950–54	I
	1955	II
	1956–58	I

*Change at 0:01 A.M.

ILLINOIS (cont.)

Place	Year	Designation
Toluca	1955	II
	1956-58	I
Tonica	1941, 6/8-9/28	II
	1946-54	I
	1955	II
	1956-58	I
Topeka	1957	II
	1958, 5/1-8/31	I
Torin	1955-58	II
Toronto	1955-56	I
	1957-58	II
Towanda	1950-54	I
	1955-56	II
	1957-58	I
Tower Hill	1957-58	II
Tremont	1940-41	I
	1946-54	I
	1955	II
	1956-58	I
Trenton	1955-58	II
Troy	1955-57	II
	1958	I
Troy Grove	1955-58	I
Tuscola	1946-54	I
	1955-58	II
Union	1947-54	I
	1955-58	II
Union Grove	1952-54	I
Union Hill	1955-58	II

Place	Year	Designation
Urbana	1940, 5/26-9/29	I
	1946-54	I
	1955	II
	1956-58	I
Utica	1952-54	I
	1955-58	II
Valmeyer	1955-58	II
Vandalia	1946	I
	1947, 5/1-9/1	II
	1955-56	I
	1957-58	II
Varna	1955-58	II
Venice	1949-54	I
	1955-58	II
Verona	1955-58	II
Versailles	1957-58	II
Vevay Park	1955-56	II
	1957-58	I
Villa Grove	1953-54	I
	1955-58	II
Villa Park	1946-54	II
	1955-58	I
Virden	1947-54	I
	1955-58	II
Virginia	1957-58	I
Wadsworth	1941	II

Place	Year	Designation
Waggoner	1957-58	II
Walnut	1947-54	I
	1955-58	II
Walshville	1958	I
Wann	1955	II
Wapella	1955-58	II
Warren	1955-58	II
Warrensburg	1955	I
	1956-58	II
Warrenville	1946-54	II
	1955	I
	1956-58	II
Washburn	1955-58	II
Washington	1947-54	I
	1955	II
Washington Park	1940-41	I
	1946-54	I
	1955-56	II
	1957-58	I
Waterloo	1952-54	I
	1955	II
	1956-58	I
Waterman	1950-54	I
	1955	II
	1956-58	I
Watseka	1946-54	I
	1955-58	II

Place	Year	Designation
Wauconda	1941	II
	1955-58	I
Waukegan	1920	I
	1921, 4/27-10/3	II
	1922-41	I
	1946-54	II
Waverly	1955	II
	1955-58	I
Wayne	1946-54	I
	1955	II
	1956-58	I
Waynesville	1955-58	II
Weber	1949-54	I
Wedron	1946	I
Weldon	1951-52	I
Wellington	1955-58	II
Wenona	1946-54	I
	1955-58	II
West Brooklyn	1955-56	II
	1957-58	I
Westchester	1955-58	I
West Chicago	1955-58	II
West Dundee	1920-41	I
	1946-58	II

Place	Year	Designation
Western Springs	1920-41	I
	1946-58	I
West Lake Forest	1955	II
West Martinsville	1955-56	II
	1957-58	I
Westmont	1938-40	I
	1941	II
	1955	II
	1956-57	I
Westville	1949-54	II
	1955-58	I
Wheaton	1920-41	I
	1946-54	II
	1955	I
	1956-58	II
Wheeling	1941	II
	1955	II
	1956-58	I
White City	1957-58	II
White Hall	1955-58	II
Wichert	1946-50	I
Williamson	1957-58	I
Williamsville	1951-54	I
	1955-56	I
	1957-58	II
Willow Springs	1920-41	I
	1946-58	I

Place	Year	Designation
Wilmette	1920-41	I
	1946-58	I
Wilmington (Green County)	1954	I
	1955-58	II
Wilmington (Will County)	1947-54	I
	1955	II
	1956-58	I
Wilsonville	1957-58	II
Winchester	1957-58	II
Windsor (Shelby County)	1957-58	II
Winfield	1947-54	I
	1955	II
	1956-58	I
Wing	1952	I
	1955, 5/1-9/25	II
	1956-58	II
Winnebago	1952-54	II
	1955	I
	1956-58	II
Winnetka	1920-41	I
	1946-54	II
	1955	I
	1956-58	II
Winslow	1957-58	I
Winthrop Harbor	1946-54	II
	1955	II
	1956-58	I

ILLINOIS (cont.)

Witt
1957-58 II

Woodbury
1955-56 II
1957-58 I

Wood Dale
1938-39 I
1955-56 II
1957-58 I

Woodland
1947-54 I
1955-58 II

Woodridge
1951-54 I
1955 II
1956-58 I

Wood River
1947-54 I
1955-58 II

Woodson
1958 II

Woodstock
1920-31 I
1938-40 I
1941 II
1946-54 I
1955 II
1956-58 I

Worden
1952-54 I
1955-58 II

Worth
1938-40 I
1941 II
1946-54 I
1955 II
1956-58 I

Yorksville
1957-58 II

Zion
*1920, 6/21-10/4 I
1921-41 I
1946-54 I
1955 II
1956-58 I

*Change at 0:01 A.M.

INDIANA

1733		Area settled
1752	9/14	Gregorian (NS) Calendar adopted in U.S.A.
1816	12/11	State entered the Union
1883	11/18	Noon, Central Standard Time (90°W) adopted
1955		From this year until 1965, more and more communities began observing EST year round. The Map Section for these years will show the increasing areas observing EST.
1958	11/2	Franklin adopted EST (75°W)
1961	7/23	Official Eastern Standard Time Zone Line was moved westward into Indiana for the first time. This Interstate Commerce Commission order encompassed 43 counties, but all or parts of 20 counties which had been observing informal EST (75°W) were omitted. See Map Section.

NOTE: INDIANA, without doubt, presents the most confused time picture in all of the 50 states. Some eastern borderline communities observed informal EST before 1955, and local authorities should be checked for specific information.

| 1969 | 1/1 | Relocation of Eastern and Central Time Zone Boundary. Until this date 29 counties observed CST and 43, EST. The whole State went into the Eastern Time Zone with the exception of 12 counties clustered in the northwest and southwest corners of the State bordering on Illinois. Effective 4/27. |

DAYLIGHT (OR WAR) TIME OBSERVED:
(Changes at 2 A.M.)

1918	3/31 – 10/27	World War I
1919	3/30 – 10/26	World War I
1920	To 1941	Not observed state-wide. See Local Ordinance Listing.
1942	2/9 – 9/30/45	World War II
1946	To 1948	Not observed state-wide. See Local Ordinance Listing.

TABLE

Year		Year	
1918	War Time	1940	4/28-9/29
1919	War Time	1941	4/27-9/28
1920	6/13-10/31	1942-45	War Time
1921	3/27-10/30	1946	4/28-9/29
1922	4/30-9/24	1947	4/27-9/28
1923	4/29-9/30	1948	4/25-9/26
1924	4/27-9/28	1949	4/24-9/25
1925	4/26-9/27	1950	4/30-9/24
1926	4/25-9/26	1951	4/29-9/30
1927	4/24-9/25	1952	4/27-9/28
1928	4/29-9/30	1953	4/26-9/27
1929	4/28-9/29	1954	4/25-9/26
1930	4/27-9/28	1955	4/24-9/25
1931	4/26-9/27	1956	4/29-9/30
1932	4/24-9/25	1957	4/28-9/29
1933	4/30-9/24	1958	4/27-9/28
1934	4/29-9/30	1959	4/26-9/27
1935	4/28-9/29	1960	4/24-9/25
1936	4/26-9/27	1961	4/30-10/29
1937	4/25-9/26	1962	4/29-10/28
1938	4/24-9/25	1963	4/28-10/27
1939	4/30-9/24	1964	4/26-10/25
		1965	4/25-10/31

INDIANA (cont.)

1949 To 1955 State law called for CST all year, but business establishments (in towns listed in Local Ordinance Listing for these years) opened and closed one hour earlier. However, most of the clocks remained on CST. For communities observing EST all year, see Map Section.

1956 Not observed state-wide. See Local Ordinance Listing and Map Section.

1957 To 1965 DST obligatory by state law. Refer to Table for dates. Local communities continued to observe their own desired DST times, with some communities observing fast time (EST) all year. See Local Ordinance Listing and Map Section issued by the Indiana State Chamber of Commerce.

1966 See Chapter VII

1967 To 1968 Legislature enacted a law requiring one clock in the Capitol and in each courthouse or city hall to be marked "official time" in compliance with the federal act. But it left residents free to observe whatever time was set by local ordinance. The Indiana statute also prohibited the 43 counties in the Eastern Time Zone from observing Daylight Saving Time. These counties remained on Eastern Standard Time year round.
Some of the Central Time Zone counties ignored the act and moved their clocks up an hour during the summer to conform with Indianapolis, the capitol.
But Lake County, in the northwestern corner of the State and close to Chicago, moved its clocks ahead to Daylight Saving Time. Union City, across the State on the Ohio boundary, also went on Daylight Saving Time.

1969 To 1979 Voted exemption from Daylight Saving Time, except for the 12 counties in the Central Time Belt clustered in the northwest and southwest corners of the State adjoining Illinois. See Map Section, pages 65-71.

OBSERVATION BY LOCAL ORDINANCE:
(Refer to Table for Month and Day if not shown)

NOTE: In 1920, DST was discontinued as a state ordinance but continued by local ordinances as noted below. This information is incomplete; however, it may be used as a key to DST observance. Information on all communities is not known, and therefore not all years are included.

Adams	Anoka	Atwood	Bargersville
1953-55	1953-55	1953-55	1947, 4/27-9/6
Adamsboro	Arcola	Auburn	Belshaw
1953-55	1953-55	1929-41	1947-48
Akron	Argos	Austin	Bendix Drive
1954	1953-55	1946-54	1948
Albany	Ari	Aurora	1951
1946-54	1953-55	1953-55	Ben Grove
Albion	Ashland	Avilla	1946-49
1946-54	1953-55	1949-54	Berne
Aldine	Athens	Avondale	1953-55
1954	1953-55	1946-54	Bass Lake
Alexandria	Attica	Aylesworth	1954-55
1946-48	1954	1953-55	Bass Lake Junction
1952-55	1952-53		1954-55
Amboy	1956, 4/29-10/28		Batesville
1953-55			1946-54
Ames			Bippus
1953-55			1954
Amity			Bicknell
1953-55			1953-55
Amo			Bedford
1953-55			1947
Anderson			1948, 4/2-9/26
1933-41			1950-56
Andrews			1956, 4/29-9/2
1953			Bee Hunter
Angola			1953-55
1939-41			Bloomer
			1953-55

INDIANA (cont.)

Bloomfield
1955
1956, 4/29-9/2
Bloomington
1946
1951-56
Bolivar
1954
Boone
1953-55
Boone Grove
1954
Booneville
1955
1956, 4/29-10/28
Boswell
1948
1950
1955
1956, 4/29-10/28
Bourbon
1948
1953-55
Bowews
1953-55
Brazil
1946
1953-56
Bremen
1939-41
1946-55
1956, 4/29-10/28
1957, 4/28-10/27
1958, 4/27-10/26
1959, 4/26-10/25
1960, 4/24-10/30
Bridgeport
1953-55
Bringhurst
1953-55
Broadway
1954

Brooklyn
1953-55
Brownstown
1955-56
Browns Valley
1953-55
Bruce Lake
1953-55
Bruceville
1953-55
Bryant
1953-55
Buck Creek
1958, 4/27-10/26
Bunker Hill
1953-55
Burket
1947, 5/1-9/16
1948-49
1953
Burnettsville
1953-55
Burr Oak
1949
Burrows
1953-55
Butler
1953-55
Calumet
1946-48
1957, 4/28-10/27
Cambridge City
1953-55
Camby
1953-55
Camden
1953-55
Campbells
1953-55
Cannelton
1955, 5/1-9/25
1956

Carmel
1955
Carmelton
1955, 5/1-9/25
Carter
1953-55
Cartersburg
1953-55
Cass
1953-55
Catlin
1953-55
Cayuga
1946, 5/1-9/29
1953-56
Cedar Lake
1948
1952-56
Center
1953-55
Centerville
1953-55
Centreton
1953-55
Chain O'Lakes
1946-49
Charlestown
1952-56
1959, 4/26-10/25
1960, 4/24-10/30
Charlottesville
1953-55
Chebanse
1949
Chesterfield
1953-55
Chesterton
1929-41
1946-55
1958, 4/27-10/26
Chili
1953-55

Churubusco
1953-55
Clanricade
1954
Clarks Hill
1955
1956, 4/29-9/28
Claypool
1947-53
Clayton
1953-55
Clear Creek
1953-55
Clermont
1953-55
Clifford
1953-55
Clinton
1946
1952-56
1958, 4/27-10/27
(1) 1959, 4/26-10/5
Clymers
1953-55
Coatesville
1953-55
Colfax
1953-55
Collett
1953-55
Collins
1953-55
Columbia City
1946-54
Columbus
1941, 6/29-10/26
1947
1956, 4/29-10/28
Connersville
1939-41
1950-54

Converse
1947
1953-55
Cook
1946
Corydon
1955
1956, 4/29-10/28
1959, 4/26-10/25
Covington
1948
1955-56
Crawfordsville
1946
1948
1950-55
1956, 4/29-10/28
Crocker
1947-48
1953-56
1958, 4/27-10/26
1960, 4/24-10/30
Cromwell
1946-53
Crooked Creek
1953-55
Crothersville
1953-55
Crown Point
1925-41
1946, 5/1-10/1
1947-55
1956, 4/29-10/28
1959, 4/26-10/25
1960, 4/24-10/30
Cudahy
1946-48
Culver
1941
1946
1947, 4/27-10/25
1948-56

Cumberland
1953-55
Curtisville
1953-55
Cutler
1953-55
Danville
1948
Darlington
1953-55
Davis
1953-55
Dayton
1947
1949
1950, 4/23-9/9
Decatur
1931
*1932, 5/1-9/25
1933-41
1946-54
Deerfield
1953-55
Delong
1953-55
Delphi
1952-56
1958, 4/27-10/26
Denham
1953-55
Denver
1953-55
Deputy
1953
Dewey
1953-55
Dillsboro
1949-53

*Change at 0:01 A.M.
(1) Ending date change at 0:01 A.M.

INDIANA (cont.)

Disko
1954

Doleville
1952-56
1958, 4/27-10/26

Donaldson
1953-55

Dune Acres
1946-49

Dunkirk
1948-55

Dunrieth
1953-55

Dupont
1953-55

Durbin
1953-55

Dyer
1920-41
1954-56

Eagletown
1953-55

East Chicago
1925-41
1946-54
1955, 4/24-10/30
1956, 4/29-10/28

East Gary
1920-41
1946-54
1957, 4/28-10/27
1958, 4/27-10/26
1959, 4/26-10/25
1960, 4/24-10/30

Eddy
1941

Eden
1955-56

Edinburg
1953-56

Edwardsport
1953-55

Effner
1953-55

Elizabethtown
1953-55

Elkhart
*1928-32
*1933, 4/30-10/1
*1934-35
1936-41
1946-48
1949, 5/1-9/25
1950-54

English
1955-56

English Lake
1953-55

Etna Green
1953-55

Evansville
1948, 5/2-10/26
1951
1955-56
1961, 4/30-9/24

Farmersburg
1953-55

Fenns
1953-55

Fillmore
1953-55

Flat Rock
1953-55

Flora
1953-55

Florida
1953-55

Foltz Fork Station
1953-55

Foraker
1946
1948

Fort Benjamin Harris
1941, 6/22-9/28
1946-54

Fort Branch
1958, 4/27-10/1

Fort Wayne
*1928-32
*1933, 4/30-10/1
*1934-35

Fountain City
1953-55

Fowler
1956

Frankfort
1946-48
1949, 4/24-9/10
1950-55
1956, 4/2-10/27

Franklin
1946-47
1953-55

Frankton
1953-55

Freedom
1953-55

French Lick
1954-56

Gadsden
1953-55

Galveston
1953-56

Garfield
1953-55

Garrett
1920-41
1946-54

Gary
1920-41
1946-54
1957, 4/28-10/27
1958, 4/27-10/26
1959, 4/26-10/25
1960, 4/24-10/30

Gas City
1948-55

Geneva
1953-55

Germantown
1953-55

Goldsmith
1951
1953

Goodland
1956, 4/29-10/28

Goshen
1920-41
1946-54

Gosport
1953-55

Grasmere
1953-55

Grass Creek
1953-55

Grayford
1953-55

Green Castle
1946-56

Greenfield
1953-55

Greensburg
1946
1951-55

Greens Fort
1953-55

Greentown
1947
1953-55

Greenwood
1953-55

Griffith
1946-48
1953-55
**1956, 4/29-(?)

Grovertown
1953-55

Guion
1953-55

Hadley
1953-55

Hagerstown
1948-55

Hamlet
1953-55

Hammond
1920-41
1946-54
1955, 4/24-10/30
1956, 4/29-10/28
1959, 4/26-10/25
1960, 4/24-10/30

Hanna
1953-55

Harris
1953-55

Hartford City
1947
1952-54

Heath
1953-55

Hebron
1953-55

Hege
1953-55

Helmsburg
1951

Hemlock
1953-55

Henryville
1953-55

Herr
1953-55

Hibbard
1946
1947, 4/27-10/25
1948-54
1956, 3/25-10/27

Highland
1953-55

Hillisburg
1953-55

Hillsburg
1947, 5/29-9/28
1948
1951

Hillsborough
1948

Hoagland
1953-55

Hobart
1920-41
1946-55
1959
1960, 4/24-10/30

Hobbs
1951-55

Holland
1956

Homer
1953-54

Hoover
1953-55

Hope
1955

Howe
1947-55
1956, 4/29-10/28

Hudson Lake
1946-49

Huntingburg
1956

----
* Change at 0:01 A.M.
** Check with local authorities

INDIANA (cont.)

Huntington
1929-30, 5/1-10/1
1946-54
Hurlburt
1954
Hynds
1953-55
Idaville
1953-55
Indiana Harbor
1920-41
1946-55
1956, 4/29-10/28
1958, 4/27-10/26
1959, 4/26-10/25
1960, 4/24-10/30
Indianapolis
1941, 6/22-9/28
1946-54
Inwood
1953-55
Irvington
1953-55
Ivanhoe
1953-55
Jasper
1951
1955-56
Jeffersonville
1946
1950-55
1956, 4/29-10/28
1959, 4/26-10/25
Jessups
1953-55
Jolieville
1947-59
Jonesville
1953-55

Jonesville
1953-55
Judson
1953-55
Kempton
1950-51
1953
Kendallville
* 1931-32
* 1933, 4/30-10/1
* 1934-35
1936-41
1946-54
Kentland
1953-55
1956, 4/29-10/28
Kenneth
1953-55
Kewanna
1948-55
Kingsbury
1946-55
1956, 4/29-10/28
1960, 4/24-10/30
Kingsland
1953-55
Kirklin
1954
Kirkpatrick
1954-55
1956, 4/29-10/28
Knightstown
1953-55
Knightsville
1953-55
Knox
1947-59
1960, 4/24-10/30
Kokomo
1946-55
1956, 4/29-11/15
1961, 4/30-10/29

Kouts
1953-55
La Crosse
1953-56
Ladoga
1955-56
Lafayette
(1)1941, 6/29-10/26
1946, 5/4-10/5
1947-49
1950, 4/23-9/9
1951-55
1956, 4/29-10/28
1958, 4/27-10/26
La Fontaine
1948
Lagrange
1939-41
1947-55
Lake Cicott
1954
Lake Park
1953-55
Laketon
1954
Lakeville
1940, 5/5-9/29
1946, 5/1-10/1
1947-55
1960, 4/24-10/30
La Otto
1947-48
1953-55
La Paz
1946-55
1956, 4/29-10/28
1958, 4/27-10/26
1959, 4/26-10/25
1960, 4/24-10/30
Lapel
1953-55

La Porte
* 1930-32
* 1933, 4/30-10/1
* 1934-35
1936-41
1946-55
1956, 4/29-10/28
Larwill
1953-55
Lawrence
1941, 6/22-9/28
1946-54
Lawrenceburg
1947-54
Lebanon
1946-55
Leesburg
1948
Leiters Ford
1954
Lena Park
1953-55
Leroy
1953-55
Lewis
1953-55
Lewisville
1953-55
Liberty
1948
1950
Liberty Mills
1953-55
Liggett
1953-55
Lincoln
1953-55
Linden
1947
1952-56

Linton
1955
1956, 4/29-10/28
1959, 4/26-10/25
Liverpool
1953-55
Logansport
1946, 4/7-9/1
1947-55
1956, 4/29-10/28
1958, 4/27-10/26
1961
Loogootee
1947
1955
1956, 4/29-9/1
lomax
1954
Lowell
1950-56
Lucerne
1953-55
Lydick
1946-48
Lynn
1953-55
Lyons
1953-55
Madison
1953-55
Magley
1954
Mahoning
1958, 4/27-10/26
Manson
1953-55
Manilla
1953-55
Maples
1953-55
Marco
1953-55

Marengo
1951
Marion
1946-54
Markles
1953-55
Marshall
1956
Marshfield
1958, 4/27-10/26
Martinsville
1953-55
Maywood
1953-55
McGrawsville
1953-55
Medaryville
1956, 4/29-10/28
Mellott
1953-55
Memphis
1953-55
Mexico
1953-55
Meyersville
1953
Michigan City
1930-41
1946-55
1956, 4/29-10/28
1957, 4/28-10/27
1958, 4/27-10/26
1959, 4/26-10/25
Middletown
1953-55
Mier
1953-55

*   Change at 0:01 A.M.
(1) Change at 1:00 A.M.

INDIANA (cont.)

Milan 1947-54
Milford 1948
Mill City 1956, 4/29-10/28
Miller 1920-41
 1946-54
 1957, 4/28-10/27
 1958, 4/27-10/26
 1959, 4/26-10/25
 1960, 4/24-10/30
Mill Grove 1953-55
Millville 1953-55
Milltown 1951-55
Mishawaka 1929, 5/15-9/30
 1930, 5/10-9/27
 1931, 4/26-9/28
 1932, 4/24-10/1
 1933-41
 1946-54
 1956, 4/29-10/28
 1958, 4/27-10/26
Mitchell 1951-55
Monon 1952-56
Monroeville 1953-55
Montdale 1953-55
Monticello 1948
 1952-56
Monterey 1954
 1956, 4/29-10/28
 1959, 4/26-10/25
 1960, 4/24-10/30

Montezuma 1952
Montmorenci 1950, 5/1-9/30
Moore 1953-55
Mooresville 1953-55
Moran 1953-55
Morgantown 1947, 4/27-10/1
 1948
Morris 1948
Mount Vernon 1955-56
Mulberry 1947, 4/27-9/30
 1949, 4/24-9/10
Muncie 1940
 1946-54
 1956, 4/29-10/28
 1959, 4/26-10/25
 1960, 4/24-10/30
Munster 1956
Nappanee 1940-41
 1946-53
Nashville 1955-56
Nelson 1953-55
Nevada 1953-55
New Albany 1946
 1950-54
 1956, 4/29-10/28
 1959, 4/26-10/25
 1960, 4/24-10/30

New Carlisle 1939-41
 1946-50
New Castle 1947-54
New Chicago 1953-55
New Haven 1948-49
New Market 1953-55
New Paris 1940
 1946-47
Newton 1953-55
Newport 1955-56
New Waverly 1958, 4/27-10/26
Noble 1933-41
 1946-54
Noblesville 1946
 1953-55
North Grove 1953-55
North Hayden 1947-48
North Indianapolis 1941, 6/22-9/28
 1946-54
North Judson 1947-55
 1956, 4/29-10/28
 1959, 4/26-10/25
 1960, 4/24-10/30
North Liberty 1947-54
North Madison 1953-55

North Manchester 1953-55
North Terre Haute 1953-55
North Vernon 1953-56
Nutwood 1953-55
Oakland City 1954-56
Oak Thornhope Station 1953-55
Odesse 1953-55
Ogden Dunes 1946-49
Olive Hill 1953-55
Onoka 1953-55
Onward 1953-55
Oakland City 1956
Ora 1954
Orleans 1952-56
Osgood 1947
 1953-55
Otis 1946-48
 1960, 4/24-10/1
 1961, 4/30-10/1
Otterbein 1949-50
Otto Creek Junction 1953-55
Oxford 1947
 1950

Paragon 1953-55
Palmer 1954
Parry 1953-55
Paoli 1954-56
Perkins 1953-55
Pershing 1953-55
Peru 1946
 1948-49
 1953-56
 1958, 4/27-10/26
Peters 1953-55
Petersburg 1955-56
Pettysville 1953-55
Philadelphia 1953-55
Pierceton 1953-55
Pike 1953-55
Plainfield 1953-56
Plymouth 1953-55
 1939, 4/23-10/1
 1946-55
 1956, 4/29-10/28
 1959, 4/26-10/25
 1961
Port Chester 1946-48
Porter 1929-41
 1946-48
 1956, 4/29-10/28
 1958, 4/27-10/26

Portland 1946-54
Powers 1953-55
Prairie View 1953-55
Preble 1954
Princeton 1956, 4/29-10/28
Puckett 1953-55
Queensville 1953-55
Ravenwood 1953-55
 1941, 6/22-9/28
 1946-54
Rays Crossing 1953-55
Reagan 1953-55
Red Key 1951
 1953-55
Reelsville 1953-55
Renner 1953-55
Rensselaer 1953-56
Remington 1953-55
Reynolds 1953-55
Richmond (1) 1932, 6/1-9/5
 1933, 6/2-9/4
 1934, 6/3-9/3
 1935, 6/2-9/2
 1946-54

(1) Many farmers and townspeople did not advance clocks

INDIANA (cont.)
Ridgeville
1947
1950-55
Rincon
1953-55
Ripley
1953-55
Rushville
1947-48
1953-55
Richvalley
1958, 4/27-10/26
Rivare
1954
Riverside
1958, 4/27-10/26
Roachdale
1955
Roann
1953-55
Rochester
1946-48
1952-54
1956, 4/2-11/1
1959, 4/26-10/25
1960, 4/24-10/30
Rockfield
1958, 4/27-10/26
Rockford
1953-55
Rockport
1955-56, 5/1-9/25
Rockville
1953-56
Rolling Prairie
1946
1948
Rome City
1938-39
1941, 4/27-11/23
1953-55
Romona
1954
Rosedale
1941, 6/29-10/26
1950-56

Rosston
1953-55
Rossville
1955-56
Royal Center
1953-55
Rushville
1953-55
Saint John
1951-55
Saint Louis Crossing
1953-55
Salem
1955-56
Sand Creek
1953-55
Santa Claus
1955-56
Saratoga
1953-55
Saxony
1954
Scipio
* 1932, 4/30-10/2
Scircleville
1951
Scottsburg
1953-56
Seafield
1953-55
Sedalia
1953-55
Seelyville
1953-55
Sellersburg
1953-55
Servia
1954
Seymour
1941, 6/29-10/26
1950-56

Sharps
1953-55
Shelburn
1946
Shelby
1954-56
Shelbyville
1946
1947, 5/1-10/1
1951-55
Sheridan
1953-55
Sidney
1947-48
1952-53
Simpson
1954
Smith (Knox Co.)
1946-48
1953-55
Snow Hill
1953-55
South Bend
* 1932, 4/30-10/2
* 1933
1934-41
1946
1947, 4/28-9/29
1948-55
1956, 3/25-10/27
1958, 4/27-10/26
1959, 4/24-10/30
South Gary
1946-47
1948, 4/25-10/30
1949-52
1957, 4/28-10/27
1958, 4/27-10/26
1959, 4/26-10/25
1960, 4/24-10/30

South Kokomo
1946-55
1956, 4/29-11/15
1961, 4/30-10/29
Southport
1953-55
South Whitley
1946-47
1952-54
Speed
1951-55
Speedway
1941, 6/22-9/28
1946-54
Spencer
1953-55
Sponsler
1953-55
Star City
1953-55
State Line
1958, 4/27-10/26
Staunton
1953-55
Stone
1953-55
Straughn
1953-55
Sullivan
1952
1955-56
Sulphur Springs
1953-55
Sunman
1948
Swayzee
1953-55
Sweetsers
1953-55
Switz City
1953-55

Syracuse
1946-54
Taylorsville
1953-55
Tecoma
1953-55
Tefft
1946-48
Tell City
1955, 5/1-9/25
1956
Terre Haute
1946
1950-55
1956, 4/29-10/28
Tippecanoe
1946-52
Tipton
1946-54
Tocsin
1954
Topeka
*1941, 5/4-9/1
1947
Tremont
1946-49
Turner
1953-55
Underwood
1953-55
Union City
1945, 4/20-9/21
1954
Uniondale
1954
Upland
1950-55
Valentine
1953-55
Valparaiso
1927, 5/13-9/25
1928-41
1946-56
1959, 4/26-10/25

Van Buren
1955
1956, 4/29-10/30
Veedersburg
1946, 5/5-9/27
1947
1954-56
Vernon
1953-56
Verona
1953-55
Vienna
1953-55
Vincennes
1946
1953-56
1960, 4/24-10/30
1961, 4/30-9/24
Wabash
1947-48
1950
1953-54
Wakarusa
1946
1948
1951-54
Walesboro
1953-55
Walkerton
1946-55
1956, 4/29-10/28
1958, 4/27-10/26
1959, 4/26-10/25
1960, 4/24-10/30
Wallen
1953-55
Walton
1953-55
Warsaw
1946-54
1959, 4/26-10/25

* Change at 0:01 A.M.

INDIANA MAP SECTION

Presented on the following pages are Indiana Time Maps for the Fall and Winter months between Daylight Saving Time Dates from 1955 through 1965.

LEGEND

Maps 1955 through 1961: Communities indicated by a full dot observed Eastern Standard Time all year. Those represented by an open dot observed Central Standard Time in the Fall and Winter months, then switched to Central Daylight Saving Time in the Spring and Summer.

Maps 1961 through 1965: Dots same as in above paragraph. Further, the light broken line in the 1961 map running from Michigan to Kentucky designates the Interstate Commerce Commission official Eastern Standard Time Zone Boundary adopted July 23, 1961.

Maps 1966 through 1973: The Fall-Winter 1970-71 was not available for publication. In this group appear four Summer Maps to show the general picture of time in this state. Further, the broken line in the 1969 Summer Map, running from Michigan to Kentucky, designates the Interstate Commerce Commission official Eastern Standard Time Zone Boundary which became effective April 27, 1969.

INDIANA (cont.)

Washington	Wheatfield	Wolcottville
1956	1947-48	1941, 4/27-10/26
Waterloo	Wheeler	1946-48
1946-54	1953-55	1953-55
Waveland	Whitaker	Woodcraft
1953-55	1953-55	1941, 6/22-9/28
Waynesville	Whiteland	1946-54
1953-55	1953-55	Woods
Wellsboro	Whiting	1953-55
1946-55	1922-41	Worthington
1956, 4/29-10/28	1946-55	1953-56
1958, 4/27-10/26	1956, 4/29-10/28	Wyatt
1959, 4/26-10/25	1958, 4/27-10/26	1940
1960, 4/24-10/30	1959, 4/26-10/25	1948
1961	Whitney	1954
Wenatah	1933-41	1960, 4/24-10/30
1953-55	Wilder	Yorktown
West Baden	1954	1953-55
1954-56	Williams	
Westfield	1953-55	
1953-55	Williamsport	
West Indianapolis	1953	
1941, 6/22-9/28	1955-56	
1946-54	Wilson	
West Lafayette	1946-49	
1955	Winamac	
1956, 4/29-10/28	1946-55	
West Lebanon	Winchester	
1958, 4/27-10/26	1946-54	
Westphalia	Windfall	
1953-55	1953-55	
Westpoint	Winfield	
1958, 4/27-10/26	1953-55	
West Terre Haute	Winona Lake	
1953-55	1953-55	
Westville	1956, 4/29-10/28	
1940-41	1961, 4/30-9/24	
1946-48	Wirt	
1952-54	1953-55	
1959, 4/26-10/25	Wolcott	
1960, 4/24-10/30	1953-55	
	1956, 4/29-10/28	

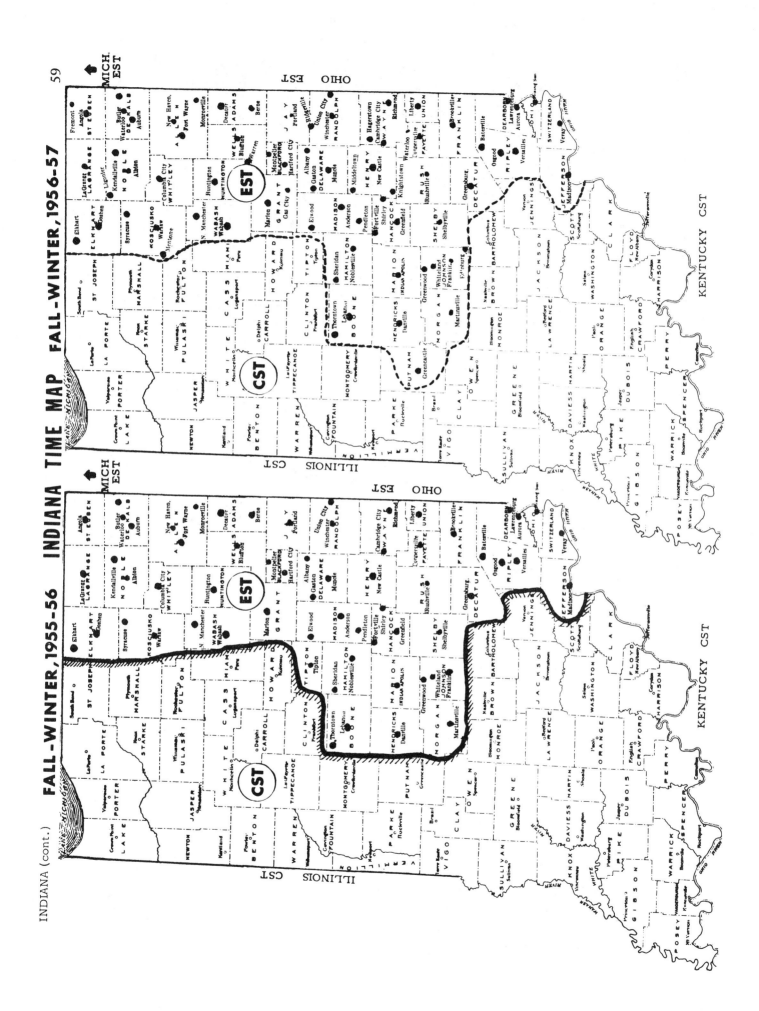

INDIANA TIME MAP

FALL-WINTER, 1956-57

FALL-WINTER, 1955-56

59

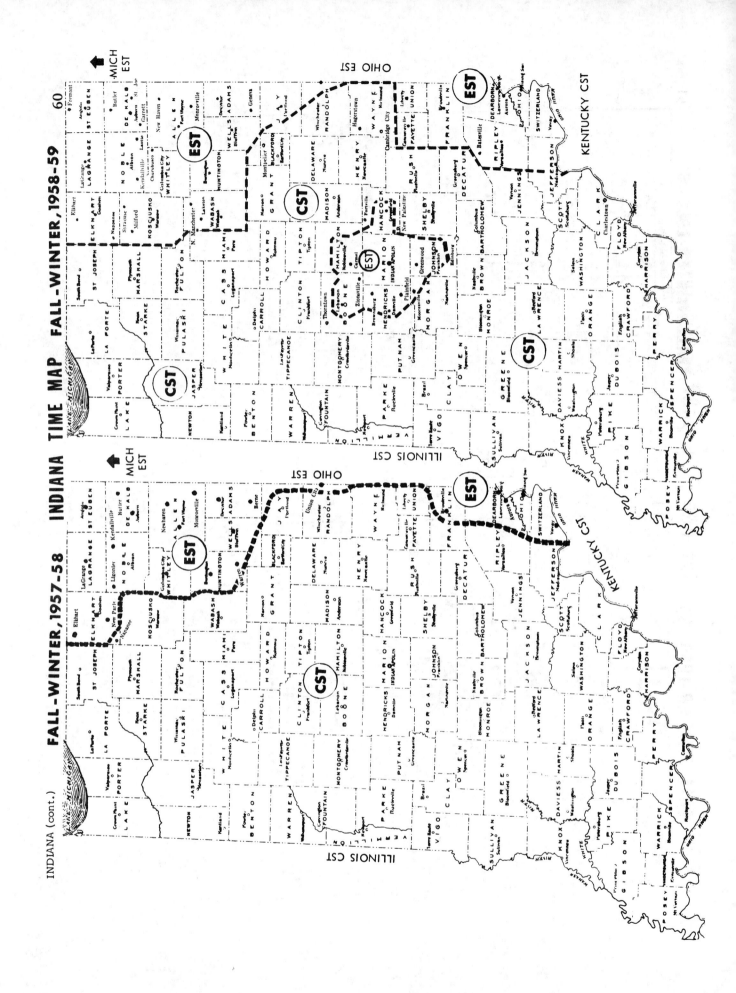

FALL-WINTER, 1957-58   INDIANA TIME MAP   FALL-WINTER, 1958-59

60

INDIANA (cont.)   INDIANA TIME MAP

FALL-WINTER 1959-60

FALL-WINTER 1960-61

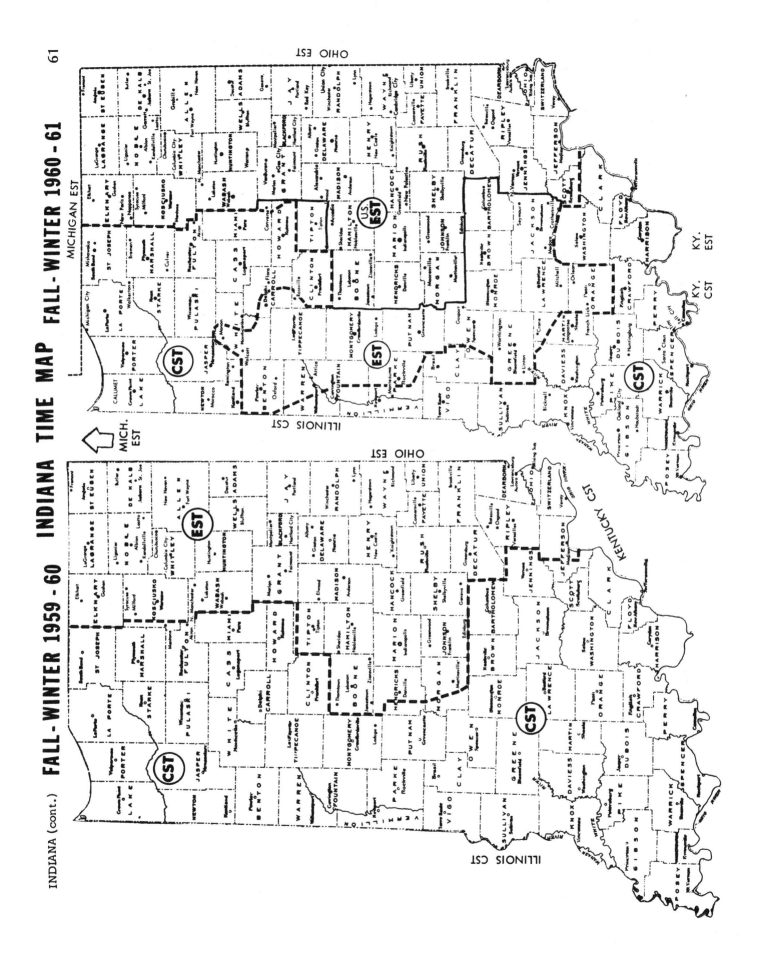

INDIANA TIME MAP

FALL-WINTER 1962-63

62

MICHIGAN EST

OHIO EST

ILLINOIS CST

KY. EST

KY. CST

CST

Informal EST

U.S. EST

FALL-WINTER 1961-62

MICHIGAN EST

OHIO EST

ILLINOIS CST

KY. EST

KY. CST

CST

Informal EST

U.S. EST

INDIANA TIME MAP

FALL-WINTER, 1963-64

FALL-WINTER, 1964-65

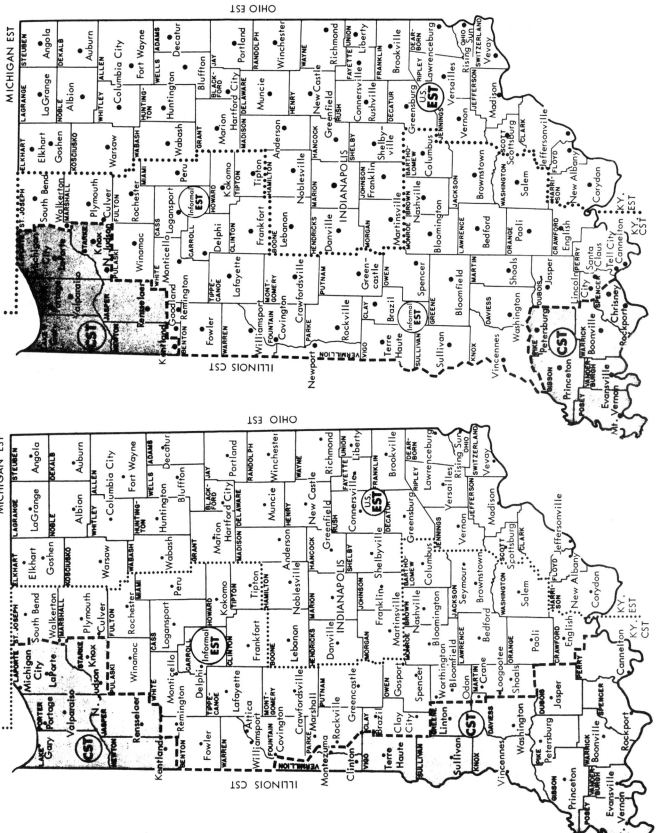

FALL-WINTER, 1966-67

FALL-WINTER, 1965-66

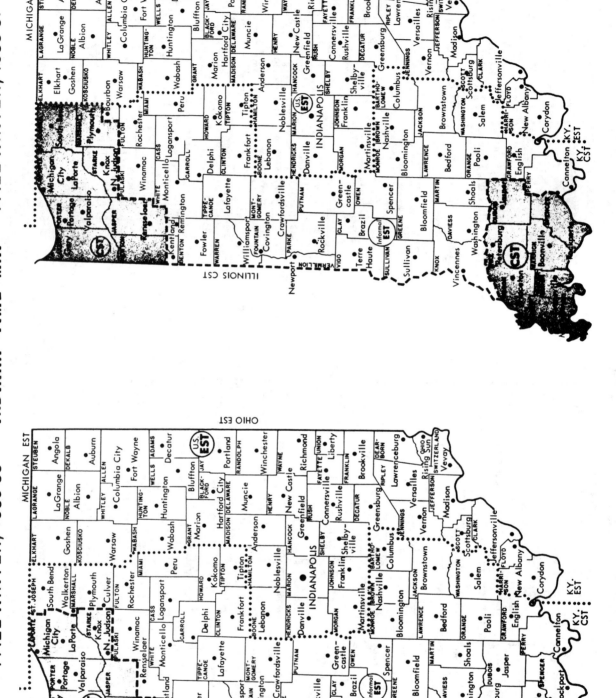

INDIANA TIME MAP

INDIANA (cont.)

FALL-WINTER, 1967-68

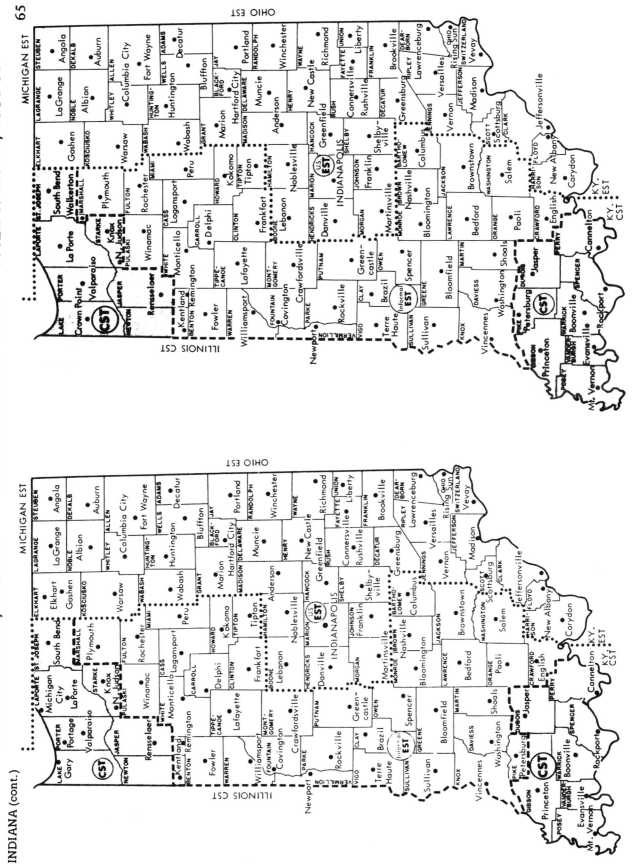

FALL-WINTER, 1968-69

INDIANA TIME MAP

SUMMER, 1970

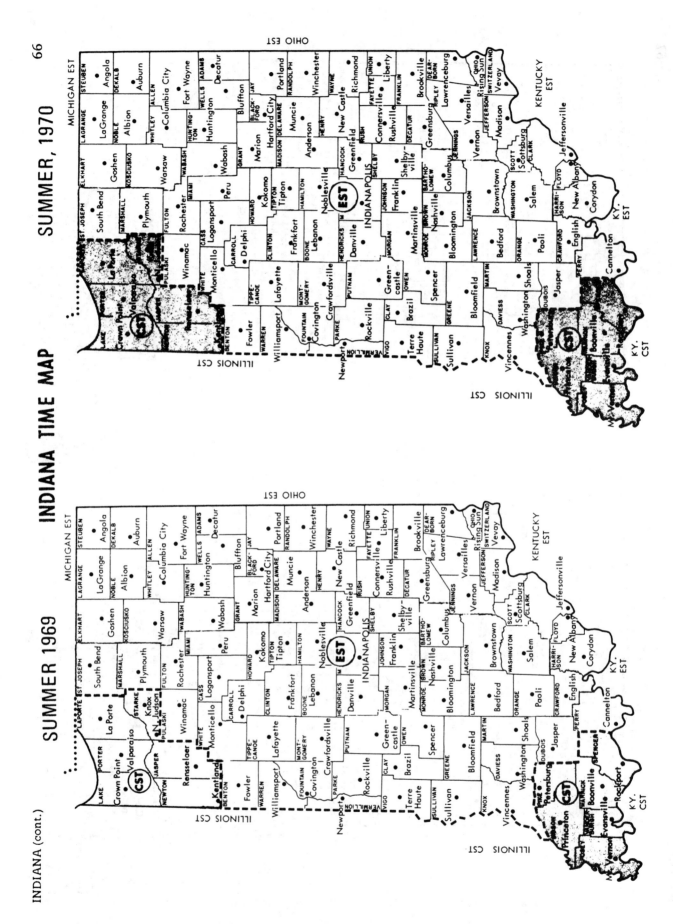

SUMMER 1969

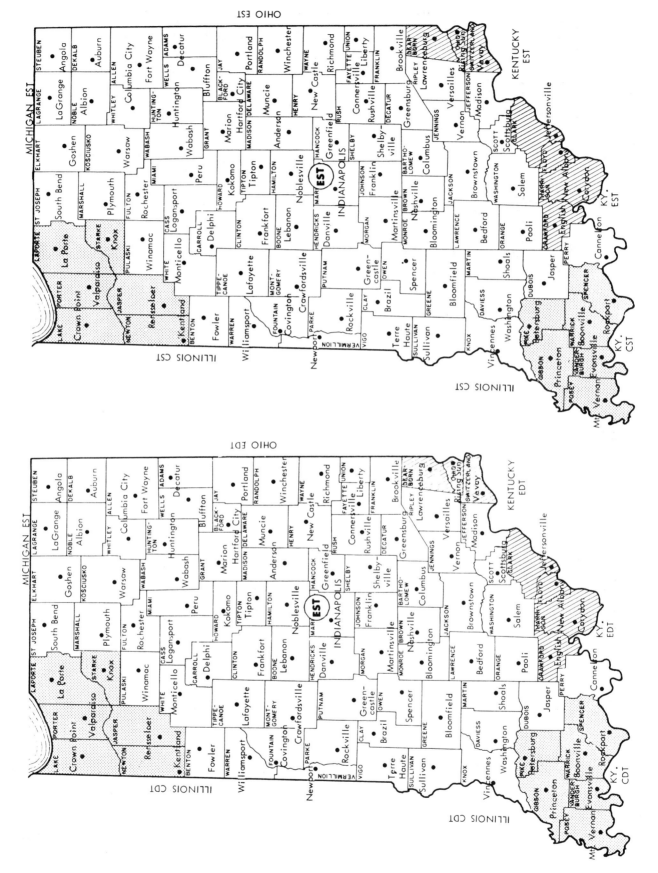

INDIANA (cont.)

INDIANA TIME MAP

SUMMER 1971

FALL-WINTER, 1971-72

INDIANA TIME MAP

FALL-WINTER, 1972-73

SUMMER 1972

INDIANA (cont.)

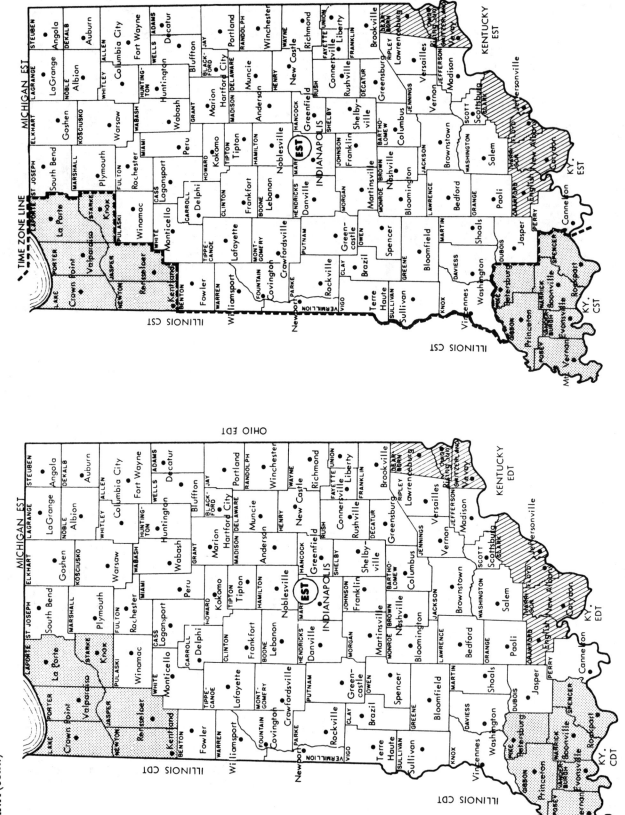

INDIANA TIME MAP: 1975

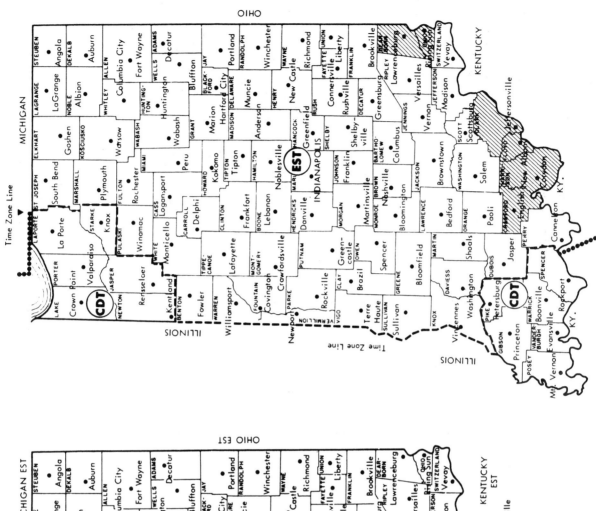

INDIANA TIME MAP: WINTER, 1974-75

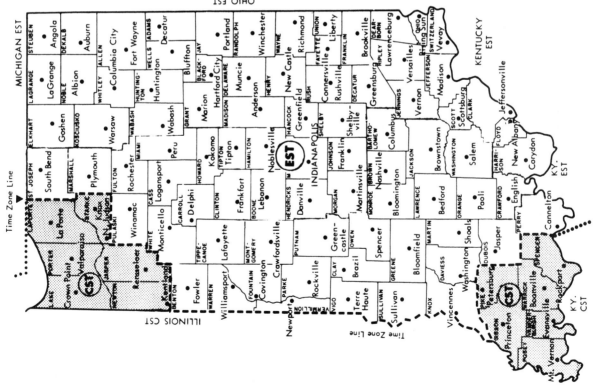

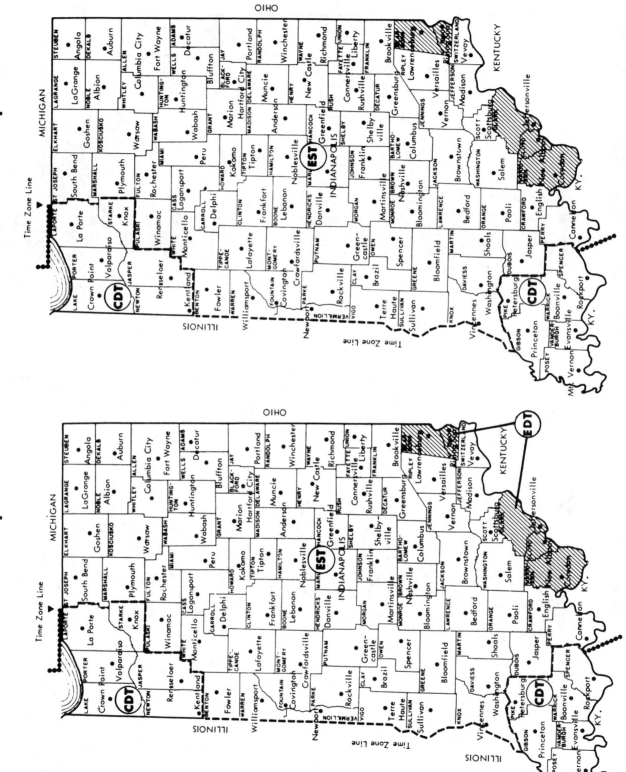

Indiana Time Map: 1977

Indiana Time Map: 1976

Indiana Time Map 1977-78

Indiana Time Map 1978-79

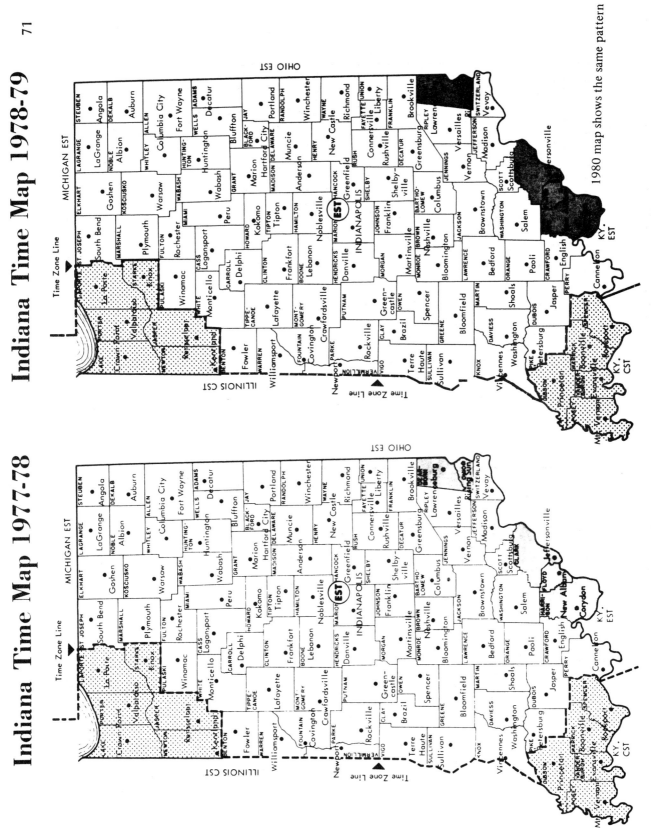

1980 map shows the same pattern

TABLE	
1918	War Time
1919	War Time
1941	4/27-9/28
1942-45	War Time
1946	4/28-9/29
1947	4/27-9/28
1957	4/28-9/29
1958	4/27-10/26
1959	4/26-9/28
1960	4/24-10/30
1961	4/30-10/29
1962	4/29-10/28
1963	4/28-10/27
1964	4/26-10/25
1965	5/30-9/6

** Check with local authorities

IOWA

1752	9/14	Gregorian (NS) Calendar adopted in U.S.A.
1788		Area settled
1846	12/28	State entered the Union
1883	11/18	Noon, Central Standard Time (90°W) adopted

DAYLIGHT (OR WAR) TIME OBSERVED:
(Changes at 2 A.M.)

1918	3/31 - 10/27	World War I
1919	3/30 - 10/26	World War I
1920	To 1941	Not observed except in Davenport. See Local Ordinance Listing.
1942	2/9 - 9/30/45	World War II
1946	To 1963	Local option by communities and varying dates of observance presents a picture of utter confusion. Dates and places not listed below should be checked with local agencies. Local Ordinance Listing is incomplete. **
1964		DST generally observed in Eastern Iowa from 4/26 to various termination dates in August, September and October; some localities started DST in May, some in June. Some cities and towns in Central and Western Iowa also on DST. Local Ordinance Listing is incomplete. **
1965	5/30 - 9/6	Observed state-wide. Refer to Table for dates.
1966	To 1979	For dates, see Table, page 181.

OBSERVED BY LOCAL ORDINANCE:
(Refer to Table for Month & Day if not shown)

IOWA (cont.)

Agency City
  1960
Batavia
  1960
Bellevue
  1963, 6/3-8/26
Bettendorf
  1959
  1960-64
Blue Grass
  1963
Buffalo
  1963
Burlington
  1960-64
  1962, 4/29-9/16
  1963, 4/28-9/29
  1964, 4/26-10/31
Clinton
  1946-47
  1960, 4/24-10/23
  1961
  1962, 4/29-9/15
  1963, 4/28-9/1
  1964, 4/26-9/27
Danville
  1960
  1961, 4/30-9/3
  1963, 4/28-8/25
  1964, 4/26-10/31
Davenport
  1941
  1957, 4/28-10/29
  1958, 4/27-10/28
  1959, 4/26-10/27
  1960-64
De Witt
  1963, 6/1-9/1
Dixon
  1963
Donnellson
  1962, 6/3-8/26

Dubuque
  1946
  1957
  1962
  1963, 6/2-9/1
  1964
Durant
  1963, 6/1-9/1
Eldridge
  1963
Fairfield
  1960
Fort Madison
  1960-61
Hamill
  1963, 4/28-9/1
Houghton
  1963, 4/28-9/1
Keokuk
  1960-61
  1962, 4/29-9/2
  1963, 4/28-9/1
  1964, 4/26-9/6
Le Claire
  1960
  1963
Lockridge
  1960
Maquoketa
  **1963
McCausland
  1963
Mediapolis
  1963, 5/26-9/1
Middleton
  1963
Montpelier
  1963
  1963

Montrose
  1961
  1962, 4/29-9/2
  1963, 4/28-9/1
  1964, 4/26-10/31
Mount Pleasant
  1960
  1961, 4/30-9/3
  **1962, 4/29-(?)
  1963, 4/28-9/29
  1964, 4/26-10/31
Muscatine
  1963
New London
  1960
  1961, 4/30-9/3
Ottumwa
  1960
Princeton
  1963
Rome
  1960
Sabula
  1963, 5/26-9/1
Spring Grove
  1963
Stockton
  1963
Viele
  1963, 4/28-9/29
Walcott
  1963
Wapello
  1963, 5/26-8/26
West Burlington
  1960
  1963
West Point
  1960
  1962, 4/29-9/16
  1963, 4/28-9/15

Wever
  **1962, 4/29-(?)
  1963, 4/28-9/29
Wilton Junction
  **1963, (?)

TABLE

1918	War Time
1919	War Time
1942-45	War Time

KANSAS

1727		Area settled
1752	9/14	Gregorian (NS) Calendar adopted in U.S.A.
1861	1/29	State entered the Union
1883	11/18	Noon, two standards of time adopted. Most of the state adopted Central Standard Time (90°W), including the boundary-line communities of:

Dodge City	Jetmore
Elkhart	Lenora
Ellis	Philippsburg
Englewood	Plainville
Great Bend	Satanta
Hugoton	Stockton

Northwestern portion adopted Mountain Standard Time (105°W), including the boundary-line communities of:

Almena	Ness City
Garden City	Syracuse

1927	8/7	CST boundary moved westward to include the southwest portion of Kansas. (This portion which had been on MST swtiched to CST)
1967	11/25	Boundary between MST and CST Zones moved to coincide with the western boundary of the State, placing entire State in the Central Standard Time Zone.

DAYLIGHT (OR WAR) TIME OBSERVED:
(Changes at 2 A.M.)

1918	3/31 - 10/27	World War I
1919	3/30 - 10/26	World War I
1920	To 1941	Not observed
1942	2/9 - 9/30/45	World War II
1946	To 1965	Not observed
1966		See Chapter VII
1967	To 1979	For dates, see Table, page 181.

TABLE I

1918	War Time	1959	4/26-10/25
1919	War Time	1960	4/24-10/30
1941	4/27-9/28	1961	4/30-10/29
1942-45	War Time	1962	4/29-10/28
1950	4/30-9/24	1963	4/28-10/27
1951	4/29-9/30	1964	4/26-10/25
1952	4/27-9/28	1965	4/25-10/31
1953	4/26-9/27		
1954	4/25-9/26	**TABLE II**	
1955	4/24-9/25		
1956	4/29-10/28	1956	4/29-9/30
1957	4/28-10/27	1957	4/28-9/29
1958	4/27-10/26		

** Check with local authorities

KENTUCKY

1752	9/14	Gregorian (NS) Calendar adopted in U.S.A.
1765		Area settled
1792	6/1	State entered the Union
1883	11/18	Noon, Central Standard Time (90°W) adopted
1920	**	Covington adopted EST (75°W)
1927	4/3	Newport adopted EST (75°W)
1947	9/28	The Interstate Commerce Commission moved the EST boundary line to include additional portions of Kentucky.
1960	4/3	Eastern Standard Time (75°W) effective in most of the State. New line started at the southwest corner of Ohio, and follows the Ohio River along the Indiana border to the mouth of the Kentucky River. Following the Kentucky River, the line passes through Carroll County and then follows a generally southward direction along the westward borders of Owen, Franklin, Anderson, Mercer, Boyle, Lincoln, Pulaski and McCreary Counties. This line puts all of the Blue Grass section on Eastern Time as well as Gallatin County and half of Carroll County, including the City of Carrollton.
1961	7/23	Louisville and Lexington area adopted EST (75°W)

DAYLIGHT (OR WAR) TIME OBSERVED:
(Changes at 2 A.M.)

1918	3/31 - 10/27	World War I
1919	3/30 - 10/26	World War I

KENTUCKY (cont).

1920	To 1941	Not observed state-wide. See Local Ordinance Listing.
1942	2/9 - 9/30/45	World War II
1946	To 1965	Not observed state-wide. See Local Ordinance Listing.

**1957-60: Fifteen Central Kentucky communities (not all listed in Local Ordinance Listing) observed DST all year.
**1961-65: Various communities in the western part of the State observed DST starting April 30, and ending on varying dates of 9/4, 9/24, and 10/29.
**1964: The Cities of Calhoun, Madisonville and Owensboro observed DST, varying dates.

1966		See Chapter VII
1967		State got a year of grace because its legislature had not met since the Uniform Time Act was passed on April 13, 1966 and would not convene until January, 1968. Some towns observed Daylight Saving Time voluntarily. The result was that the State had four different times, as it straddles the line between Eastern and Central Time Zones.
1968	To 1979	For dates, see Table, page 181.

OBSERVATION BY LOCAL ORDINANCE:
(Refer to Table for Month & Day if not shown)

COUNTY

Jefferson County: 1958, 4/27-6/19 I

COMMUNITIES

Anchorage: 1960-61 I

Berea: 1955 I; 1956 II

Brodhead: 1941, 4/27-9/1 I

Buechel: 1951 I; 1954-55 I; 1956 II

Carrollton: 1953 I; 1957-59 All yr.

Cynthiana: 1953 I; 1953-55 I; 1956 II

Danville: 1954 I; 1955, 4/24-9/6 I; 1956, 4/29-9/4 I; 1957 I; 1959, 4/26-10/31 I

Dry Ridge: 1953 I; 1954, 4/25-9/6 II

Elizabethtown: 1955 I; 1956 II

Eminence: 1955 I; 1956 II

Fisherville: 1951 I; 1956 II

Frankfort: 1951 I; 1954-55 I; 1956 II; 1957-59 All yr.

Franklin: 1953 I

Georgetown: 1953 I; 1954, 4/25-9/6 I; 1957-59 All yr.

Glencoe: 1953 I

Harrodsburg: 1951 I; 1956-57 II

Irvine: 1941, 4/27-9/13 I

Jeffersontown: 1951 I; 1955 I; 1956-57 II

Junction City: 1957 II

La Grange: 1953 I; 1955 I; 1956 II

Lawrenceburg: 1951 I; 1955 I; 1956-57 II

Lebanon Jct.: 1953 I

Lexington: 1941 I; 1950, 5/7-9/24* I; 1951 I; 1952, 4/27-6/18 I; 1953 I; 1954, 4/25-9/5 I; 1955, 4/24-9/5 I; 1956 II; 1957-59 All yr.

Louisville: 1950-57 II; 1958, 4/27-6/18 I; 1959 I; 1960, 4/30-10/29 I; 1961, 4/30-10/29 II

Maysville: 1953 I

Midway: 1941 I

Millersburg: 1941 I

Milton: 1953 I

Mount Sterling: 1955 I; 1956-57 II; 1959 I

Nicholasville: 1955, 4/24-9/5 I; 1956, 4/29-9/4 I

Paris: 1941 I; 1951 I; 1953 I; 1954, 4/25-9/5 I; 1955 I; 1956 II

Richmond: 1955 I; 1956, 4/29-9/3 I

Shelbyville: 1955 I; 1956-57 II; 1959-61 I

Shepardsville: 1953 I; 1955 I

Somerset: 1957, 4/28-9/2 I; 1958-59 All yr.

Sparta: 1953 I

Talmage: 1957 II

Taylorsville: 1941, 4/27-8/31 I

Versailles: 1951 I; 1955 I; 1956-57 II

Warsaw: 1953 I

West Point: 1956 II

Wilmore: 1953 I; 1955 I

Winchester: 1954-55 I; 1956 II; 1957-59 All yr.

Worthville: 1956 II

*Check surrounding towns.

TABLE	
1918	War Time
1919	War Time
1942-45	War Time
1946	4/29-9/29

LOUISIANA

1699		Area settled
1752		Gregorian (NS) Calendar adopted in U.S.A.
1812	4/30	State entered the Union
1883	11/18	Noon, Central Standard Time (90°W) adopted

DAYLIGHT (OR WAR TIME) OBSERVED:
(Changes at 2 A.M.)

1918	3/31 - 10/27	World War I
1919	3/30 - 10/26	World War I
1920	To 1941	Not observed
1942	2/9 - 9/30/45	World War II
1946	To 1966	Not observed state-wide. See Local Ordinance Listing.
1967	To 1979	For dates, see Table, page 181.

OBSERVATION BY LOCAL ORDINANCE:
(Refer to Table for Month & Day)

Kenner   1946
New Orleans 1946

TABLE

1918	War Time	1940	4/28-9/29
1919	War Time	1941	4/27-9/28
1920	4/14-9/26	1942-45	War Time
1921	4/3-9/25	1946	4/28-9/29
1922	4/2-9/24	1947	4/27-9/28
1923	4/29-9/30	1948	4/25-9/26
1924	4/27-9/28	1949	4/24-9/25
1925	4/26-9/27	1950	4/30-9/24
1926	4/25-9/26	1951	4/29-9/30
1927	4/24-9/25	1952	4/27-9/28
1928	4/29-9/30	1953	4/26-9/27
1929	4/28-9/29	1954	4/25-9/26
1930	4/27-9/28	1955	4/24-10/30
1931	4/26-9/27	1956	4/29-10/28
1932	4/24-9/25	1957	4/28-10/27
1933	4/30-9/24	1958	4/27-10/26
1934	4/29-9/30	1959	4/26-10/25
1935	4/28-9/29	1960	4/24-10/30
1936	4/26-9/27	1961	4/30-10/29
1937	4/25-9/26	1962	4/29-10/28
1938	4/24-10/1	1963	4/28-10/27
1939	4/30-9/24	1964	4/26-10/25
		1965	4/25-10/31

MAINE

1624		Area settled
1752	9/14	Gregorian (NS) Calendar adopted in U.S.A.
1820	3/15	State entered the Union
1886	12/15	Eastern Standard Time (75°W) adopted by Belfast only
1887		Eastern Standard Time (75°W) adopted state-wide

DAYLIGHT (OR WAR) TIME OBSERVED:
(Changes at 2 A.M.)

1918	3/31 - 10/27	World War I
1919	3/30 - 10/26	World War I
1920	To 1941	Not observed state-wide. See Local Ordinance Listing.
1942	2/9 - 9/30/45	World War II
1946	To 1954	Not observed state-wide. See Local Ordinance Listing.
1955	To 1965	Adopted state-wide. Refer to Table for dates.
1966	To 1979	For dates, see Table, page 181.

OBSERVATION BY LOCAL ORDINANCE:
(Refer to Table for Month and Day if not shown)

Adams	Auburn	Bangor	Bath	Belgrade	Biddeford Pool
1949-54	1923-35, 6/15-9/15	1920-22	1931-33	1946-54	1920-22
Alfred	1936-41	1923-38	1934, 4/29-10/30	Bemis	1923-38
1946-54	1946-54	1939, 4/30-10/15	1935-37	1946-54	1939, 4/30-10/15
Alton	Augusta	1940-41	1938, 4/30-9/25	Biddeford	1940-41
1949-54	1946-54	1946-54	1939-41	1923-37	Biddeford
Anson	Ayers	Bar Harbor	Bayside	1938, 4/28-10/1	1946-54
1946-54	1946-54	1923-41	1938-41	1939-41	Bingham
Ashland	Bancroft	Bar Mills	Belfast	1946-54	1938-41
1949-54	1946-54	1946-54	1938-41		1946-54

MAINE (cont.)

Binney 1949-54
Blackstone 1949-54
Blue Hill 1938-41
Boothbay Harbor 1938-41
Bowden 1949-54
Bowdoinham 1938-39
 1946-54
Boyd Lake 1949-54
Bradley 1938-39
 1949-54
Brewer 1946-54
Bridgton 1938-41
Bridgewater 1949-54
Bristol 1938-39
Brownville 1949-54
Brunswick 1920-22
 1923-38
 1939, 4/30-10/15
 1940-41
 1946-54
Buckfield 1938-39
 1946-54
Bucksport 1938-41
Burnham 1947-54
Buxton 1946-54

Byron 1946-54
Calais 1938-41
Camden 1938-39
Campbell 1938-41
Canton 1949-54
Cape Elizabeth 1941
Caribou 1949-54
Carmel 1946-54
Castigan 1946-54
Castine 1938-39
Cathance 1946-54
Chelsea 1946-54
Cherryfield 1946-54
Clinton 1946-54
Columbia Falls 1947-54
Corinna 1938-39
 1946-54
Cornish 1938-39
Crowleys Junction West 1946-54

Crystal 1949-59
Cumberland Mills 1938-39
Cupsuptic 1946-54
Damariscotta 1938-39
Danforth 1938-41
Danville 1938-39
Danville 1946-54
Danville Junction 1938-39
Darkharbor 1938-39
Davidson 1949-54
Deadwater 1946-54
Dennysville 1938-39
Derby 1938-41
Derring Junction 1938-41
Dexter 1938-41
Dixfield 1939-41, 6/1-10/15
Dover 1946-54
Dover-Foxcroft 1938-41
Drew 1946-54
Dudley 1949-59
Dyer Brook 1949-54

Eagle Lake 1938-39
 1949-54
East Baldwin 1946-54
East Brownfield 1946-54
East Gray 1946-54
East Hulden 1946-54
East Lebanon 1946-54
East Machias 1938-39
 1946-54
East Millinocket 1938-39
East Newport 1938-39
 1946-54
Easton 1938-39
East Peru 1949-54
Eastport 1938-41
East Sumner 1946-54
East Waterloo 1946-54
Eliot 1946-54
Ellis 1946-54
Ellsworth 1938-41
 1946-54
Ellsworth Falls 1946-54

Enfield 1938-39
 1946-54
Etna 1946-54
Fairfield 1938-41
Fairmount 1938-39
Farmington 1949-54
Forsythe 1946-54
Fort Fairfield 1938
 1939, 4/30-10/15
 1940-41
Fort Kent 1938-39
Franklin 1938-39
 1949-54
Franklin Road 1946-54
Freedom 1938-39
Freeport 1938-41
Frenchville 1938-39
Frye 1946-54
Fryeburg 1946-54
Gardiner 1938-41
 1946-54
Gilbertville 1946-54

Goodrich 1938-39
 1949-54
Goose Rocks Beach 1941, 4/27-9/28
Gordons 1946-54
Grand Isle 1938-39
Great Works 1949-54
Greenbush 1946-54
Greene 1946-54
Greenlake 1946-54
Greenville 1938-40
Grimes Mill 1941, 4/27-9/8
Grimestone 1949-54
Griswold 1949-54
Guilford 1938-41
Hale 1946-54
Hallowell 1938-41
 1946-54
Hancock 1938-39
 1946-54
Hanford 1949-54
Harmony 1946-54
Harrington 1946-54

MAINE (cont.)

Town	Year(s)
Harrison	1939-41
Hartford	1946-54
Hartland	1946-54
Harvey	1949-54
Hebron Station	1946-54
Herman	1946-54
Highmoor	1938-39
Highpine	1938-41
Hillman	1946-54
Hillside	1949-54
Hinckley	1946-54
Hiram	1946-54
Hollis Center	1946-54
Houghton	1946-54
Houlton	1947-54
Howe Brook	1949-54
Indian Pond	1946-54
Ingalls	1946-54
Island Falls	1946-54
Jackman	1938-39
Jacksonville	1946-54
Jemtland	1938-39
Jewett	1949-54
Keegan	1946-54
Kennebago	1938-39
Kennebunk	1949-54
Kennebunkport	1946-54
Kingman	1938-41
Kittery	1946-54
Lagrange	1949-54
Lake Austin	1946-54
Lake Maxie	1938-40
Lakeside	1946-54
Leeds Junction	1947-54
Lewiston	1920-22; 1923-38; 1939, 4/30-10/15; 1940-41; 1946-54
Lilly Pond	1938-39
Limestone	1949-54
Lincoln	1938-41; 1946-54
Lincoln Center	1946-54
Lisbon and Lisbon Falls	1938-40
Lisbon Center	1946-54
Littleton	1946-54
Livermore Falls	1949-54
Lucerne in Maine	1938-39; 1939, 4/30-10/1
Ludlow	1946-54
Machias	1938-40
Madawaska	1946-54
Madison	1938; 1940-41; 1946-54
Manchester	1938-41
Mapleton	1946-54
Maranacook	1941
Marion	1946-54
Mars Hill	1938-39; 1949-54
Massardis	1949-54
Mattawamkeag	1938-39
Maysville	1946-54
Mechanic Falls	1949-54
Medford	1938-39
Medford Center	1946-54
Mexico	1949-54
Michaud	1946-54
Milford	1949-54
Mill Brook	1946-54
Millinocket	1946-54
Milo	1938-54
Monmouth	1938-39
Monson	1941
Monticello	1946-54
Mount Desert	1941; 1946-54
Mount Vernon	1938-41
National Soldier's Home	1946-54
New Gloucester	1946-54
New Limerick	1949-54
Newport	1946-54
Newport Junction	1938-39
New Sweden	1938-39
Nicolin	1949-54
Nixon	1946-54
Norridgewock	1938-41
North Anson	1946-54
North Bangor	1938-41
North Berwick	1946-54
North Jay	1938-39
Northern Maine Junction	1947-54
Norway	1938-39
Nurcross	1949-54
Oak Hill	1938-41
Oakfield	1946-54
Oakland	1949-54
Ogren	1938-41
Ogunquit	1938-41
Olamon	1946-54
Old Orchard Beach	1946-54
Old Town	1938-41
Oquossoc	1946-54
Orono	1946-54
Packards	1949-54
Passadumkeag	1946-54
Patten	1949-54
Patten Junction	1949-54
Pembroke	1938-39
Perham	1947-54
Peru	1946-54
Phair	1938-39
Pittsfield	1938-41
Plaisted	1949-54
Poland	1946-54

MAINE (cont.)

Poland Spring — 1931-37; 1938, 4/24-9/25; 1939-41
Pollard Brook — 1946-54
Portage — 1920-22; 1923-38; 1939, 4/30-10/15
Portland — 1940-41; 1946-54
Porpoise — 1941, 4/27-9/38
Presque Isle — 1938; 1939, 4/30-10/15; 1940; 1949-54
Prides Mill — 1949-54
Rand Cove — 1920-22; 1923-38; 1939, 4/30-10/15
Randolph — 1940-41; 1946-54
Rangeley — 1941, 4/27-10/28
Raymond — 1938-41; 1946-54
(1) 1920-41
Readfield — 1938-41; 1946-54
Richmond — 1938-41; 1946-54
Robinsons — 1949-54
Rockland — 1938-41
Roxbury — 1946-54

Rumford — 1938-41; 1946-54
Sabattus — 1946-54
Saco — 1920-22; 1923-38; 1939, 4/30-10/15; 1940-41; 1946-54
Saint Croix — 1949-54
Saint Luce — 1938-39
Saint Francis — 1938-39
Sanford — 1920-22; 1923-38; 1939, 4/30-10/15; 1940-41
Sangerville — 1941, 4/27-10/28
Scarboro Beach — 1938-41; 1946-54
Schoodic — 1949-54
Sebago Lake — 1946-54
Sebec — 1941, 4/27-10/28
Shawmut — 1946-54
Sheridan — 1949-54
Sherman Station — 1949-54
Silvers Mills — 1946-54

Skerry — 1949-54
Skowhegan — 1938-41
Smyrna Mills — 1949-54
Soldier Pond — 1938-39
Solon — 1938-40; 1941, 4/27-9/7
South Berwick — 1946-54
South Lagrange — 1949-54
South Paris — 1938-39
South Poland — 1941
Southport — 1938-39
South Portland — 1931-37; 1938, 4/24-9/25; 1939-41
South Rangely — 1946-54
South Windham — 1938-41
Spaulding — 1949-54
Springvale — 1920-22; 1923-38; 1939, 4/30-10/15; 1940-41; 1946-54
Squapan — 1949-54

Stacyville — 1949-54
Steep Falls — 1938-54
Stillwater — 1946-54
Stockholm — 1949-54
Stratton — 1938-39; 1949-59
Summit — 1938-39
Tapsham — 1946-54
Thomaston — 1938-41
Timoney — 1949-54
Troutdale — 1946-54
Unionville — 1946-54
Van Buren — 1938, 4/24-9/25; 1939-41
Vanceboro — 1946; 1938-39; 1939-41
Vassalboro — 1948-54
Veazie — 1946-54
Wallagarss — 1949-54
Waldoboro — 1938-41; 1947-54
Walnut Hill — 1946-54
Warren — 1938-39; 1940, 4/28-9/24

Waterboro — 1946-54
Waterford — 1938-41
Waterville — 1920-22; 1923-38; 1939, 4/30-10/15; 1940-41; 1946-54
Waukeag — 1938-39
Weeksboro — 1946-54
Wells and Wells Beach — 1938-40; 1946-54
West Baldwin — 1946-54
Westbrook — 1931-37; 1938, 4/24-9/25; 1939-41
West Enfield — 1946-54
West Farmington — 1938-40
Westfield — 1949-54
West Kennebunk — 1946-54
Westman Land — 1949-54
West Minot — 1938-39
West Outlet — 1946-54
West Peru — 1946-54

West Seboeis — 1949-54
Whitneyville — 1946-54
Wilton — 1938-40
Windham — 1946-54
Winn — 1938-39; 1946-54
Winslow — 1938-39
Winterport — 1938-39
Winterville — 1949-54
Winthrop — 1938-41
Wiscasset — 1938-41
Woodfords — 1938-40
Woodland — 1938-39
Woolwich — 1938-41
Wytopitlock — 1946-54
Yarmouth — 1938-39
York Harbor — 1938-41

(1) Not observed; but natives went to work an hour earlier--no clocks turned back.

82

MARYLAND

1634		Area settled
1752	9/14	Gregorian (NS) Calendar adopted in U.S.A.
1788	4/28	State entered the Union
1883	11/18	Noon, Eastern Standard Time (75°W) adopted

DAYLIGHT (OR WAR) TIME OBSERVED:
(Changes at 2 A.M.)

1918	3/31 – 10/27	World War I
1919	3/30 – 10/26	World War I
1920	To 1941	Not observed
1942	2/9 – 9/30/45	World War II
1946	To 1957	Not observed state-wide. See Local Ordinance Listing.
1958		Observed state-wide, except Garrett County. Refer to Table I for dates.
1959	To 1966	Observed state-wide. Refer to Table I for dates.
1967	To 1979	For dates, see Table, page 181.

OBSERVATION BY LOCAL ORDINANCE:
(Refer to Table for Month & Day)

COUNTIES

(1) Communities adjacent to Washington, D.C. in Montgomery County and Prince Georges County

1952	I
1953	II
1954-65	I

COMMUNITIES

TABLE I

1918	War Time
1919	War Time
1942-45	War Time
1946	4/28-9/29
1947	4/27-9/28
1948	4/25-9/26
1949	4/24-9/25
1950	4/30-9/24
1951	4/29-9/30
1952	4/27-9/28
1953	4/26-9/27
1954	4/25-9/26
1955	4/24-9/25
1956	4/29-10/28
1957	4/28-10/27
1958	4/27-10/26
1959	4/26-10/25
1960	4/24-10/30
1961	4/30-10/29
1962	4/29-10/28
1963	4/28-9/27
1964	4/26-10/25
1965	4/25-10/31
1966	4/24-10/30

TABLE II

1953	4/30-9/26
1956	4/29-9/30
1957	4/28-9/29

(1) See map of Washington, D.C.

MARYLAND (cont.)

- Aberdeen: 1949-55 I; 1956 II; 1957-66 I
- Aikin: 1948-55 I; 1956 II; 1957-66 I
- Aireys: 1953-66 I
- Allens: 1953-66 I
- American Stores: 1953-66 I
- Anderson: 1947 I
- Annapolis: 1947-55 I; 1956 II; 1957-66 I
- Antietam: 1949 I
- Annapolis Junction: 1953-66 I
- Ardmore: 1953-66 I
- Arnold: 1947-55 I; 1956 II; 1957-66 I
- Arundel: 1953-66 I
- Ardwick: 1953-66 I
- Ashland: 1947 II; 1953-66 I
- Bacon Hill: 1948-66 I
- Bainbridge: 1953 I; 1955 I; 1956 II; 1957-66 I

- Baltimore & Suburbs: 1947-55 I; 1956 II; 1957-66 I
- Barclay: 1953-66 I
- Bare Hills: 1954 I
- Barnes: 1953-66 I
- Basket: 1953-66 I
- Bay View: 1953-66 I
- Beaverdam: 1953-66 I
- Bee Tree: 1953-66 I
- Bel Alton: 1956 II; 1957-66 I
- Belvedere: 1953-66 I
- Bengies: 1953-66 I
- Berlin: 1947-55 I; 1956 II; 1957-66 I
- Biggs: 1953-66 I
- Big Spring: 1954-55 I; 1956 II; 1957-66 I
- Bishop: 1948-66 I
- Black: 1953-66 I
- Blue Mount: 1953-66 I

- Bowie: 1953-66 I
- Bowie Road: 1953-66 I
- Brandywine: 1953-66 I
- Brooklynville: 1953-66 I
- Bush River: 1953-66 I
- Cambridge: 1948-55 I; 1956 II; 1957-66 I
- Carville: 1953-66 I
- Cavetown: 1950 I
- Cedarhurst: 1947-55 I; 1956 II; 1957-66 I
- Centerville: 1953-55 I; 1956 II; 1957-66 I
- Chapel: 1953-66 I
- Charlestown: 1953-66 I
- Cheltenham: 1953-66 I
- Chase: 1953-66 I
- Chestertown: 1953-55 I; 1956 II; 1957-66 I
- Cheverly: 1954 I
- Chewsville: 1948-50 I

- Clarke: 1953-66 I
- Cockeysville: 1947 I; 1953-55 I; 1956 II; 1957-66 I
- Collington: 1953-66 I
- Conway: 1953-66 I
- Corbett: 1953-66 I
- Cordova: 1948-66 I
- Costen: 1953-66 I
- Crisfield: 1947-48 I; 1953-66 II
- Croom Station: 1953-66 I
- Crownsville: 1953-66 I; 1956 II; 1957-66 I
- Cullen: 1955 I; 1956 II; 1957-66 I
- Cumberland: 1947-55 I; 1956-57 II; 1958-66 I
- Davis: 1953-66 I
- Dericksons: 1953-66 I
- Dessard: 1953-66 I
- Douglas: 1953-66 I
- Duley: 1953-66 I

- Earleigh Heights: 1953-66 I
- East New Market: 1953-66 I
- Easton: 1947-55 I; 1956 II; 1957-66 I
- Eccleston: 1953-66 I
- Eckhart Junction: 1953-66 I
- Edgeview: 1953-66 I
- Eden: 1953-66 I
- Edgewood: 1949-51 I; 1953-55 I; 1956 II; 1957-66 I
- Elkton: 1953-66 I
- Elvaton: 1953-66 I
- Ennols: 1953-66 I
- Faulkner: 1953-66 I
- Federalsburg: 1948-66 I
- Ferndale: 1953-66 I
- Flemings: 1953-66 I
- Fort George G. Meade: 1947 I; 1950 I; 1952-55 I; 1956 II; 1957-66 I

- Fountain Rock: 1953-66 I
- Frederick: 1947-55 I; 1956 II; 1957-66 I
- Frederick Road: 1954 I
- Freeland: 1953-66 I
- Friendship: 1953-66 I
- Frostburg: 1947-55 I; 1956-57 II; 1958-66 I
- Fruitland: 1953-66 I
- Funkstown Station: 1953-66 I
- Galt: 1953-66 I
- Gambrills: 1953-66 I
- Garrison: 1953-66 I
- Girdletree: 1948-66 I
- Glenburnie: 1953-66 I
- Glencoe: 1953-66 I
- Glenn Dale: 1953-66 I
- Glyndon: 1947-55 I; 1956 II; 1957-66 I
- Goldsboro: 1948-66 I
- Golts: 1953-66 I

MARYLAND (cont.)

Place	Years	Zone
Graystone	1953-66	I
Greenmount	1947-55	I
	1956	II
	1957-66	I
Greensboro	1948-66	I
Gunpowder	1953-66	I
Hagerstown	1946-55	I
	1956	II
	1957-66	I
Hagerstown Junction	1953-66	I
Halethorpe	1954	I
Hall	1953-66	I
Hampstead	1947-55	I
	1956	II
	1957-66	I
Hancock	1948-55	I
	1956	II
	1957-66	I
Harewood Park	1954	I
Harmans	1947	I
	1953-66	I
Harmony Grove	1953-66	I
Havre de Grace	1949-55	I
	1956	II
	1957-66	I
Hayden	1953-66	I
Henderson	1953-66	I
Hematite	1953-66	I
Highfield	1947-55	I
	1956	II
	1957-66	I
Hill	1953-66	I
Holly Grove	1953-66	I
Hollins	1947	II
	1957-66	I
Hopewell	1953-66	I
Hurlock	1948-66	I
Ironhill	1953-66	I
Ironshire Station	1953-66	I
Jericho Park	1953-66	I
Jessups	1950-55	I
	1956	II
	1957-66	I
Keymar	1948-55	I
Kennedyville	1948-66	I
Kingston	1948-49	I
Kitts Mill	1953-66	I
Ladiesburg	1953-66	I
Lake	1954	I
Lambson	1953-66	I
Landover	1953-66	I
Lanham	1953-66	I
Lankfords	1953-66	II
Lansdowne	1953-66	I
La Plata	1953-66	I
Laurel	1949-50	I
	1952-55	I
	1956	II
	1957-66	I
Le Gore	1953-66	I
Leland	1953-66	I
Linkwood	1953-66	I
Linthicum Heights	1953-66	II
Lineboro	1947-55	I
	1956	II
	1957-66	I
Llandoff	1956	II
	1957-66	I
Lona coning	1954-56	I
	1957	II
	1958-66	I
Loretto	1948-49	I
Luke	1948-55	I
	1956	II
	1957-66	I
Lutherville	1947	I
	1953-66	I
Lynch	1953-66	I
Magnolia	1953-66	I
Marion Station	1948-49	II
	1953-66	I
Marsh	1953-66	I
Maryvel	1953-66	I
Massey	1953-66	I
Mattawoman	1953-66	I
Maugansville	1953-66	I
Middleburg	1948-66	I
Middle River	1947-50	I
Mitchellville	1954-66	I
Millersville	1953-66	I
Millington	1947-55	I
	1956	II
	1957-66	I
Monkton	1953-66	I
McAleer	1953-66	I
McCoole	1954-56	I
	1957	II
	1958-66	I
Mount Savage	1948-50	I
Mount Washington	1947	I
	1953-66	I
Neubert	1953-66	I
Newark	1953-66	I
New Midway	1953-66	I
New Windsor	1953-66	I
North East	1953-66	I
Notre Dame	1953-66	I
Oakington	1953-66	I
Oakland	1950	I
Ocean City	1954-55	II
	1956-57	I
Odenton	1953-66	I
Ohlers Grove	1953-66	I
Old Town	1947-55	I
Otter Point	1953-66	I
Owings Mills	1947-55	I
	1956	II
	1957-66	I
Oxford	1954-55	I
	1956-57	II
	1957-66	I
Padonia	1947	I
	1954	I
Parkton	1953-66	I
Parole	1953-66	I
Pasadena	1953-66	I
Patapsco	1947	I
	1953-66	I
Patuxent	1947	I
	1953-66	I
Pearre	1950	I
Peninsula Junction	1954-55	II
	1956-57	I
Perryman	1953-66	I
Perryville	1947	I
	1953-66	I
Phoenix	1953-66	I
Piney Creek	1953-66	I
Pocomoke (City)	1953-66	II
Popes Creek	1948-55	I
	1956	II
Portland	1957-66	I
	1953-66	I

MARYLAND (cont.)

Place	Years	Class
Port Tobacco Station	1953-66	I
Powell	1953-66	I
Price	1953-66	I
Rosedale	1953-66	I
Princess Anne	1947-66	I
Princeton	1953-66	I
Principio Furnace	1953-66	I
Queen Anne	1947-55	I
	1956	II
Queenstown	1957-66	I
Queponco	1953-66	I
	1948-52	I
Ridgely	1947, 5/11-9/2	I
	1948-55	I
Ralphs	1956	II
	1957-66	I
Reid	1953-66	I
	1948-55	I
	1956	II
	1957-66	I
Reids Grove	1953-66	I
Revell	1953-66	I
Rhodesdale	1953-66	I
Riderwood	1947	I
	1953-66	I
Roberts	1953-66	I
Rockland	1953-66	I

Place	Years	Class
Rocky Ridge	1948-54	I
	1956	II
	1957-66	I
Rogers	1953-66	I
Rosedale	1953-66	I
Rosewick	1953-66	I
Ruarks	1953-66	I
Ruxton	1947-55	I
	1956	II
	1957-66	I
Ruxton Lake	1953-66	I
Salisbury	1948-52	I
Saint Denis	1953-66	I
Saint James	1957	I
Sanatorium	1948-54	I
Scarboro	1953-66	I
Seabrook	1953-66	I
Security	1947-55	I
	1956	II
	1957-66	I
Severn	1947	I
	1953-66	I

Place	Years	Class
Severna Park	1953-66	I
Sharretts	1953-66	I
Shipley	1953-66	I
Short Lane	1953-66	I
Showell	1953-66	I
Silver Spring	1955	I
Smithsburg	1947-55	I
	1956	II
	1957-66	I
Snow Hill	1948-55	I
	1956	II
South Salisbury	1957-66	I
Sparks	1953-66	I
Springfield	1953-66	I
Springs	1953-66	I
Stemmers Run	1953-66	I
Stevenson	1953-66	I
Still Pond	1953-66	I
Stockton	1948-66	I
Stoney Run	1953-66	I
Sudlersville	1953-66	I

Place	Years	Class
Swan Lake	1953-66	I
Talbert	1953-66	I
Taneytown	1953-66	I
Texas	1947	I
	1953-66	I
Thompson	1953-66	I
Thurmont	1947-55	I
	1956	II
	1957-66	I
Timonium	1947	I
	1953-66	I
Townshend	1953-66	I
Trappe	1948-51	I
	1953-66	I
Turnpike	1953-66	I
Tuxedo	1953-66	I
Union Bridge	1947-55	I
	1956	II
	1957-66	I
Vienna	1953-55	I
	1956	II
	1957-66	I
Waldorf	1953-66	I
Walker	1953-66	I
Walkersville	1953-66	I

Place	Years	Class
Waterbury	1953-66	I
Websters	1953-66	I
Wesley	1953-66	I
Westernport	1953-66	I
	1948-55	I
	1956-57	II
Westminister	1947-55	I
	1956	II
	1957-66	I
Westover	1948-66	I
White Hall	1953-66	I
White Plains	1953-66	I
Williams	1953-66	I
Williamsburg	1953-66	I
Williamsport	1947-55	I
	1956	II
	1957-66	I
Willoughby	1953-66	I
Woodberry	1954	I
Woodsboro	1953-66	I
Worton	1953-66	I
Wye Mill Station	1953-66	I

MASSACHUSETTS

1620		Area settled
1752	9/14	Gregorian (NS) Calendar adopted in U.S.A.
1788	2/6	State entered the Union
1883	11/18	Noon, Eastern Standard Time (75°W) adopted

DAYLIGHT (OR WAR) TIME OBSERVED:
(Changes at 2 A.M.)

1918	3/31 - 10/27	World War I
1919	3/30 - 10/26	World War I
1920	To 1941	Observed state-wide. Refer to Table for dates.
1942	2/9 - 9/30/45	World War II
1946	To 1965	Observed state-wide. Refer to Table for dates.
1966	To 1979	For dates, see Table, page 181.

TABLE

Year	Dates	Year	Dates
1918	War Time	1940	4/28-9/29
1919	War Time	1941	4/27-9/28
1920	3/28-10/31	1942-45	War Time
1921	4/24-9/25	1946	4/28-9/29
1922	4/30-9/24	1947	4/27-9/28
1923	4/29-9/30	1948	4/25-9/26
1924	4/27-9/28	1949	4/24-9/25
1925	4/26-9/27	1950	4/30-9/24
1926	4/25-9/26	1951	4/29-9/30
1927	4/24-9/25	1952	4/27-9/28
1928	4/29-9/30	1953	4/26-9/27
1929	4/28-9/29	1954	4/25-10/31
1930	4/27-9/28	1955	4/24-10/30
1931	4/26-9/27	1956	4/29-10/28
1932	4/24-9/25	1957	4/28-10/27
1933	4/30-9/24	1958	4/27-10/26
1934	4/29-9/30	1959	4/26-10/25
1935	4/28-9/29	1960	4/24-10/30
1936	4/26-9/27	1961	4/30-10/29
1937	4/25-9/26	1962	4/29-10/28
1938	4/24-10/1	1963	4/28-10/27
1939	4/30-9/24	1964	4/26-10/25
		1965	4/25-10/31

TABLE

1918	War Time		1942-45	War Time
1919	War Time		1946	4/28-9/29
1920	6/13-10/31		1947	4/27-9/28
1921	3/27-10/31		1948	4/25-9/26
1922	4/30-9/24		1949	4/24-9/25
1923	4/29-9/30		1950	4/30-9/24
1924	4/27-9/28		1951	4/29-9/30
1925	4/26-9/27		1952	4/27-9/28
1926	4/25-9/26		1953	4/26-9/27
1927	4/24-9/25		1954	4/25-9/26
1928	4/29-9/30		1955	4/24-9/25
1929	4/28-9/29		1956	4/29-9/30
1930	4/27-9/28		1957	4/28-9/29
1931	4/26-9/27		1958	4/27-9/28
1932	4/24-9/25		1959	4/26-9/27
1933	4/30-9/24		1960	4/24-10/30
1934	4/29-9/30		1961	4/30-9/24
1935	4/28-9/29		1962	4/29-9/30
1936	4/26-9/27		1963	4/28-9/29
1937	4/25-9/26		1964	4/26-9/27
1938	4/24-9/25		1965	4/25-10/31
1939	4/30-9/24		1966	4/24-10/30
1940	4/28-9/29			
1941	4/27-10/26			

MICHIGAN

1650		Area settled
1752	9/14	Gregorian (NS) Calendar adopted in U.S.A.
1837	1/26	State entered the Union

STANDARD TIME ZONE SHIFTS

1885	9/18	Central Standard Time (90°W) legalized
1915	5/15	Eastern Standard Time (75°W) adopted in Detroit and Highland Park. Time confused through the 'teens,--check carefully. **
1920		EST adopted in Bay City (4/15) and Ypsilanti (?)
1921	11/24	EST adopted in Ann Arbor
1922	11/14	EST adopted in Saginaw
1923	12/1	EST adopted in Jackson *
1924		EST adopted in Albion (4/1) and Lansing (5/1 *)
1925	5/4	EST adopted in Allegan
1927	4/1	EST adopted in Battle Creek
1928		EST adopted in Alma (?) / Sault Ste. Marie (12/23) / South Haven (?)
1930	1/4	EST adopted in Monroe
1931	4/26	EST legalized by State, but some cities continued on their own desired standard time, as below.

* Change at 0:01 A.M.
** Check with local authorities

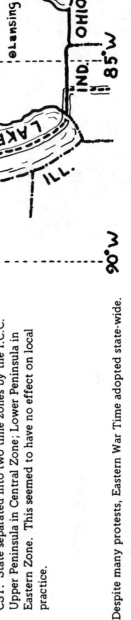

MICHIGAN (cont.)

1931 EST adopted in:

Adrian, 4/26	Kalamazoo, 2/28
Benton Harbor, 4/26	Manistee, 10/6
Big Rapids, 4/26	Muskegon, 4/11
Cadillac, 4/26	Newberry, 6/1
Calumet, 4/26	Onaway, 4/26
Coldwater, 4/26	Paw Paw, 2/28
Eagle River, 4/26	Pontiac, 4/26
Flint, 4/26	Sturgis, 3/29

1932 EST adopted in:

Fremont, (?)	Hastings, (?)
Grand Haven, 11/10	Holland, 3/10
Grand Rapids, 4/4	Petoskey, 4/17

1933 EST adopted in Mackinaw City, 6/(?)

1935 EST adopted in Bridgman, 4/7
Buchanan, 9/29
* Dowagiac, 4/2

1936 9/27 EST adopted in Hancock, L'Anse, Manistique and Saint Ignace. Only upper peninsular places remained on CST. State separated into two time zones by the I.C.C. Upper Peninsula in Central Zone; Lower Peninsula in Eastern Zone. This seemed to have no effect on local practice.

1942 2/9 - 9/30/45 Despite many protests, Eastern War Time adopted state-wide.

1945 9/30 EST in effect state-wide.

1967 12/10 At 0 hour Grand Marais, small town in Upper Peninsula, adopted EST in defiance of federal time act.

1969 4/27 I.C.C. extends the Eastern Zone to include all of Michigan.

1973 4/29 Relocation of Standard Time Zone boundary in Upper Peninsula places Gogebic, Iron, Dickinson and Menominee counties in the Central Time Zone.

* Change at 0:01 A.M.
(?) No record could be found by local authorities

MICHIGAN (cont.)

DAYLIGHT (OR WAR) TIME OBSERVED:
(Changes at 2 A.M.)

1918	3/31 - 10/27	World War I
1919	3/30 - 10/26	World War I
1920	To 1941	Not observed state-wide. See Local Ordinance Listing.
1942	2/9 - 9/30/45	World War II (See Addenda on page 184)
1943	2/5	Switched to Central War Time except cities which made materials for war protection.
1946	To 1965	Not observed state-wide. See Local Ordinance Listing.
1966		See Chapter VII
1967	6/14	Adopted Daylight Saving Time at 12:01 a.m. But the Upper Peninsula rebelled and kept to Standard Time, except the county of Chippewa, which switched to Daylight Saving Time with the rest of the state.
1968	To 1973	Not observed according to State law.

OBSERVATION BY LOCAL ORDINANCE:
(Refer to Table for Month & Day if not shown)

COUNTY

Dickison
1960-64
1965, except Breen, Felch and West Branch

COMMUNITIES

Adrian	Battle Creek	Calumet	Daggett	Escanaba
1921-30	1921-26	1946, EST all year	1946	*1928, 4/29-9/28
1948	Beaton	Campbell	Dearborn	*1930, 4/27-9/28
Albion	1946	1946	1948	*1931-41
1921-23	Beechwood	Carbondale	Defiance	1946-47
Alpha	1946	1946	1946	Faunus
1946	Benton Harbor	Carlton	Detroit	1946
Antoine	1921-30	1948	1946	Felch
1946	Bessemer	Carney	Dianne	1946
Bagley	1946	1946	1948	Flat Rock
1946	Birmingham	Cascade	Diorite	1948
Baraga	1948	1946	1946	Florence
1946	Brampton	Caspian	Dowagiac	1946
Barkley	1946-47	1946	*1932-34, 4/2-10/2	Ford River Station
1946	Buchanan	Cassopolis	Dunham	1946
Bark River	1921-35	1935, 4/8-9/2	1946	Forsyth
1946-47	Cadillac	Champion	Elmwood	1946
Basswood	1920, 4/10-9/18	1949	1946	
1946	1921, 5/1-10/2	Cheboygan		
	1926, 5/1-9/4	1921-26		
	1927, 4/30-9/3	1927, 3/2-11/5		
	1928-30	Choate		
		1946		
		Clowry		
		1946		
		Clytie		
		1946		
		Coldwater		
		1921-30		
		Connorville		
		1946		
		Covington		
		1946		
		Crystal Falls		
		1949		
		1950, 5/1-10/1		
		1952		

*Change at 0:01 A.M.

MICHIGAN (cont.)

Foster City
  1946
Fremont
  1921-31
Gaastra
  1946
Gibbs City
  1946
Gladstone
  1929-41
Gogebic
  1946
  1947
Grand Haven
1925, 4/12-9/27
1926, 4/11-9/26
1927, 4/10-9/25
1928, 4/8-9/30
1929, 4/14-9/29
1930, 4/13-9/28
1931, 4/12-9/27
Grand Rapids
1920, 4/4-9/26
1921, 4/3-9/25
1922, 4/2-9/24
1923, 4/1-9/30
1924, 4/6-9/28
1925, 4/5-9/27
1926, 4/4-9/26
1927, 4/3-9/25
1928, 4/1-9/30
1929, 4/7-9/29
1930, 4/6-9/28
1931, 4/5-9/27
Gwinn
  1941
Hancock
1946, EST all year
Hansen
  1946

Hardwood
  1946
Harris
  1946
Hartleys
  1946
Hastings
1931, 4/12-9/27
Hazel
  1946
Helps
  1946
Hemetite
  1946
Hermansville
  1946
Highland Park
  1948
Holland
*1920, 3/17-10/2
*1921, 4/17-10/2
*1922, 4/16-10/2
*1923, 4/15-9/3
*1924, 5/4-10/4
*1925, 4/11-10/11
*1926, 4/10-9/26
*1927, 4/9-9/25
*1928, 3/21-9/30
*1929, 3/20-9/29
*1930, 4/12-9/28
*1931, 4/11-9/27
Houghton
*1932, 10/2-12/31
*1933, 1/1-3/26
1946, EST all year
Hylas
  1946
Ingalls
  1946
Iron Mountain
1946, 5/5-9/29
  1950

Iron River
1935, 5/15-9/1
1946, 5/1-9/29
  1947
1950, 5/1-10/1
Ironwood
  1946
1961-64
(1) 1965
Ishpeming
1932, 5/1-10/2
1933, 4/30-10/1
1934-41
1946-47
Kalamazoo
1920, 4/11-10/10
1921, 4/17-10/9
1922, 4/30-10/1
1923, 4/15-10/7
1924, 4/13-10/5
1925, 4/12-12/31
1926, 1/1-11/14
*1927, 3/27-10/31
*1928, 3/18-11/11
*1929, 3/17-11/10
*1930, 3/16-11/9
Kew
  1946
Kloman
  1946
Labranche
  1946
Lambertville
  1948
L'Anse
1925, 4/29-9/30
  1949
Lansing
1923, 5/1-12/31
1924, 1/1-5/1

Larch
  1946
Lathrop
  1946
Leaper
  1946
Little Lake
1946-47
Loretto
  1946
Ludington
1927, 5/1-9/25
1931, 4/5-10/4
McFarland
  1946
Manistique
1931-35
Mansfield
  1946
Marenisco
  1946
Marquette
1930, 5/4-9/28
1931, 5/3-9/27
1933, 6/1-9/3
1934, 6/1-9/2
1935-41
1946-49
Martins Landing
  1946
Mastodon
  1946
Maybee
  1948
Melvindale
  1948
Menominee
  1946
Metropolitan
  1946

Milan
  1948
Monroe
1920-29
Munising
*1930, 5/4-9/28
*1931, 5/3-9/27
*1932, 5/1-9/25
*1933, 5/7-10/1
*1934, 5/6-9/30
*1935, 5/5-9/29
1936-41
Muskegon
*1927, 4/10-9/25
*1928, 4/8-9/30
*1929, 4/14-9/29
*1930, 4/13-9/28
Nadau
  1946
Narenta
  1941
Nauets
  1948
Nagunee
1930, 5/4-9/28
1931, 5/3-9/27
1933, 6/1-9/3
1934, 6/1-9/2
1935-41
1946-49
Newberry
1928-30, 6/1-10/1
New Buffalo
1930-41
Niagara
  1946
Niles
*1932, 4/30-10/2
1933, 4/30-9/24
(Changes at 1:00
A.M.)
1934-41

Norway
  1946
Onaway
1920-30
Oro
  1946
Palmer
  1946
Panola
  1946
Partridge
  1946
Paulding
  1946
Pentoga
  1946
Perronville
  1946
Petersburg
  1948
Pontiac
  1948
Powers
  1946
Princeton
  1946
Quinnesec
  1946
Richards
  1946
Riversiding Siding
  1946
Robbins
  1946
Rock
  1947
Romulus
  1948

* Change at 0:01 A.M.
(1) By local option

MICHIGAN (cont.)

Saint Anthonys	1948	Trenton	1948
Saint Ignace	1946, EST all year	Trout Creek	1949
Sands	1946	Turin	1946
Sault Ste. Marie	1946, EST all year	Verona	1946
Sawyer	1920-41	Vulcan	1946
Schaffer	1946	Wakefield	1946
Scofield	1948	Wallace	1946
Scott Lake	1946	Watersmeet	1946
Shingleton	1947	Waucedah	1946
Siemens	1946	Wellington	1946
Spaulding	1946	Wells	1946
Stack	1946	Whitney	1946
Stager	1946	Wilson	1946
Stambaugh	1946	Windee	1946
Stephenson	1946	Wyandotte	1948
Stickley	1946		
Sturgeon	1946		
Swanzy	1946		
Talbot	1946		
Toledo	1948		

TABLE

1918	War Time
1919	War Time
1942-45	War Time
1946	4/28-9/29
1957	4/28-10/27
1958	4/27-9/2
1959	5/24-9/8
1960	5/22-9/6
1961	5/28-9/5
1962	5/27-9/4
1963	5/26-9/3
1964	5/24-9/8
1965	5/23-9/7

CANADA — WIS. — N. DAK. — S. DAK. — IOWA — Duluth — 90°W — 92°W

MINNESOTA

1752	9/14	Gregorian (NS) Calendar adopted in U.S.A.
1805		Area settled
1858	5/11	State entered the Union
1901	2/26	Central Standard Time (90°W) adopted

DAYLIGHT (OR WAR) TIME OBSERVED:
(Changes at 2 A.M.)

1918	3/31 - 10/27	World War I
1919	3/30 - 10/26	World War I
1920	To 1941	Not observed
1942	2/9 - 9/30/45	World War II
1942	July	Repealed War Time
1946	To 1956	Not observed except in Duluth. See Local Ordinance Listing
1957	To 1958	DST obligatory by State law. Refer to Table for dates.
1959	To 1965	DST legalized state-wide from the fourth Sunday in May to Tuesday following Labor Day. Refer to Table for dates. Bordering communities were allowed to observe DST the same dates as adjoining states.** For exceptions, see Local Ordinance Listing.
1966		See Chapter VII
1967	To 1979	For dates, see Table, page 181

OBSERVATION BY LOCAL ORDINANCE:
(Refer to Table for Month & Day if not shown)

Bayport 1965, 5/9-10/31
Birchwood 1965, 5/9-10/31
Dakota 1965, 4/25-10/31

Duluth 1946
1959, 4/26-9/27
1965, 4/25-10/31
East Oakdale 1965, 5/9-10/31

Excelsior 1959, 4/26-9/27
Goodview 1965, 4/25-10/31
Hamburg 1959, 4/26-9/27

Hibbing 1965, 5/9-10/31
Hokah 1965, 4/25-10/31
Hopkins 1959, 4/26-9/27

Houston 1965, 4/25-10/31
La Crescent 1965, 4/25-10/31
Lake Elmo 1965, 5/9-10/31

Lauderdale 1965, 5/9-10/31

** Check local authorities

MINNESOTA (cont.)

Mahtomedi
  1965, 5/9-10/31
Minneapolis
  1959, 4/26-9/27
Minneiska
  1965, 4/25-10/31
Newport
  1965, 5/9-10/31
Norwood
  1959, 4/26-9/27
Rochester
  1965, 5/9-10/31
Rollingstone
  1965, 4/25-10/31
Roseville
  1965, 5/9-10/31
Saint Louis Park
  1959, 4/26-9/27
Saint Paul
  1959, 4/26-9/27
  1965, 5/9-10/31
Shoreview
  1965, 5/9-10/31
Stillwater
  1965, 5/9-10/31
Sunfish Lake
  1965, 5/9-10/31
Two Harbors
  1965, 4/25-10/31
Vadnais Heights
  1965, 5/9-10/31
Victoria
  1959, 4/26-9/27
Wayzata
  1959, 4/26-10/25
Waconia
  1959, 4/26-9/27
West Saint Paul
  1965, 5/9-10/31
Winona
  1959, 4/26-9/27
  1965, 4/25-10/31
Young America
  1959, 4/26-9/27

TABLE		
1918	War Time
1919	War Time
1942-45	War Time

MISSISSIPPI

1710		Area settled
1752	9/14	Gregorian (NS) Calendar adopted in U.S.A.
1817	12/10	State entered the Union
1883	11/18	Noon, Central Standard Time (90°W) adopted

DAYLIGHT (OR WAR) TIME OBSERVED:
(Changes at 2 A.M.)

1918	3/31 – 10/27	World War I
1919	3/30 – 10/26	World War I
1920	To 1940	Not observed
1941	7/31 –2/9/42	Observed by State Offices only
1942	2/9 – 9/30/45	World War II
1946	To 1965	Not observed
1966		See Chapter VII
1967	To 1979	For dates, see Table, page 181.

MISSOURI

1752	9/14	Gregorian (NS) Calendar adopted in U.S.A.
1764		Area settled
1821	8/10	State entered the Union
1883	11/18	Noon, Central Standard Time (90°W) adopted

DAYLIGHT (OR WAR) TIME OBSERVED:
(Changes at 2 A.M.)

1918	3/31 - 10/27	World War I
1919	3/30 - 10/26	World War I
1920	To 1941	Not observed
1942	2/9 - 9/30/45	World War II
1946	To 1965	Not observed state-wide. See Local Ordinance Listing.
1966		See Chapter VII
1967	To 1979	For dates, see Table, page 181.

TABLE I

1918	War Time
1919	War Time
1942-45	War Time
1946	4/28-9/29
1947	4/27-9/28
1948	4/25-9/26
1949	4/24-9/25
1950	4/30-9/24
1951	4/29-9/30
1952	4/27-9/28
1953	4/26-9/27
1954	4/25-9/26
1955	4/24-9/25
1956	4/29-10/28
1957	4/28-10/27
1958	4/27-10/26
1959	4/26-10/24
1960	4/24-10/30
1961	9/30-10/29
1962	4/29-10/28
1963	4/28-10/27
1964	4/26-10/25
1965	4/25-10/31

TABLE II

1956	4/29-9/30
1957	4/28-9/29
1958	4/27-9/28
1959	4/26-9/27
1960	4/24-9/25
1961	4/30-9/24
1962	4/29-9/30
1963	4/28-9/29
1964	4/26-9/28
1965	4/25-9/26

OBSERVATION BY LOCAL ORDINANCE:
(Refer to Table for Month & Day if not shown)

Alexandria
1965, 4/25-9/5

Annada
1962, 4/29-9/30
1963, 4/28-9/8
1964, 4/26-9/6
1965, 4/25-10/3

Ashburn
1963, 4/28-9/8 — II
1964 — II

Bourbon
1965 — I

Canton
1961-62 — I
1963, 4/28-8/31
1964, 4/26-8/29

Clarksville
1960 — I
1962 — II
1963, 4/28-9/8 — I
1964, 4/26-9/6 — I
1965, 4/25-10/3 — I

Crystal City
1956 — II

De Soto
1957-65 — I

Dixon
1958 — I
1962-65 — I

Durham
1963, 4/28-9/1 — I

East Prairie
1965 — II

Elsberry
1960 — I
1962 — II

Ethlyn
1963-64 — I

Ewing
1963, 4/28-9/1 — I
1964, 5/1-9/31 — I
1965, 5/7-9/5 — II

Festus
1956 — II
1957-65 — I

Foley
1963 — I

Foristell
1960-65 — I

Fort Leonard Wood
1956 — II
1958 — I

Gilmore
1963-65 — I

Hannibal
1960 — I
1961, 4/30-9/10 — I
(Cont.)

Hannibal (Cont.)
1962, 4/29-9/9
1963, 4/28-9/8
1964, 4/26-9/13
1965, 4/25-9/12

Hawk Point
1964, 4/26-10/31
1965 — I

Helton
1963, 4/28-9/8 — I

Hermann
1965 — I

Hunnewell
1964, 4/26-9/6 — I

Illmo
1965 — I

Kahoka
1961 — I
1962, 5/20-8/25
1963, 5/19-8/25
1964, 5/17-9/1
1965, 5/23-9/4

Kirkwood
1954 — I

La Belle
1964, 5/17-9/1
1965, 5/23-8/22

La Grange
1962, 4/29-9/9 — I
1963-65 — I

Lebanon
1956 — II

MISSOURI (cont.)

Lewistown — I
1963
1964, 5/18-9/1
1965, 5/22-8/28

Louisiana
1961, 4/30-9/9 — I
1962 — II
1963, 4/28-9/8 — II
1964 — II
1965 — I

Machens
1960 — I
1963 — I

Maplewood
1954 — I

Memphis
1963 — I
1965, 4/25-9/5 — II

Monroe City
1960 — I
1962, 4/29-9/2 — I
1964, 4/26-9/6 — I
1965, 4/25-9/5 — I

Moscow
1963-64 — II
1965, 4/30-10/31 — I

O'Fallon
1947 — I
1949-55 — I
1956 — II
1957-65 — I

Old Monroe
1956 — II
1959 — I

Orchard Farm
1959 — I
1963-65 — I

Pacific
1954 — I
1956-65 — I

Palmyra
1949-55 — I
1956 — II
1957-59 — I
1960 — I
1962, 4/29-9/9
(Cont.)

Palmyra (Cont.)
1963, 4/28-9/8
1964, 4/26-9/13
1965, 4/25-9/5

Peruque
1963-64 — I

Poplar Bluff
1958 — I

Princeton
1954-55 — I
1956 — II
1957-59 — I

Quincy
1965 — I

Reading
1963 — I
1964 — II

Richland
1956 — II

Rolla
1956 — II
1957 — I

Saint Charles
1947 — I
1949-55 — II
1956 — II
1957-65 — I

Saint Clair
1957-65 — I

Saint James
1960-65 — I

Saint Louis
1956 — II
1957 — I

Saint Louis County
1963-65 — I

Saint Peters
1947 — I
1949-55 — II
1956 — I
1957-65 — I

Saverton
1963, 4/28-9/8
1964, 4/26-9/13

South River
1963, 4/28-9/8
1964, 4/26-9/13

Troy
1963 — II
1965, 4/30-10/31 — II

Truesdail
1960-65 — I

Warrenton
1960-65 — I

Wayland
1962, 4/20-8/25 — I
1964, 5/15-9/1 — I
1965, 4/25-9/5 — I

Waynesville
1956 — II

Webster Groves
1954 — I

Wentzville
1955 — I
1956 — II
1957-65 — I

Westalton
1954 — I
1964-65 — I

Winfield
1959-65 — I

Wright City
1960-65 — I

MONTANA

1752	9/14	Gregorian (NS) Calendar adopted in U.S.A.
1809		Area settled
1883	11/18	Noon, Mountain Standard Time (105°) adopted, except towns west of 112W30, which adopted PST (120°W)
1889	11/8	State entered the Union
1895		Mountain Standard Time adopted state-wide. (Communities west of 112W30 switched from PST to MST)

DAYLIGHT (OR WAR) TIME OBSERVED:
(Changes at 2 A.M.)

1918	3/31 – 10/27	World War I
1919	3/30 – 10/26	World War I
1920	To 1941	Not observed
1942	2/9 – 9/30/45	World War II
1946	To 1965	Not observed state-wide. See Local Ordinance Listing.
1966		See Chapter VII
1967	To 1979	For dates, see Table, page 181.

TABLE

1918	War Time		1954	War Time
1919	War Time		1955	War Time
1942-45	War Time		1956	War Time
1946	5/15-9/28		1957	5/26-9/29
1947	5/12-8/31		1958	4/27-9/28
1948	5/2-9/6		1959	5/31-9/13
1949	4/24-9/5		1960	5/29-9/6
1950	5/1-9/4		1961	5/30-9/4
1951	5/6-9/3		1962	5/30-9/5
1952	4/27-9/28		1963	5/30-9/2
1953	4/26-9/7		1964	5/30-9/8
			1965	5/30-9/6

OBSERVATION BY LOCAL ORDINANCE:
(Refer to Table for Month & Day if not shown)

COUNTY	COMMUNITIES	Billings	Butte (Cont)
Silver Bow	Anaconda	1963	1954, 4/25-9/6
1946	1946		1955-56
1947, 5/31-8/31	1947, 5/31-8/31	Bozeman	1957, 4/28-9/1
1948	1948-49	1964	1958-66
1953	1950, 4/30-9/24	Butte	Deer Lodge
	1951, 4/29-9/30	1946-51	1955, 4/25-9/25
	1956-65	1952, 4/27-9/1	1956, 4/29-9/3
		1953	
		(Cont)	

Livingston	1964
Philipsburg	1952
	1953, 5/31-9/6
Warm Springs	1952

TABLE	
1918	War Time
1919	War Time
1942-45	War Time
1956	4/29-9/29

NEBRASKA

1752	9/14
1850	
1883	11/18

Gregorian (NS) Calendar adopted in U.S.A.

Area settled

Noon, two standards of time adopted, with time change at North Platte, which observes CST.

Eastern portion adopted Central Standard Time (90°W), including the boundary-line communities of:

Albion	Elm Creek	O'Neill
Alma	Endicott	Ord
Amherst	Fairbury	Orleans
Ashland	Fremont	Osceola
Beatrice	Fullerton	Overton
Bloomfield	Genoa	Plainview
Blue Springs Jct.	Gibbon	Pleasanton
Boelus	Gothenburg	Polk
Brady	Grand Island	Poole
Burwell	Hastings	Princeton
Cedar Rapids	Hayland	Raymond
Central City	Humphrey	St. Edward
Chapman	Kearney	St. Paul
Clarks	Lane	Schuyler
Columbus	Lexington	Scribner
Cortland	Long Pine	Seward
Cozad	Loup City	Shelton
Crofton	Madison	Silver Creek
Curtis	Maxwell	Spalding
Dannebrog	McCook	Stromsburg
David City	Norfolk	Superior
Eddyville	North Bend	Valley
Edgar	North Loup	Valparaiso
Elba	Oakdale	Wahoo
	Oconee	York

Western portion adopted Mountain Standard Time (105°W), including the boundary-line communities of:

NEBRASKA (cont.)

Ainsworth	Gering	Northport
Alliance	Haig	O'Fallons
Bailey	Hershey	Ogallala
Benkelman	Imperial	Oshkosh
Big Springs	Keystone	Paxton
Broadwater	Kimball	Pine Ridge
Brule	Lemoyne	Poole
Bushnell	Lewellen	Potter
Chappell	Lodgepole	Sarben
Crawford	Lisco	Scottsbluff
Culbertson	McGrew	Sidney
Dakota Junction	Melbeta	Sutherland
Dix		Thedford
		Valentine

1968 1/1 Relocation of Central and Mountain Time Zone Boundary. Until this date the boundary split several counties. The new arrangement conforms with county Boundary-Lines thus:

CST Counties		MST Counties	
Blaine	Lincoln	Arthur	Hooker
Brown	Logan	Chase	Keith
Hayes	McPherson	Cherry	Perkins
Hitchcock	Thomas	Dundy	
Keyapaha			

DAYLIGHT (OR WAR) TIME OBSERVED:
(Changes at 2 A.M.)

1918	3/31 - 10/27	World War I
1919	3/30 - 10/26	World War I
1920	To 1941	Not observed
1942	2/9 - 9/30/45	World War II
1946	To 1965	Not observed except in Ainsworth and Valentine. See Local Ordinance Listing.
1966		See Chapter VII
1966	To 1979	For dates, see Table, page 181.

OBSERVATION BY LOCAL ORDINANCE:
(Refer to Table for Month & Day)

Ainsworth
1955, All year
1956

Valentine
1955, All year
1956

TABLE

1918	War Time	1955	4/24-9/25
1919	War Time	1956	4/29-9/30
1942-45	War Time	1957	4/28-9/29
1948-49	Power Shortage	1958	4/27-9/28
		1959	4/26-9/27
1950	4/30-9/24	1960	4/24-9/25
1951	4/29-9/30	1961	4/30-9/24
1952	4/27-9/28	1962	4/29-10/28
1953	4/26-9/27	1963	4/28-10/27
1954	4/25-9/26	1964	4/26-10/25
		1965	4/25-10/31

OREG.   IDAHO   UTAH   ARIZ.   CALIF.   Caliente   PST   MST   114°24'

** Check with local authorities

NEVADA

1752	9/14	Gregorian (NS) Calendar adopted in U.S.A.
1850		Area settled
1864	10/31	State entered the Union
1883	11/18	Noon, Pacific Standard Time (120°W) adopted, except Caliente, which observed Mountain Standard Time (105°W)
1930	To 1960	Parts of Elko, White Pine, Clark and Lincoln Counties observed Mountain Standard Time (105°W) year round. Each locality in these Counties should be investigated as the official time (Government and Railroads) was PST (120°W).**
1961	9/24 - 1965	Eureka, Lincoln and White Pine Counties on MST (105°W) year round. Some portions of Humboldt, Elko and Clark also observed MST year round. **

DAYLIGHT (OR WAR) TIME OBSERVED:
(Changes at 2 A.M.)

1918	3/31 - 10/27	World War I
1919	3/30 - 10/26	World War I
1920	To 1941	Not observed
1942	2/9 - 9/30/45	World War II
1946	To 1947	Not observed
1948	3/14 - 1/1/49	Observed state-wide due to power shortage
1949		Not observed
1950	To 1965	Observed state-wide. Refer to Table for dates.
1966	To 1979	For dates, see Table, page 181.

NEW HAMPSHIRE

1623		Area settled
1752	9/14	Gregorian (NS) Calendar adopted in U.S.A.
1788	6/21	State entered the Union
1883	11/18	Noon, Eastern Standard Time (75°W) adopted

DAYLIGHT (OR WAR) TIME OBSERVED:
(Changes at 2 A.M.)

1918	3/31 – 10/27	World War I
1919	3/30 – 10/26	World War I
1920	To 1936	Not observed
1937	To 1941	Observed state-wide. Refer to Table for dates.
1942	2/9 – 9/30/45	World War II
1946	To 1965	Observed state-wide. Refer to Table for dates.
1966	To 1979	For dates, see Table, page 181.

TABLE

1918	War Time
1919	War Time
1937	5/11–9/26
1938	4/24–10/2
1939	4/30–9/24
1940	4/28–9/29
1941	4/27–9/28
1942–45	War Time
1946	4/28–9/29
1947	4/27–9/28
1948	4/25–9/26
1949	4/24–9/25
1950	4/30–9/24
1951	4/29–9/30
1952	4/27–9/28
1953	4/26–9/27
1954	4/25–10/27
1955	4/24–10/30
1956	4/29–10/28
1957	4/28–10/27
1958	4/27–10/26
1959	4/26–10/25
1960	4/24–10/30
1961	4/30–10/29
1962	4/29–10/28
1963	4/28–10/27
1964	4/26–10/25
1965	4/25–10/31

NEW JERSEY

1664		Area settled
1752	9/14	Gregorian (NS) Calendar adopted in U.S.A.
1787	12/18	State entered the Union
1883	11/18	Noon, Eastern Standard Time (75°W) adopted
1902	4/2	Swedesboro adopted EST (75°W)

DAYLIGHT (OR WAR) TIME OBSERVED:
(Changes at 2 A.M.)

1918	3/31 - 10/27	World War I
1919	3/30 - 10/26	World War I
1920	To 1941	No law regulating DST; much confusion. Local ordinances put into effect. For these years check the list below carefully. By 1941, most of the state was observing DST.
1942	2/9 - 9/30/45	World War II
1946	To 1966	Observed state-wide. Refer to Table for dates.
1967	To 1979	For dates, see Table, page 181.

OBSERVATION BY LOCAL ORDINANCE:
(Refer to Table for Month & Day if not shown)

Asbury Park
  1920-36
 *1937-41
 *1946-66
Atlantic City
  1921, 6/5-9/25
  1922-41
  1946-66
Atlantic Highlands
  1920-41
  1946-66
Barnegat
  1920-41
  1946-66
Bayonne
  1920-41
  1946-66

Belleville
  1920-41
  1946-66
Belmar
  1920-41
  1946-66

(1) Bernardsville
  1920-31
  1932-35
  1936-41
  1946-66
Bloomfield
  1920-41
  1946-66

Boonton
  1920-41
  1946-66
Bordentown
  1920-41
  1946-66
Bound Rock
  1920-41
  1946-66

Bradley Beach
  1920-41
  1946-66
Brewster
  1920-41
  1946-66

* Change at 0:01 A.M.
(1) Optional by Natives

TABLE

1918	War Time		1941	War Time
1919	War Time		1942-45	War Time
1920	3/28-10/31		1946	4/28-9/29
1921	4/24-9/25		1947	4/27-9/28
1922	4/30-9/24		1948	4/25-9/26
1923	4/29-9/30		1949	4/24-9/25
1924	4/27-9/28		1950	4/30-9/24
1925	4/26-9/27		1951	4/29-9/30
1926	4/25-9/26		1952	4/27-9/28
1927	4/24-9/25		1953	4/26-9/27
1928	4/29-9/30		1954	4/25-9/26
1929	4/28-9/29		1955	4/24-10/30
1930	4/27-9/28		1956	4/29-10/28
1931	4/26-9/27		1957	4/28-10/27
1932	4/24-9/25		1958	4/27-10/26
1933	4/30-9/24		1959	4/26-10/25
1934	4/29-9/30		1960	4/24-10/30
1935	4/28-9/29		1961	4/30-10/29
1936	4/26-9/27		1962	4/29-10/28
1937	4/25-9/26		1963	4/28-10/27
1938	4/24-9/25		1964	4/26-10/25
1939	4/30-9/24		1965	4/25-10/31
1940	4/28-9/29		1966	4/24-10/30

NEW JERSEY (cont.)

Bridgeton	1920-41 / 1946-66
Burlington	1920-41 / 1946-66
Butler	1920-41 / 1946-66
Caldwell	1920-41 / 1946-66
Camden	1921-41
Cape May	1920-41 / 1946-66
Carlstadt	1921-41 / 1946-66
Cateret	1920-41 / 1946-66
Chatham	1920-41 / 1946-66
Clifton	1922-66
Collingswood	1920-41 / 1946-66
Cranbury	1920-41 / 1946-66
Cranford	1920-41 / 1946-66
Dover	1920-41 / 1946-66
East Orange	1920-41 / 1946-66

Egg Harbor City	1921, 6/5-9/25 / 1922, 6/4-9/24 / 1923, 6/3-9/30 / 1924, 6/1-9/28 / 1925-31 / 1932, 6/26-9/25 / 1933-41 / 1946-66
Elizabeth	1920-41 / 1946-66
Elmer	1920-41 / 1946-66
Englewood	1920, 4/18-10/31 / 1921-41 / 1946-66
Fair Haven	1920-41 / 1946-66
Flemington	1920-41 / 1946-66
Fort Lee	1920-41 / 1946-66
Freehold	1920-41 / 1946-66
Garfield	1920-41 / 1946-66
Glassboro	1920-41 / 1946-66
Glen Ridge	1921-41 / 1946-66
Gloucester	1920-41 / 1946-66

Hackensack	1920-41 / 1946-66
Hackettstown	1920-41 / 1946-66
Haddonfield	1921-41 / 1946-66
Hammonton	1921-41 / 1946-66
Harrison	1920-41 / 1946-66
Hasbrouck Heights	1920-41 / 1946-66
Hawthorne	1920-41 / 1946-66
Highlands	1920-41 / 1946-66
Hightstown	1920-41 / 1946-66
Hoboken	1920-41 / 1946-66
Irvington	1921-41 / 1946-66
Jersey City	1920-41 / 1946-66
Kearney	1921-41 / 1946-66
Keyport	1921-41 / 1946-66

Lakehurst	1920-41 / 1946-66
Lakewood	1920-41 / 1946-66
Lambertville	1920-41 / 1946-66
Lodi	1920-41 / 1946-66
Long Branch	1920-41 / 1946-66
Lyndhurst	1920-41 / 1946-66
Madison	1920-41 / 1946-66
Manasquan	1920-41 / 1946-66
Milltown	1921-41 / 1946-66
Millville	1921-41 / 1946-66
Monmouth Beach	1921-41 / 1946-66
Montclair	1920-41 / 1946-66
Mount Holly	1920-41 / 1946-66
Netcong	1920-41 / 1946-66

Newark	1920-41 / 1946-66
New Brunswick	1920-41 / 1946-66
North Bergen	1920-41 / 1946-66
Nutley	1930-41 / 1946-66
Ocean City	1920-41 / 1946-66
Ocean Grove	1920-41 / 1946-66
Orange	1920-41 / 1946-66
Park Ridge	1920-41 / 1946-66
Passaic	1920-41 / 1946-66
Paterson	1928-41 / 1946-66
Penns Grove	1920-41 / 1946-66
Perth Amboy	1920-41 / 1946-66
Pitman	1921-41 / 1946-66
Plainfield	1921-41 / 1946-66

Pleasantville	1921-41 / 1946-66
Point Pleasant	1921-41 / 1946-66
Princeton	1921-41 / 1946-66
Rahway	1921-41 / 1946-66
Raritan	1921-41 / 1946-66
Red Bank	1921-41 / 1946-66
Ridgewood	1921-41 / 1946-66
Riverton	1921-41 / 1946-66
Roosevelt	1921-41 / 1946-66
Roselle	1920-41 / 1946-66
Rumson	1920-41 / 1946-66
Rutherford	1921-41 / 1946-66
Sea Bright	1921-41 / 1946-66
Sea Isle City	1921-41 / 1946-66

NEW JERSEY (cont.)

Seacaucus
1921-41
1946-66

Somerville
1922-41
1946-66

South Amboy
1921-41
1946-66

South Orange
1920-41
1946-66

Spring Lake
1920-41
1946-66

Summit
1920-41
1946-66

Sussex
1920-41
1946-66

Swedesboro
1922, 6/10-9/24
1923, 6/3-9/30
1924, 6/1-9/28
1925, 6/7-9/27
1926, 6/6-9/26
1927, 6/5-9/25
1928, 6/3-9/30
1929, 6/2-9/29
1930, 6/1-9/28
1931, 6/6-9/26
1932, 6/3-9/25
1933, 6/4-9/24
1934, 6/5-9/30
1935, 6/6-9/29
1936-41
1946-66

Tenafly
1920-41
1946-66

Toms River
1920-41
1946-66

Trenton
1920-41
1946-66

Tuckerton
1921-41
1946-66

Union
1920-41
1946-66

Vineland
1920-41
1946-66

Weehawken
1920-41
1946-66

Westfield
1920-41
1946-66

West New York
1920-41
1946-66

West Orange
1920-41
1946-66

Wildwood
* 1920-41
* 1946-66

Williamstown
1920-41
1946-66

Woodbury
1920-41
1946-66

Wrightstown
1920-41
1946-66

*Change at 0:01 A.M.

TABLE

1918	War Time
1919	War Time
1942-45	War Time
1953	4/26-9/27
1954	4/25-9/26
1955	4/24-9/25
1956	4/29-9/30
1957	4/28-9/29
1958	4/27-9/28
1959	4/26-9/27
1960	4/24-9/25
1961	4/30-9/24
1962	4/29-9/30
1963	4/28-9/29
1964	4/26-9/27
1965	4/25-9/26

UTAH COLO. OCLA. CST MST TEX. ARIZ. MEXICO Los Alamos 106°W19'

NEW MEXICO

1537		Area settled
1752	9/14	Gregorian (NS) Calendar adopted in U.S.A.
1883	11/18	Noon, Mountain Standard Time (105°W) adopted
1912	1/6	State entered the Union

DAYLIGHT (OR WAR) TIME OBSERVED:
(Changes at 2 A.M.)

1918	3/31 - 10/27	World War I
1919	3/30 - 10/26	World War I
1920	To 1941	Not observed
1942	2/9 - 9/30/45	World War II
1946	To 1952	Not observed
1953	To 1965	Not observed state-wide. See Local Ordinance Listing.
1966		See Chapter VII
1967	To 1979	For dates, see Table, page 181.

OBSERVATION BY LOCAL ORDINANCE:
(Refer to Table for Month & Day if not shown)

COUNTY

Los Alamos
1953-65

COMMUNITIES

Santa Fe
1955, 4/24-5/8

TABLE

Year	Dates		Year	Dates
1918	War Time		1918	War Time
1919	War Time		1919	War Time
1921	4/24-9/25		1941	War Time
1922	4/30-9/24		1942-45	War Time
1923	4/29-9/30		1946	4/28-9/29
1924	4/27-9/28		1947	4/27-9/28
1925	4/26-9/27		1948	4/25-9/26
1926	4/25-9/26		1949	4/24-9/25
1927	4/24-9/25		1950	4/30-9/24
1928	4/29-9/30		1951	4/29-9/30
1929	4/28-9/29		1952	4/27-9/28
1930	4/27-9/28		1953	4/26-9/27
1931	4/26-9/27		1954	4/25-9/26
1932	4/24-9/25		1955	4/24-10/30
1933	4/30-9/24		1956	4/29-10/28
1934	4/29-9/30		1957	4/28-10/27
1935	4/28-9/29		1958	4/27-10/26
1936	4/26-9/27		1959	4/26-10/25
1937	4/25-9/26		1960	4/24-10/30
1938	4/24-9/25		1961	4/30-10/29
1939	4/30-9/24		1962	4/29-10/28
1940	4/28-9/29		1963	4/28-10/27
			1964	4/26-10/25
			1965	4/25-10/31

NEW YORK

1614		Area settled
1752	9/14	Gregorian (NS) Calendar adopted in U.S.A.
1788	7/26	State entered the Union
1883	11/18	Noon, Eastern Standard Time (75°W) adopted.

DAYLIGHT (OR WAR) TIME OBSERVED:
(Time changes at 2 A.M., unless otherwise indicated by asterisk)

1918	3/31 - 10/27	World War I
1919	3/30 - 10/26	World War I
1920	3/28 - 10/31	Observed state-wide
1921	To 1941	Not observed state-wide. See Local Ordinance Listing.
1942	2/9 - 9/30/45	World War II
1946	To 1954	Not observed state-wide. See Local Ordinance Listing.
1955	To 1965	Observed state-wide. Refer to Table for dates.
1966	To 1979	For dates, see Table, page 181.

OBSERVATION BY LOCAL ORDINANCE:
(Refer to Table for Month & Day if not shown)

Accord
1938-39
Adams
1940, 6/2-9/2
1948
Addison
1946
1951-54

Adrian
1951-54
Afton
1941, 6/20-9/1
1946-54
Akron
1939, 6/4-9/10
1940

Albany
1921-41
·1946-54
Albertson
1946-54
Albion
1939, 5/6-9/30
1940-41
1946, 4/28-9/20
1947-52

Alden
1921-41
1946
Alexander
1941
Alexandria Bay
1948-54
Alfred
1946

Allegany
1951-54
Almond
1938-41
1951-54
Alsen
1948

Altamont
1946-54
Altona
1947
1949-54
Amenia
1938-39
1946
1948
1951-53

NEW YORK (cont.)

Amhurst 1939
Amityville 1923-41, 1946-54
Amsterdam 1923-41, 1946-54
Andover 1941, 1951-54
Angola 1938-39, 1946-48, 1953-54
Apalachin 1947-50
Apulia 1947-54
Aquebogue 1946-54
Arcade 1940, 6/23-9/2; 1941; 1953-54
Arden 1946-54
Ardsley 1938-39, 1947-54
Ardsley-on-Hudson 1947-54
Arkport 1951-54
Arkville 1953
Ashokan 1938-39, 1946
Ashville 1951-54
Athens 1938-39
Athol Springs 1938-39, 1947-48
Atlanta 1947-54
Attica 1939; 1940, 4/28-9/2; 1941; 1951-54
Auburn 1939-41, 1946-54
Auburndale 1951-54
Auriesville 1953-54
Ausable Forks 1946
Avoca 1947-54
Avon 1951-54
B. & O. Junction 1947
Babylon 1921-41, 1951-54
Bainbridge 1940, 6/2-9/1; 1941, 6/20-9/1; 1946-54
Baldwin 1938-39, 1947-54
Baldwin Place 1948
Baldwinsville 1939-41, 1947-48
Ballston Spa 1928-41, 1946-54
Bangor 1947-48
Bangor Station 1950
Barker 1953-54
Barneveld 1951
Barrytown 1951
Barryville 1951-54
Barton 1951-54
Batavia 1939-41, 1946-54
Bath 1940-41, 1946-54
Bayport 1946-54
Bayshore 1921-41, 1951-54
Bayside 1946-54
Bayville 1925-41
Beacon 1925-41, 1947-54
Bedford 1925-41
Bedford Hills 1947-54
Belfast 1951-54
Bellaire 1946-54
Bellerose 1946-54
Bellmore 1925-41, 1951-54
Bellona 1947
Bellport 1925-41
Belmont 1941, 1951-54
Belmont Park 1946-54
Belvidere 1951-54
Benton 1953-54
Bergen 1941, 1947-48
Berlin 1950-52
Bethpage 1950-54
Big Flats 1947
Big Indian 1949
Big Moose 1938, 1949
Binghamton 1930, 6/15-8/30; 1939, 5/7-9/24; 1940, 5/5-9/29; 1941; 1946-54
Black Creek 1951-54
Black Rock 1946-54
Blauvelt 1947
Blodgett Mills 1947-50
Bloomingburg 1938-39
Blooming Grove 1951-54
Bloomville 1951
Bluepoint 1931-41, 1946-54
Bolivar 1940-41
Bolton 1931-41
Bomansville 1946-54
Boonville 1948
Brainard 1947
Brentwood 1946-50; 1951, 4/29-9/23; 1952-54
Brewster 1938-39, 1947-51, 1954
Briarcliff Manor 1921-41, 1949, 1951
Brico 1941
Brighton 1947
Brisben 1947-48, 1951-54
Broadway 1946-54
Brockport 1939-41, 1946-54
Brocton 1941, 1946-54
Bronxville 1925-41, 1948-49, 1952-54
Brooklyn 1921-41, 1946-54
Brushton 1931-41; 1941, 6/20-9/8; 1947; 1949-50; 1953-54
Bryn Mawr Park 1947-48
Buffalo 1921-41, 1946-50
Burke 1948-49, 1951-54

NEW YORK (cont.)

Burns	1951–54
Burnside	1938–39
Burt	1938–39
Buskirk	1938–39; 1946–54
Cadosia	1951–54
Cadyville	1939–41; 1946–54
Cairo	1928–41
Caledonia	1946–54
Callicoon	1951–54
Calverton	1946–54
Cambridge	1938–39; 1946–54
Camden	1948; 1951–54
Cameron	1951–54
Cameron Mills	1951–54
Camillus	1938–39
Campbell	1947; 1951–54
Campbell Hall	1938–39; 1948; 1951–54
Canaan	1951
Canajoharie	1921–41; 1947; 1951; 1953–54
Canandaigua	1940–41; 1946–54
Canaseraga	1951–54
Canastota	1939–41; 1950–54
Candor	1941, 5/4–9/28; 1947–50
Canisteo	1940–41; 1951–54
Canton	1940, 6/2–9/1; 1941, 6/1–8/31; 1947–54
Cape Vincent	1948
Carlton	1941
Carle Place	1946–54
Carmel	1948
Carrollton	1951–54
Carthage	1940, 5/12–9/3; 1941; 1948–54
Castleton	1947–48
Castle-on-Hudson	1938–39; 1951
Catskill	1921–41; 1946–54
Cattaraugus	1951–54
Cedarhurst	1925–41; 1946–54
Cemetery	1948–54
Center Avenue	1946–54
Centereach	1946–54
Center Moriches	1921–41; 1946–54
Center Port	1921–41
Central Bridge	1948–54
Central Islip	1946–54
Central Square	1947
Ceres	1953–54
Chadwicks	1947–50
Chaffee	1953–54
Champlain	1941, 6/20–9/8; 1947; 1950–54
Chappaqua	1921–41; 1947–54
Charlotte	1947–49
Chateaugay	1947–54
Chatham	1930–41; 1946–54
Chauncey	1951
Chautauqua	1938, 6/16–9/5; 1939–40; 1947
Chazy	1925–41; 1946–54
Chelsea	1951
Chemung	1951–54
Chenango Bridge	1947–54
Chenango Forks	1947–54
Cherry Creek	1941; 1951–54
Cherry Valley	1947–54
Chester	1946–54
Chestertown	1927–29, 6/1–10/1; 1930–41
Childwold	1949
Chotranghy	1941, 6/20–9/8
Churchville	1941, 6/1–9/26; 1946–48; 1950–51
Churubusco	1946–54
Claremont	1941, 5/1–9/30
Clarence	1938–39
Clark Mills	1938–39
Claverack	1938–39; 1951–54
Clayton	1940, 6/23–9/3; 1941, 6/22–8/31
Clayville	1947–50
Clifton Mills	1951–54
Clifton Springs	1940–41; 1946–54
Clinton	1938–39
Clyde	1941; 1948
Clymer	1953–54
Cobleskill	1940–41; 1946–54
Cochecton	1951–54
Coeymans	1921–41
Cohocton	1946–47; 1949–54
Cohoes	1921–41; 1946–54
Cold Spring	1947; 1954
Cold Spring Harbor	1921–41; 1946–54
Coldwater	1946–48; 1950–52
Colemans	1948
Colliers	1950–54
Collins	1951–54
Colonie	1946–54
Commack	1938–39
Comstock	1946–54
Conesus	1951–54
Conewaugo	1951–54
Congers	1925–41
Cooper Plains	1951–54
Cooperstown	1940–41; 1946–54
Copake	1938–39
Copiague	1946–54
Coran	1946–54
Corfu	1946–47; 1949–54
Corinth	1940, 4/28–9/2; 1941, 4/27–9/7; 1925–41; 1946–54
Corning	1939–41; 1946–54

NEW YORK (cont.)

Cornwall
1925-31
* 1932, 4/30-10/1
* 1933, 4/29-9/30
*1934-41
Cortland
1939-41
1946-54
Cortland Junction
1947
Cottekill
1938-39
Country Life Press
1946-54
Coventry
1947-48
Coxsackie
1950-54
Craryville
1951
Crestwood
1948
1950
1953-54
Croton Falls
1947-48
1951
1953-54
Croton Lake
1951
Croton-on-Hudson
1925-31
1932, 4/3-9/25
1933, 4/2-9/24
1934, 4/1-9/30
1935, 4/7-9/29
1936-41
1948
Crown Point
1946-54

Crystal Run
1938-39
Cuba
1951-54
Cutchogue
1946-54
Dale
1951-54
Dalton
1951-54
Dannemora
1938-41
Dansville
1946-54
Davenport Center
1948
1951
Dayton
1938-39
1951-54
Deer Park
1950-51
1953
Delanson
1940-41
1947-48
Delevan
1941
1953-54
Delmar
1938-41
1946-54
Depew
1925-41
1946-54
Deposit
1941, 6/1-8/31
1946, 6/2-9/1
1951-54
Derby
1938-39
1946-48
1953-54

Dewitt
1951-54
Dobbs Ferry
1925-41
1947-49
1952-54
Dolgeville
1923, 5/6-9/30
1924, 5/4-9/28
1925, 5/3-9/27
1926, 5/2-9/26
1927, 5/8-9/25
1928, 5/6-9/30
1929, 5/5-9/29
Douglaston
1940
1946-54
Dover Plains
1938-39
Dresden
1946
1947-53
Dundee
1940, 5/19-9/22
1941
Dunkirk
1940-41
1946-54
Eagle Bridge
1938-39
1946-54
Eagle Harbor
1946-48
1953-54
Earlville
1947-50
East Aurora
1930, 6/15-8/30
1939, 5/7-9/24
1940, 5/5-9/29
1941
1946-48
1953-54

East Bethany
1947
East Clarence
1938-39
East Greenbush
1938-39
East Hampton
1921-41
1946-54
East Meredith
1923-41
1948
East New York
1951-52
East Northport
1946-54
Easton Station
1938-39
East Rochester
1939
1947-48
East Rockaway
1946-54
East Salamanca
1946-54
East Syracuse
1939
East Williston
1946-54
East Worcester
1946-48
1950-54
Eden
1951-54
Elba
1941, 6/1-9/7
Elizabethtown
1938-39
Ellenburg
1940-41
1949-54
Ellenville
1923-41
1948

Ellicottville
1939, 6/4-9/4
Elmhurst
1946-54
Elmira
1953-54
Elmsford
1940-41
1946-54
Elnora
1923-41
Elsmer
1947
Endicott
1951-52
Erwin
1946-54
Esopus
1938-39
1946
Essex
1946-54
Evans Mills
1940
1951-54
Fair Oaks
1938-39
Fairport
1921-41
1946-54
1947-48
1950-52
Fairville
1953-54
Falconer
1940-41
1951-54
Fallsburgh
1948
Fancher
1946-48
1950-52

Farmingdale
1938-39
1946-54
Farnham
1953-54
Far Rockaway
1921-41
1946-54
Fayetteville
1939
Ferndale
1938-39
1948
Firthcliffe
1938-39
Flatbush
1946-54
Fleetwood
1951
Fleischmanns
1938-39
1953
Floral Park
1923-41
1946-54
Florida
1951-54
Flushing
1921-41
1946-54
Fly Summit
1946-54
Fonda
1923, 5/6-9/30
1924, 5/4-9/28
1925, 5/3-9/27
1926, 5/2-9/26
1927, 5/8-9/25
1928, 5/6-9/30
1929, 5/5-9/29
1950-54

* Change at 0:01A.M.

NEW YORK (cont.)

Forest 1951-54
Forest Hills 1923-41, 1946-54
Forks 1951-54
Fort Ann 1946-54
Fort Edward 1921-41, 1946-54
Fort Erie 1948, 1950-51
Fort Plain 1925-41, 1947, 1949-54
Fort Solanga 1938-39
Fort Ticonderoga 1946-54
Frankfort 1930-41, 1948
Franklin Springs 1938-39
Franklinville 1941, 1953-54
Fredonia 1940, 1946-48
Freeport 1921-31, 1932, 4/24-10/30, 1933-41, 1946-54
Fresh Pond 1946-54

Friendship 1941, 1951-54
Fulton 1923-41, 1946-54
Gabriels 1947, 1948, 5/17-9/26, 1949
Gage 1953-54
Galena 1947-48
Gallatinville 1941
Garden City *1921-41
Gardiner 1938-39
Gardenville 1953-54
Garrison 1925-41, 1947-54
Gasport 1938, 1939, 1946-50, 1954
Geneva 1939-41, 1946-54
Genesco 1940-41
Germantown 1951
Ghent 1938-41, 1951-54
Gibson 1946-54

Glendale 1946-54
Glen Cove 1923-41, 1946-54
Glen Head 1946-54
Glen Station 1938-39, 1946-54
Glens Falls 1923-41, 1946-54
Gloversville 1921-41, 1951, 1953-54
Goldens Bridge 1947, 1951
Golf Summit 1951-54
Goshen 1925-41, 1946-54
Gouverneur 1941, 5/5-9/11, 1948-54
Gowanda 1938-41, 1951-54
Grand Gorge 1947-50, 1953
Grand Hotel Station 1946, 1949-50, 1953
Granville 1938-41, 1946-54

Great Neck 1925-41, 1946-54
Great River 1946-54
Greenburgh 1939
Greendale 1938-39, 1946
Greene 1941, 1947-54
Green Island 1925-31, 1932-41, 4/2-9/24, 1946-47
Greenlawn 1938-39, 1946-54
Greenport 1921-41, 1946-54
Greenvale 1925-41, 1946-54
Greenwich 1921-41, 1946-54
Greigsville 1947
Greycourt 1951-54
Groton 1951
Groveland 1947
Grumman 1946-54
Haberman 1946-54

Hadley 1938-39, 1946, 1948-54
Haines Falls 1921-41
Hale Eddy 1951-54
Hall 1948, 1953-54
Hamburg 1921-41, 1951-54
Hamilton 1939, 6/25-9/3, 1940-41, 1948
Hammond 1952-54
Hammondsport 1940, 5/12-10/20, 1941, 4/26-9/1
Hampton Bays 1946-51
Hamptonburgh 1938-39
Hancock 1946-54
Hankins 1951-54
Harmon-on-Hudson 1946-54

Harpursville 1948-54
Harrison 1925-41
Hartsdale 1925-41, 1948-54
Hastings-on-Hudson 1923-41, 1947, 1950, 1952-54
Hauppauge 1946-54
Haverstraw 1923-41, 1948, 1953-54
Hawthorne 1923-41, 1947-48, 1951
Hempstead 1923-41, 1946-54
Hempstead Gardens 1946-54
Herkimer 1923, 5/6-9/30, 1924, 5/4-9/28, 1925, 5/3-9/27, 1926, 5/2-9/26, 1927, 5/8-9/25, 1928, 5/6-9/30, 1929, 5/5-9/29, 1946, 1948-54
Hewlett 1921-41, 1946-54

Hicksville
1946-54
High Falls
1948
Highland
1921-41
1946
1951
Highland Falls
1921-41
1951
Hillsdale
1939-41
1946-54
Hillside
1946-54
Hilton
1939
Himrod
1953-54
Hinsdale
1951-54
Hobart
1941
Holbrook
1946-54
Holland
1953-54
Holland Patent
1951
Holley
1946-48
1950-51
Hollis
1923-41
1951-54
Holtsville
1946-54
Homer
1939-40
1947-54

Hoosick
1938-39
1946-54
Hoosick Falls
1931-41
1946-54
Hornell
1940-41
1946
1951-54
Horseheads
1947-48
1951-54
Howells
1946-54
Howes Cave
1940-41
1946-54
Hubbardsville
1947-48
1951-54
Hudson
1921-41
1946-54
Hudson Falls
1921-41
1946-54
Hunt
1951-54
Hunter
1938-39
Hunterspoint
1946-54
Huntington
1923-41
1946-54
Hurley
1938-39
Hyde Park
1938-41
1947-54

Ilion
1921
1922, 4/23-9/24
1923, 4/29-9/2
1924, 5/30-9/1
1925, 5/30-9/5
1926, 5/30-9/6
*1927, 5/8-9/25
*1928-31
*1932, 5/2-9/27
1933-41
1948
1953-54
Interlaken
1941
1951
Inwood
1946-54
Iona Island
1947
Irona
1947-54
Irondequoit
1940
1941, 4/27-10/4
Irving
1953-54
Irvington
1921-41
1947-48
1951
Ischua
1953-54
Island Park
1939
1946-54
Islip
1923-41
1946-54
Itaska
1951-54

Ithaca
1921, 5/8-9/11
1922, 5/14-9/10
1923, 5/13-9/9
1924, 5/11-9/14
1940-41
1946-54
Jamaica
1921-41
1946-54
Jamesport
1946-54
Jamestown
1932, 6/25-9/25
1938, 6/5-9/4
1939, 6/4-9/3
1940-41
1946-47
1951-54
Jamesville
1947-50
Jamison Road
1953-54
Jericho
1925-41
Johnson City
1940, 5/5-9/29
1941, 5/4-9/28
1947-54
Johnsonville
1938-39
1946-54
Johnstown
1921-41
1951-54
Jonesville
1946-54
Kanona
1951-54
Katonah
1921-41
1947-54

Keeseville
1951-54
Kendall
1947-48
Kenmore.
(1) 1921-41
Kennedy
1951-54
Kerhonkson
1938-39
1948
Kew Gardens
1946-54
Killawog
1947-54
Kill Buck
1951-54
Kinderhook
1938-39
Kings Park
1946-54
Kingston
1946-54
Kirkwood
1951-54
Kitchawan
1951
Knapps
1947-48
Knowlesville
1946-47
Kyserike
1938-39
Lackawanna
1939-41
1951-54
Lafayette
1951-54
Lake Clear
1949
Lake Clear Junction
1948

Lake George
1921-41
1946-54
Lake Katrine
1946-47
Lake Mahopac
1921-41
1947-54
Lake Placid
1921-41
1946-54
Lake View
1938-39
1946-54
Lakeville
1951-54
Lakewood
1951-54
Lamson
1947-48
Lancaster
1925-41
1946-54
Landis
1946-54
Langdon
1951-54
Larchmont
1921-41
La Salle
1946-48
Laurel
1946-54
Laurelton
1946-54
Lawrence
1921-41
1946-54

* Change at 0:01 A.M.
(1) Termination date only, change at 0:01 A.M.

NEW YORK (cont.)

Lawtons
1951-54
Lebanon Springs
1951-54
Lees
1946-54
Le Roy
1931-41
1947-48
1951-54
Liberty
1921, 5/22-9/25
1922, 5/21-9/30
1923, 5/6-9/30
1925, 5/17-9/13
1926, 5/16-9/12
1927, 5/15-9/10
1928-41
Lime Lake
1953-54
Limestone
1951-54
Lincolndale
1947
1951
Linden
1951-54
Lindenhurst
1929-41
1946-54
Lindley
1951-54
Lisbon
1947-54
Lisle
1947-54
Little Falls
1925-41
1946
1949-54
Little Neck
1946-54

Little Rock
1951-54
Little Valley
1951-54
Livingston
1941
Livingston Manor
1941
1948
Livonia
1951-54
Lloyd Harbor
1938-39
Lockport
1927, 6/1-8/31
1929, 5/23-9/3
1930, 5/25-9/2
1931-41
1946-54
Locust Manor
1946-54
Locust Valley
1925-41
1946-54
Long Beach
1921-41
1946-54
Long Eddy
1951-54
Long Island City
1921-41
1946-54
Long Lake
1948-49
Loon Lake
1949
Lordville
1951-54
Lowville
1940, 5/26-9/29
1941
1948-54

Luzerne
1938-39
Lynbrook
1925-41
1946-54
Lyon Mountain
1938-39
1941
1948
**1949, 5/(?)-10/1
1950-54
Lyons
1940-41
1947-54
Lyons Falls
1950-54
Machias
1953-54
Madrid
1947
Mahopac
1949
1951-54
Malden
1951
Malden-on-Hudson
1946-48
Malone
1925-38
1939, 6/18-9/3
1940, 6/16-9/1
1941, 6/15-9/7
1947-54
Malverne
1933, 4/30-10/1
1934-41
1946-54
Mamakating
1939
Mamaroneck
1921-41
Manchester
1946
1950-54

Manhasset
1923-41
1946-54
Manorville
1946-54
Marathon
1946-54
Marcy
1938-39
1946-48
Markham
1951
Massapequa
1923-41
1946-54
Massapequa Park
1946-54
Massena
1940, 6/2-9/1
1941
1948-54
Mastic-Shirley
1946-54
Mattituck
1946-54
Mattydale
1939
Mayville
1941
1953-54
Meadowbrook
1951-54
Mechanicville
1925-41
1946-54
Medford
1946-54
Medina
1931-41
1946-51

Mellenville
1938-39
Melrose
1938-39
Menands
1946-54
Merillon
1946-54
Merrick
1921-41
1946-54
Messengerville
1947-54
Middle Granville
1946-54
Middle Island
1946-54
Middleport
1946-54
Middletown
1946-51
Middleville
1938-39
Milford
1946-47
Millbrook
1921-41
1948
Millerton
1938-39
Mill Neck
1951-54
Millport
1946-54
Millwood
1948
1951
Milo
1953-54

Mineola
1931-41
1946-54
Minetto
1947-48
Mohawk
1923, 5/6-9/30
1924, 5/4-9/28
1925, 5/3-9/27
1926, 5/2-9/26
1927, 5/8-9/25
1928, 5/6-9/30
1929, 5/5-9/29
1930-41
1948
Moira
1947
1950-54
Mongaup
1951-54
Monroe
1921-41
1946-54
Montgomery
1951-54
Monticello
1927, 5/15-9/12
1932
1933, 5/7-9/24
1934, 4/22-9/23
1935-41
Montour Falls
1947-48
1951-54
Montrose
1925-41
1947
Montvale
1946-54

**Check with local
authorities

NEW YORK (cont.)

Mooers
1941, 5/1-9/1
1948-50
Mooers Forks
1951-54
Morrisville
1948
Morton
1947-48
Mountain Dale
1950-51
Mountain View
1949
Mount Ivy
1946-54
Mount Lebanon
1938-39
Mount Kisco
1923-41
1947-54
Mount Morris
1940
1946-54
Mount Vernon
1923-41
1946
1948
1952-54
Murray Hill
1946-54
Nanuet
1946-54
Napanoch
1938-39
1948
Narrowsburg
1951-54
Nassau
1946-54
Newark
1940-41
1946-54

Newburgh
1921-41
1947-54
Newburgh Junction
1946-54
New Castle
1939
New Hamburg
1947-48
New Hartford
1938-39
1946-50
New Hyde Park
1946-50
New Lebanon
1938-39
1946-50
New Paltz
1938-39
New Rochelle
1921-41
Newton Hook
1938-39
New York City
& Suburbs
1921-41
1946-54
New York Mills
1946-54
Niagara Falls
1941
1921, 3/24-9/25
1923
1926, 5/30-9/26
1929, 6/9-9/1
1930, 6/8-9/7
1931, 6/14-9/4
1932, 5/14-9/5
1933, 5/21-9/24
1934-41
1946-54

Nichols
1947-50
Niobe
1951-54
Niverville
1938-39
North Brookfield
1947-54
North Clymer
1953-54
North Collins
1951-54
North Creek
1946-54
North Evans
1953-54
North Hempstead
1921-41
North Judson
1948
North Lawrence
1947-54
North Macedon
1950-52
North Norwich
1951-54
North Petersburg
1951-54
Northport
1925-41
1946-54
North Rose
1947-48
North Stephentown
1951-54
North Stockholm
1951-54
North Tarrytown
1925-41
North Tonawanda
1921-41
1946-54

Northville
1925-41
Norwich
1939
1940, 5/11-9/14
1941
1946-54
Norwood
1941
1947-54
Nostrand
1946-54
Nyack
1941
Oakdale
1946-54
Oakfield
1940
Oaks Corners
1947-52
Oceanside
1946-54
Ogdensburg
1925
1939, 5/28-9/3
1940, 5/26-9/1
1941
1946-54
Old Chatham
1948
1950
Old Forge
1950
Olean
1940-41
1946-48
1951-54
Oneida
1925
1939-41
1946-54
Oneida Castle
1939

Oneonta
1940-41
1946-54
Ontario
1947-48
Orangeburg
1946-54
Orchard Park
1938-39
1946-54
Oriskany
1921-26
1927, 6/5-8/28
1928-41
Orleans
1953-54
Oscawanna
1948
Ossining
1921-41
1946
1952-54
Ostego
1940, 6/2-9/1
1941, 5/18-9/7
Oswego
1925-41
1927, 6/12-9/11
1928-41
1946-54
Otego
1946-54
Otisville
1946-54
Otter Lake
1949
Owego
1921-40
1941, 5/4-9/28
1946-54
Owls Head
1948-49
Oxford
1941
1948-54

Oyster Bay
1925-41
1946-54
Painted Post
1941
Palatine Bridge
1938-39
1946-54
Palmyra
1940-41
1947-54
Paris
1947-48
1951-54
Park Ridge
1946-54
Parksville
1938-39
Patchogue
1921-41
1946-54
Paul Smith's
1949
Pawling
1925-41
1947-49
1952-54
Pearl River
1946-54
Peconi
1946-54
Peekskill
1921-41
1948-54
Pelham
1921-41
1941, 5/4-9/28
1946-54
Pelham Manor
1921-41
Penn Yan
1940-41
1946-54

NEW YORK (cont.)

Penny Bridge
1946-54
Perry
1940, 5/5-9/1
1941
Persia
1925-41
1951-54
Peru
1946
Petersburg
1931-41
1946-54
Petersburg Junction
1938-39
1947-48
Philadelphia
1948
Philipse Manor
1947-48
Phillipsport
1938-39
Philmont
1921-41
1951
Phoenicia
1938-39
1949
Phoenix
1951-54
Piermont
1925-41
Pine-Aire
1946-54
Pinebush
1951-54
Pine Hill
1938-39
Pinelawn
1946-54
Pine Valley
1951-54

Pitcher Hall
1939
Pittsford
1947-52
Plandome
1925-41
1946-54
Plattsburg
1931-41
1946-54
Pleasantville
1925-41
1947-54
Point O'Woods
1923-41
Poland
1951-64
Pomona
1946-54
Poolville
1947-48
1951-54
Portageville
1951-54
Port Chester
1921-41
Port Ewen
1946
1950
Port Henry
1921-41
1946-54
Port Jefferson
1921-41
1946-54
Port Jervis
1921-41
1946-54
Port Kent
1946-54
Port Washington
1921-41
1946-54

Potsdam
1940, 6/16-9/1
1941
1947-54
Poughkeepsie
1921-41
1946-54
Preble
1951-54
Presho
1951-54
Protection
1925-41
1953-54
Pulaski
1940
1948
Pulvers
1938-39
Purchase
1925-41
Purdys
1947-48
1951-54
Putnam
1948
Queens Village
1921-41
1946-54
Quogue
1951
Ramapo
1946-54
Randolph
1921-41
1951-54
Rathbone
1946-54
Ravena
1925-41
1953-54
Red Creek
1947-48

Red Hook
1941
Red House
1951-54
Redwood
1948
1950-54
Remsen
1946-47
1949
Rensselaer
1930, 4/6-9/28
1931-41
Republic
1946-54
Rexford
1946-50
Reynolds
1946-54
Rhinebeck
1925-41
1947-48
1953-54
Rhinecliff
1941
1946-54
Richburg
1941
1946-54
Richfield
1951-54
Richfield Junction
1947-48
Richmond Hill
1921-41
1946-54
Richmondville
1947-54
Ridge
1946-54
Ridgefield Park
1951

Ripley
1941
1947
Riverhead
1921-41
Riverside
1938-39
1946-54
Riverside Junction
1953-54
Rochester
1926, 5/30-9/12
1927, 5/29-9/11
1930, 5/18-9/28
1939-41
1946-50
1951, 4/29-9/23
1952-54
Rock Glen
1951-54
Rock Stream
1953-54
Rockville
1951-54
Rockville Center
1921, 5/1-9/2
1922-41
1946-54
Rome
1927, 5/15-9/1
1946-54
Ronkonkoma
1946-54
Roosevelt
1921-27
1938-41
Roscoe
1938-39
Rosendale
1938-39
1946-54

Rosyln
1938-39
1946-54
Round Lake
1938-39
Rouses Point
1941
1946-54
Roxbury
1951
Rush
1946
Rushville
1941
Rye
*1921-41
Sabattis
1949
Sackets Harbor
1948
Sag Harbor
1923-41
Saint Albans
1946-54
Saint James
1946-54
Saint Johnsville
1931-41
1947-54
Saint Josephs
1938-39
Salamanca
1940-41
1946-54
Salem
1946, 4/28-10/31
1947-54
Salisbury Center
1941, 4/28-9/17

* Change at 0:01 A.M.

NEW YORK (cont.)

Saltaire 1925-41	**Schenevus** 1940-41 1946-54	**Shoreman** 1925-41	**South Byron** 1947-58	**Springville** 1939, 6/1-8/31 1940, 6/1-8/31 1941	**Summerdale** 1953-54
Sampson 1946-49 1952-54	**Schroon Lake** 1938-39	**Shortsville** 1947-52	**South Cambridge** 1946-54	**Springwater** 1951-54	**Summit Park** 1946-54
Sanborn 1947-48	**Schuylerville** 1921-41 1946-54	**Shushan** 1954	**South Dayton** 1941, 4/28-9/2 1951-54	**Staatsburg** 1938-39 1946, 4/28-10/27 1947-48	**Summitville** 1938-39
Sands Point 1925-41	**Scio** 1941 1951-54	**Sidney** 1940-41 1946-54	**South Farmington** 1946-54	**Stafford** 1948	**Suspension Bridge** 1946-54
Sanitaria Springs 1946-54	**Scotia** 1925-41 1947-48	**Silver Creek** 1936, 6/11-9/9 1937, 6/11-9/10 1938, 6/12-9/11 1940, 5/12-9/1 1941 1946-54	**Southfields** 1946-54	**Stamford** 1953	**Swain** 1951-54
Saranac Inn 1947 1949	**Sea Cliff** 1923-41 1946-54	**Silver Springs** 1940 1951-54	**South Glens Falls** 1925-41	**Standish** 1938-39	**Syosset** 1925-41 1946-54
Saranac Lake 1925-41 1946-54	**Seaford** 1921-41 1946-54	**Skaneateles** 1939	**South Granby** 1947-48	**Stanley** 1953-54	**Syracuse** 1939-41 1946-54
Saratoga Springs 1921-41 1946-54	**Selden** 1946-54	**Slingerlands** 1938-39 1946-54	**South Lavonia** 1951-54	**Starkey** 1948 1953-54	**Tannersville** 1931-41
Saugerties 1925-41 1946, 4/28-9/30 1947-54	**Selkirk** 1938-39	**Sloansville** 1938-40	**South Nyack** 1921-41	**Steamburg** 1951-54	**Tappan** 1947-48
Sauquoit 1947-50	**Seneca Falls** 1940-41 1946-54	**Sloatsburg** 1946-54	**Southold** 1923-41 1946-54	**Stephentown** 1946-54	**Tarrytown** 1923-41 1946 1952-54
Savona 1951-54	**Setauket** 1946-54	**Smithboro** 1951-54	**Southport** 1953-54	**Stewart Manor** 1946-54	**The Glen** 1948-54
Sayville 1925-41 1946-54	**Shandaken** 1931-41	**Smith's Basin** 1948	**South Wales** 1953-54	**Stillwater** 1946-54	**Thendara** 1949-54
Scarborough 1925-41 1948 1951	**Sharon** 1948	**Smithtown** 1923-41 1946-54	**Sparkill** 1946-54	**Stockport** 1951-54	**Thiells** 1946-54
Scarsdale 1921-41 1948-54	**Sharon Springs** 1947-54	**Sodus Center** 1953-54	**Sparrow Bush** 1951-54	**Stony Brook** 1946-54	**Thomson** 1946-54
Schaghticoke 1946-54	**Sharon Station** 1946 1949	**Sodus Point** 1953-54	**Spencerport** 1946-53	**Stony Creek** 1948-54	**Thornwood** 1947 1951
Schenectady 1923-41 1946-54	**Sherburne** 1946-54	**Southampton** 1923-41 1946-54	**Speonk** 1946-54	**Stuyvesant** 1939-41	**Thurman** 1948
	Sherman 1953-54		**Springfield Gardens** 1923-41 1946-54	**Suffern** 1925-41 1946-54	**Ticonderoga** 1923-41 1946-54
	Sherrill 1939-41		**Spring Glen** 1938-39		
			Spring Valley 1921-41 1946-54		

NEW YORK (cont.)

Tivoli 1938-39
Tonawanda 1923-41, 1946-54
Towners 1948, 1951
Troy 1932, 4/2-9/24; 1933, 4/1-9/30; 1934, 4/7-9/29; 1935, 4/6-9/28; 1936-41; 1946-54
Trumansburg 1941
Tuckahoe 1923-41, 1952-54
Tully 1939, 1947-54
Tunnel 1947, 1953-54
Tupper Lake 1938; 1939, 6/11-9/10; 1940-41; 1946-54
Tuxedo Park 1923-41, 1946-54
Ulster Park 1947
Unadilla 1940-41, 1946-54
Union 1951-54
Union Hall Station 1946-54

Union Springs 1939
Upton 1951-54
Ushers 1946-54
Utica 1921-26; 1927, 6/5-8/28; 1928-41; 1946-54
Valatie 1938-39
Valhalla 1925-41, 1947
Valley Cottage 1947-48
Valley Falls 1938-39, 1946-54
Valley Stream 1925-41, 1946-54
Vandalia 1953-54
Van Hoesen 1938-39
Vergennes 1951
Vernon 1946-54
Vestal 1947-50
Victor 1950-54
Voorheesville 1938-41, 1946-54
Walden 1923-41

Wallace 1951-54
Wallington 1953-54
Walkill 1938-39
Walloomsac 1938-39
Wantagh 1923-41, 1946-54
Wappingers Falls 1923-41
Warrensburg 1930, 4/15-10/15; 1931-41; 1946, 4/28-10/31; 1947-54
Warsaw 1940-41
Warsing 1938-39
Warwick 1923-41, 1946-54
Wassaic 1938-39
Waterboro 1946-48
Waterford 1951-54
Waterloo 1940-41, 1946-54
Waterport 1940-41
Watertown 1938-41, 1946-54
Waterville 1947-54

Watervliet 1921-41, 1946-54
Watkins Glen 1946-48, 1951-54
Watts Flats 1951-54
Waverly 1940, 1946
Wayland 1948-50
Wayneport 1947-48
Wayville 1946-54
Webster 1947-48
Webster Crossing 1951-54
Wells Bridge 1947-54
Wellsburg 1951-54
Wellsville 1941, 1946, 1951-54
Wemple 1946-54
Wende 1940-41
West Athens 1938-39
West Brookville 1939
Westbury 1925-41, 1946-54

West Chazy 1947-54
Westfield 1929; 1939, 7/2-9/3; 1940, 6/2-9/1; 1941; 1946-54
Westhampton 1923-41, 1946-54
West Haverstraw 1925-41; 1947, 5/4-9/28; 1948-54
West Hempstead 1946-54
West Henrietta 1951-54
West Hurley 1938-39, 1946
West Lebanon 1941, 1951-54
Westmoreland 1938-39
West Nyack 1947-54, 1948-49, 1953
Westons Mills 1953-54
West Point 1923-41, 1947-54
Westport 1946-54
West Salamanca 1951-54
West Waterford 1938-39, 1946-54

Westwood 1946-54
Whitehall 1923-41, 1946-54
White Plains 1921-41, 1946-54
Whitesboro 1921-26; 1927, 6/5-8/28; 1928-41
Whitney Point 1947-50
Willards Station 1951-54
Williamson 1947-48
Williamsville 1923-41
Willsboro 1946-54
Wingdale 1938-39, 1953-54
Winterton 1938-39
Winthrop 1947-54
Wolcott 1947-48
Woodard 1951-54
Woodbury 1923-41
Woodcliff Lake 1946-54
Woodfalls 1951-54
Woodhaven 1921-41, 1946-54

NEW YORK (cont.)

Woodmere
1921-41
1946-54
Woodridge
1938-39
Woodside
1946-54
Woodstock
1931-41
Worcester
1946-54
Wurtsboro
1938-39
Wyandanch
1946-54
Wymanock
1951-54
Wyoming
1941
Yaphank
1946-54
Yonkers
1921-41
1946-54
Yorktown Heights
1950
Yorkville
1940-41

TABLE

1918		War Time
1919		War Time
1942-45		War Time
1946		4/28-9/29
1957		4/28-9/29

ATLANTIC OCEAN

VA.

S.C.

TENN.

⊙Asheville.

GA.

82 W33'

NORTH CAROLINA

1650		Area settled
1752	9/14	Gregorian (NS) Calendar adopted in U.S.A.
1789	11/21	State entered the Union
1883	11/18	Noon, Eastern Standard Time (75°W) adopted east of and including Asheville (82W33). Central Standard Time (90°W) adopted west of Asheville.
1947	9/28	EST adopted state-wide. Communities west of Asheville switched from CST to EST.

DAYLIGHT (OR WAR) TIME OBSERVED:
(Changes at 2 A.M.)

1918	3/31 - 10/27	World War I
1919	3/30 - 10/26	World War I
1920	To 1940	Not observed
1941	8/1 - 2/9/42	Observed by all State Offices only
1942	2/9 - 9/30/45	World War II
1946	To 1965	Not observed state-wide. See Local Ordinance Listing.
1966	To 1979	For dates, see Table, page 181.

OBSERVATION BY LOCAL ORDINANCE:
(Refer to Table for Month & Day)

Acton	1946		Almond	1946		Balsam	1946		Beta	1946		Bushnell	1946		Canton	1946
Addie	1946		Andrews	1946		Barkers	1946		Boswell	1946		Buquo	1946		Clyde	1946
Alexander	1946		Asheville	1946		Barnard	1946		Bryson City	1946		Candler	1946		Coalville	1946

NORTH CAROLINA (cont.)

Cole	1946	Nantahala	1946	Waynesville	1946
Craggy	1946	Noland	1946	Wesser	1946
Dillsboro	1946	Olivette	1946	Whittier	1946
Ela	1946	Paintrock	1946	Willets	1946
Epps Springs	1946	Redmond	1946	Wilmington	1957
Forney	1946	Regal Peachtree	1946	Wilmot	1946
Frys	1946	Rollins	1946		
Hazelwood	1946	Runion	1946		
Hewitts	1946	Sandy Bottom	1946		
Hominy	1946	Saunook	1946		
Hot Springs	1946	Shaleville	1946		
Ivy Bridge	1946	Stackhouse	1946		
Judson	1946	Starbuck	1946		
Lake Junaluska	1946	Sulphur Springs	1946		
Luther	1946	Sylva	1946		
Maltby	1946	Talc Mountain	1946		
Marble	1946	Tomotla	1946		
Marshall	1946	Tom Thumb	1946		
Montford	1946	Topton	1946		
Murphy	1946	Turnpike	1946		
Murphy Junction	1946	Volga	1946		

NORTH DAKOTA

1752	9/14	Gregorian (NS) Calendar adopted in U.S.A.
1780		Area settled
1883	11/18	Noon, Mountain Standard Time (105°W) adopted in southwestern portion. Rest of State adopted Central Standard Time (90°W) except Flaxton, Minot and Portal (located in Northwestern portion) which adopted MST (105°W).
1889	11/2	State entered the Union.
1929	12/8	1:00 A.M., CST adopted state-wide; however, southwestern tip of State continued on MST.
1931	1/31	The 1929 Act was repealed and the 1883 picture returned to the State.
1945	9/30	At termination of War Time southwestern tip of State continued on MST, and the remainder of the State observed CST. (1)
1960	5/15	Mandan adopted CST (90°W) permanently.
1967	11/25	Boundary between MST and CST moved east to include within the Mountain Standard Time Zone those counties which have historically observed MST.

DAYLIGHT (OR WAR TIME) OBSERVED
(Changes at 2 A.M.)

1918	3/31 - 10/27	World War I
1919	3/30 - 10/26	World War I
1920	To 1941	Not observed
1942	2/9 - 9/30/45	World War II
1943	4/1	Switched to Mountain War Time.
1946	To 1960	Not observed state-wide. See Local Ordinance Listing.
1961	To 1966	Not observed. Daylight Savings Time prohibited by State legislative action.
1967	To 1979	For dates, see Table, page 181.

TABLE

1918	War Time
1919	War Time
1942-45	War Time
1957	4/28-10/27
1958	5/31-9/2
1959	5/30-9/8

(1) See heavy line on map

NORTH DAKOTA (cont.)

OBSERVATION BY LOCAL ORDINANCE:
(Refer to Table for Month & Day if not shown)

Fargo
 1957-59
Grand Forks
 1957-59
Mandan
 1952-59 , 5/15-9/15
Wahpeton
 1957-59

OHIO

1752	9/14	Gregorian (NS) Calendar adopted in U.S.A.
1788		Area settled
1803	3/1	State entered the Union

STANDARD TIME ZONE SHIFTS

1883	11/18	Central (90 W) to Standard Time. Noon. Standard Time was adopted by railroads and government offices. However, part of the general public continued the use of Local Mean Time until 1893. **
1890	1/1	Central Standard Time (90°W) adopted in Springfield
1890	6/15	Central Standard Time (90°W) adopted in Cleveland
1893	4/1	Noon, Central Standard Time (90°W) adopted state-wide
1914	5/1	Cleveland, Clyde and Milan adopted Eastern Standard Time (75°W)*
1919	1/1	(1) Western boundary of Eastern Standard Time Zone was drawn through Fremont, Clyde, Bellevue, Monroeville, Willard, Shelby, Shelby Junction, Galion, Lancaster, Dundas and Gallipolis, Ohio.
1919	5/11	Sandusky adopted EST at 2 A.M.
1919	6/1	(1) The EST Zone line was redrawn farther to the east, thus excluding the points mentioned in 1919, 1/1 above, from the eastern zone.
1920	6/6	Mount Vernon was included in the eastern zone.
1922	4/1	(1) The EST boundary line was again changed to include Toledo and other portions of northern Ohio in the eastern zone. **
1924	3/30	(1) The eastern zone was extended to include Columbus, Fostoria and Gallipolis and other points. ** NOTE: Columbus did not comply, see 1926.

TABLE

1918	War Time
1919	War Time
1920	3/28-10/31
1921	4/24-9/25
1922	4/30-9/24
1923	4/29-9/30
1924	4/27-9/28
1925	4/26-9/27
1926	4/25-9/26
1941	4/27-9/28
1942-45	War Time
1947	4/27-9/28
1948	4/25-9/26
1949	4/24-9/25
1950	4/30-9/24
1951	4/29-9/30
1952	4/27-9/28
1953	4/26-9/27
1954	4/25-9/26
1955	4/24-9/25
1956	4/29-9/30
1957	4/28-9/29
1958	4/27-10/26
1959	4/26-10/25
1960	4/24-10/30
1961	4/30-10/29
1962	4/29-10/28
1963	4/28-10/27
1964	4/26-10/25
1965	4/25-10/31

See Ohio Map under 1966 TIME PICTURE

* Change at 0:01 A.M.
** Check with local authorities

OHIO (cont.)

1924 8/31   (1) There was a further extension of the eastern zone to include Findley, Kenton and Marysville, and a portion of the State north of Columbus. * & **

1925   Fremont adopted EST

1926 9/26   EST adopted in:

Akron	Dayton	Newark
Canton	Elyria	Portsmouth
Columbus	Lima	

1927 4/4   (1) The eastern zone was extended to include all Ohio points on and east of the main line of the Baltimore and Ohio Railroad from Toledo to Cincinnati. ** This put most of the major cities, including Cincinnati, Springfield and Steubenville, on EST.

1936 9/27   (1) 2 A.M. By order of the Interstate Commerce Commission, the entire State of Ohio was put on EST, including several small borderline towns which had clung to their former Central Time despite the 1927 order. **

      (1) However, in many instances the changes in local statutes or ordinances did not coincide with the change made by the Interstate Commerce Commission in the official Federal boundaries. The dates given above are those on which the change was effective for the purposes covered by the Standard Time Act.

DAYLIGHT (OR WAR) TIME OBSERVED:
(Changes at 2 A.M.)

1918 3/31 - 10/27   World War I

1919 3/30 - 10/26   World War I

1920 To 1941   Not observed state-wide. See Local Ordinance Listing.

1942 2/9 - 9/30/45   World War II

*Change at 0:01 A.M.
**Check with local authorities

OHIO (cont.)

1943   2/21 3 A.M.   Legislative ordinances passed that put entire state on Central War Time. Not all cities complied. Central War Time was adopted by Columbus, Dayton, Springfield, Findley. Cincinnati, Green Mountain Commission, Montgomery County, Greenville was on Central War Time until April 4, 1943, after which it reverted to Eastern War Time until October 3, 1943.

Communities which stayed on Eastern War Time were Akron, Albion, Ashland, Athens, Barberton, Bucyrus, Canton, Cayahoga Falls,   Conneaut, Crestline, Dover, East Liverpool, Middleport, Mt. Vernon, Pomeroy, Salem, Sandusky, Shelby, Steubenville, Toledo, Warren, Wellsville, Xenia, Youngstown.

1945   4/29 3 A.M. CWT   The following communities changed from Central War Time to Eastern War Time: Akron, Alliance, Canton, Chardon,   Dayon, Dover, Elyria, Findlay, Lakewood, Lima, Norwalk, Oberlin, Painesville, Salem, Sandusky, Van Wert, Wooster, Warren, Youngstown.

1946 - 1965   See local ordinance listing

1966   See Map, page 179

1967   Observed state-wide (see dates page 181), except Dayton (dates listed in Observation by Local Ordinance below)

1968   To 1979   Observed state-wide, see Table on page 181

OHIO (cont.)

OBSERVATION BY LOCAL ORDINANCE:
(Refer to Table for Month & Day if not shown)

Adams Mills
1958-65
Air Hill
1958-65
Akron
1920-26
1949
1950, 4/30-9/30
1951-65
Alger
1961-65
Alliance
1948-49
1950, 4/30-9/30
1951-65
Alpha
1958-65
Alton
1958-65
Amanda
1958-65
Amherst
1958, 4/27-10/26
1959-65
Andover
1955-65
Aquilla Village
1956-57
1958, 4/27-10/26
1959-65
Ashtabula
1949-65
Athalia
1964, 4/26-10/25

Atlanta
1958-65
Attica
1958-65
Atwater
1958-65
Auburn
1961-64
Augusta
1960-61
Aurora
1948-57
1958, 4/27-10/26
1959-65
Austinburg
1958-65
Austintown
1965
Ava
1958-65
Avon
1958-65
1959-65
Avon Lake
1948-49
1951
1957-65
Baddow Pass
1958-65
Bainbridge
1961-65

Bangs
1958-65
Barberton
1949-65
Barnesville
1960, 6/1-9/30
1961, 6/4-9/3
1962, 4/29-9/30
1963, 6/1-8/31
1964, 4/26-9/27
Bartlett
1965, 4/25-9/26
Bay Village
1949
Beach City
1958, 4/27-10/26
1961-63
Beallsville
1965
Bedford
1955-65
Bedford Heights
1961-65
Bellaire
1947-65
Bellbrook
1958-65
Belle Valley
1958-65

Belmont
1955-56
Belpre
1963, 4/28-9/29
1964, 4/26-9/27
1965, 4/25-9/26
Bentleyville
1961
Berea
1948-57
1958, 4/27-10/26
1959-65
Berlin Heights
1949
Bethesda
1956
Bettsville
1958-65
Beverly
1963, 4/28-9/29
1964, 4/26-9/27
1965, 4/25-9/26
Big Prairie
1958-65
Big Walnut
1958-65
Birds Run
1958-65
Black Lick
1958-65
Blackrun
1958-65

Blissfield
1958-65
Bloomville
1958-65
Blue Ash
1958-65
Boston
1957
Bowerston
1957-65
Bradford
1960-65
Brady Lake
1961-63
Brandywine
1958-65
Brecksville
1957
Brecon
1960-65
Bremen
1958-65
Brewster
1958
Bridgeport
1948

Brier Hill
1948-65
Brighton
1965
Brilliant
1958-65
Brimfield
1961-63
Brinkhaven
1958-65
Bristolville
1958-65
Broadview Heights
1960-65
Brookfield
1951
Brooklyn
1955-57
1959-65
Brook Park
1957
Brookside
1959-65
Brookville
1956-57
Brunswick
1961-65
Brunt
1958-65
Buck Hill
1958-65

OHIO (cont.)

Burbank 1961-65
Burgoon 1958-65
Burton 1955-57, 1961-65
Byesville 1955-57, 1959-65
Cable 1958-65
Cadiz 1965
Caldwell 1958-65
Caledonia 1958, 4/27-10/26; 1961-65
Cambridge 1959-65
Campbell 1963, 4/28-9/29; 1964, 4/26-9/27; 1965, 4/25-9/26
Campbellstown 1958-65
Canal Fulton 1961-65
Canfield 1956-57, 1963-65
Cannel Spur 1958-65
Canton 1920; 1921, 4/3-9/25; 1922, 4/2-9/24; 1923, 4/1-9/30; 1924, 4/6-9/28; 1925, 4/5-9/27; 1926, 4/4-9/26; 1950-65
Carrothers 1958-65
Cedarville 1958-65
Centerburg 1958-65
Chagrin Falls 1955-57, 1961-65

Champion 1963
Chandler 1956-65
Chardon 1956-57; 1958, 4/27-10/26; 1959-65
Chesapeake 1958-65
Chesterland 1956-57, 1961-65
Chippewa Lake Village 1960-61
Cincinnati 1920-21, 1922-26
Circleville 1958-65
Clarington 1957
Clarksville 1958-65
Cleveland 1948-49; 1950, 4/30-9/30; 1951-65
Cleveland Heights 1955-65
Clinton 1958-65

Collinsville 1958-65
Columbiana 1950, 4/30-9/30; 1951-65
Columbus 1920; 1921, 4/3-9/25; 1922-26
Conesville 1958-65
Conneaut 1948-65
Conotton 1958-65
Conover 1958-65
Convoy 1958-65
Cooperdale 1958-65
Cortland 1958
Covington 1959, 4/26-9/27; 1960-65
Craig Beach 1948, 4/25-9/6; 1958-65
Creston 1958, 4/27-10/26
Crestline 1956-57, 1960-65
Cromers 1947
Crooksville 1958-65
Custaloga 1958-65
Cuyahoga Falls 1951-65

Dalton 1957
Damascus 1957
Danville 1958-65
Darrowville 1958, 4/27-10/26
Dayton 1920, 3/28-9/26; 1921, 4/3-9/25; 1922, 4/2-9/24; 1923, 4/1-9/30; 1924, 4/6-9/28; 1925, 4/5-9/27; 1926, 4/4-9/26; 1967. 4/30-10/29
Decliff 1961-65
Delaware 1958-65
Del Mount 1960-61
Delphos 1958-65
Dennison 1954-57
Derwent 1958-65
Dexter City 1958-65
Dixon 1958-65
Dodson 1958-65
Dola 1958-65
Dorset 1951
Doughton 1948-65

Dover 1957-65
Doylestown 1956-65
Dresden 1955-65
Dudley 1958-65
Dunkirk 1958-65
Dyke 1958-65
Eagleville 1961-65
East Canton 1958-65
East Cleveland 1948-57
East Columbus 1958, 4/27-10/26; 1959-65
Eastlake 1957
East Liberty 1959-65
East Liverpool 1955-56
East Orwell 1949
East Palestine 1950, 4/30-9/30; 1951-55
East Sparta 1956, 4/29-10/28; 1957, 4/28-10/27; 1958, 4/27-10/26
Eaton 1958-65

Elba 1958-65
Eldorado 1958-65
Elgin 1961-65
Elida 1958-65
Ellis 1958-65
Elyria 1920-26, 1948-65
Euclid 1955-57; 1958, 4/27-10/26; 1959-65
Evansville 1961-63
Fairport 1956
Fairport Harbor 1958-65
Fairview 1956-57
Fairview Park 1959-65
Flat Rock 1958-65
Fletcher 1958-65
Flint 1958-65
Florence 1958-65
Foraker 1961-65
Forest 1958-65
Foster 1958-65
Frank 1958-65
Frazeysburg 1958-65

OHIO (cont.)

Fredericksburg	1958-65
Freedom Station	1949-65
Galena	1958-65
Gambier	1958-65
Garfield	1956-65
Garrettsville	1948-65
Gates Mills	1958, 4/27-10/26; 1959-63
Geauga Lake	1948-65
Geneva	1948-58
Geneva-on-the-Lake	1959, 4/26-9/27; 1960-65
Georgetown	1955-65
Gettysburg	1958-65
Gibsonburg	1958-65
Gilbert	1958-65
Girard	1948-65
Glade Run	1958-65
Glendale	1958-65
Glenmont	1958-65
Glenmore	1961-65
Glenwood	1958-65

Grafton	1953-58; 1961-65
Grand River	1949-65
Greentown	1956-57; 1959-65
Greenville	1962-65
Gregory	1948-65
Guernsey	1958-65
Hageman	1958-65
Hammondsville	1958-65
Hanover	1958-65
Harbor	1958-65
Harlem Springs	1958-65
Harrod	1960-61
Hartville	1961-65
Harvey	1956-57
Hayden	1958-65
Hazelwood	1958-65
Heath	1958-65
Helena	1958-65
Helmick	1958-65
Hepburn	1961-65

Highland Heights	1958, 4/27-10/26; 1960-61
Hilliards	1958-65
Hinckley	1955-57; 1960-65
Hiram	1948-65
Holmesville	1958-65
Homeworth	1958-65
Hoover	1958-65
Hopedale	1958-65
Horatio	1958-65
Howard	1958-65
Howland	1963-65
Hubbard	1948-65
Hudson	1948-49; 1950, 4/30-9/30; 1951-65
Huntington	1956
Hunting Valley	1961-63
Huron	1948
Independence	1960-65
Irondale	1956-65
Isleta	1958-65
Jasper	1958-65

Jeddoe	1948-65
Jefferson	1951-58; 1959, 4/26-9/27; 1960-65
Jewett	1954-65
Johnsons	1958-65
Kemp Station	1961-65
Kenmore	1949-65
Kensington	1958-65
Kent	1949-65
Kidron	1958, 4/27-10/26; 1959-65
Kilgore	1963-65
Killbuck	1960-61
Kimbolton	1958-65
Kinderhook	1958-65
Kings Mills	1958-65
Kingsville	1957
Kinsman	1959-61
Kipton	1951
Kirby	1960-65
Kirtland	1960-61
Kylesburg	1958-65

La Fayette	1958-65
Lagrange	1955-57; 1958, 4/27-10/26; 1960-65
Lakeline	1962-65
Lake Milton	1954-65
Lakemore	1955-57; 1958, 4/27-10/26; 1959-65
Lakeville	1961-65
Lakewood	1948-50; 1955-57; 1958, 4/27-10/26; 1959-65
Lancaster	1958-65
Lansing	1960-65
Lawndale	1949-65
Laws	1958-65
Layland	1958-65
Leavittsburg	1949-65
Leetonia	1954-65
LeRoy	1956-57; 1960-65
Lewis Center	1958-65
Lima	1920-26
Limaville	1958-65

Lincoln Road	1958-65
Linndale	1948-57; 1958, 4/27-10/26
Lisbon	1956-57; 1960-65
Litchfield	1963-65
Lockwood	1958-65
Lodi	1955-57; 1958, 4/27-10/26; 1959-65
London	1958-65
Lorain	1948; 1951-65
Lordstown	1958; 1959, 4/26-9/27; 1960-65
Loudonville	1961-65
Louisville	1955-65
Louisville Junction	1961
Lowell	1965, 4/25-9/26
Lowellville	1956-59; 1963-65
Lowellville Junction	1960
Lucas	1958-65
Lyndhurst	1958, 4/27-10/26; 1959-65

OHIO (cont.)

Lynn 1958-65
Macedonia 1954-65
Macksburg 1958-65
Madison 1948-65
Magnolia 1958-65
Mahoning 1948-65
Malvern 1958-65
Mansfield 1952-53
Mantua 1948-65
Maplegrove 1958-65
Maple Heights 1956-65
Marble Cliff 1958-65
Marietta 1920-26, 1956-65
Mentor-on-the-Lake 1956-57, 1962-65
Marion 1964, 5/14-10/25
Marne 1958-65
Marshallville 1958-65
Martel 1961-65
Martins Ferry 1955-65
Mason 1958-65
Massillon 1950-58, 1959-65
Masury 1948-65

Maximo 1958-65
Mayfield Heights 1958, 4/27-10/26
Mayfield Village 1959-65
Mc Donald 1960-65
Mc Guffey 1957
McKinley Heights 1961-65
Medina 1955-57
Meekiers 1960-65
Melco 1958-65
Melvin 1958-65
Mentor 1948-49, 1956-65
Metz 1956-57, 1962-65
Middleburg Heights 1958-65
Middlefield 1957-65
Middle Point 1955-57, 1961, 4/30-10/1
Middletown 1965
Milford Center 1958-65, 1960-65

Millersburg 1958-65
Millersville 1958-65
Millport 1958-65
Milton 1961-65
Mineral City 1957
Mineral Ridge 1958, 1959, 4/26-9/27, 1960-65
Minerva 1956-65
Mingo Junction 1958-65
Mogadore 1959-65
Monnett 1958-65
Monroe Falls 1959
Moreland Hills 1961
Morgan Run 1958-65
Morrow 1958-65
Mount Eaton 1963
Mount Liberty 1958-65
Mount Pleasant 1957
Mount Vernon 1958-65
Nankin 1961-65
Navarre 1958, 1959, 4/26-9/2, 1960-65

Neffs 1952
Negley 1956
Nevada 1961-65
Newark 1920, 1921 4/3-9/25, 1922-26
New Athens 1959-61
Newburg 1958-65
Newbury 1961-65
Newcomerstown 1955
New Holland 1965
New Hope 1958-65
New Lexington 1958-65
New Lyme Station 1958-65
New Madison 1958-65
New Martinsville 1963, 4/28-9/29
New Metamoras 1965
New Middletown 1957
New Milford 1958-65
New Paris 1958-65
New Philadelphia (1) 1957-61, 1962, 1963-65

New Salisbury 1958-65
New Springfield 1957
Newton Falls 1955-56, 1959-65
New Waterford 1957-65
Niles 1946-49, 1950, 4/30-9/30, 1951-57, 1958, 4/27-9/7, 1959-65
North Berne 1958-65
North Broadway 1958-65
North Canton 1956-65
Northfield 1960-65
North Industry 1956-57
North Jackson 1958-65
North Kingsville 1965
North Lawrence 1963-65
North Lima 1957
North Olmsted 1961-65
North Ridgeville 1956-65
North Robinson 1960-65
North Royalton 1960-65
North Sebring 1958-65

North Warren 1949-65
Norton 1958-65
Novelty 1961-65
Oakfield 1958-65
Oakwood Village 1960-65
Oberlin 1948-65
Ogden 1958-65
Oldham 1959-65
Olmsted Falls 1958-65
Omal 1948, 1951, 1959-65
Omar 1958-65
Ontario 1961-65
Orange 1958-65
Oregonia 1958-65
Orrville 1958-65
Orwell 1957-65
Outville 1955-57, 1960-65
Painesville 1948-65
Parkman 1961-65
Parkview 1960-65

OHIO (cont.)

Parma
1956-57
1959-65
Parma Heights
1956-57
1960-65
Pataskala
1958-65
Pauls
1958-65
Pavonia
1961-65
Penfield
1965
Peninsula
1957
1958, 4/27-10/26
1959-65
Pepper Pike
1961-64
Perry
1948
1960-65
Perry Heights
1960-65
Perrysville
1958-65
Phalanx
1948-65
Phalanx Station
1948-65
Pikeville
1965, 4/25-9/26
1958-65
Piqua
1960-65
Pittsfield
1958-65
Plain City
1958-65
Pleasant Ridge
1958-65

(1) Retail outlets EST.
Industry DST

Poland
1957
1958, 4/27-10/26
1959-65
Polk
1961-65
Port Homer
1957
Portland
1950
Portsmouth
1920
1921, 4/3-9/25
1922-26
Port Washington
1958-65
Post Boy
1958-65
Powhatan Point
1956-65
Proctorville
1965
Ravenna
1949-65
Reading
1958-65
Red Bank
1958-65
Reesville
1958-65
Reno
1958-65
Richfield
1957
Richmond
1959, 4/26-9/27
1960-65
Richmond Heights
1958, 4/27-10/26
1959-61
Ridgeton
1958-65

Rittman
1949-65
Rochester
1956-57
1960-65
Rock Creek Station
1958-65
Rock Cut
1958-65
Rocky River
1948-65
Rogers
1963-65
Rome
1958-65
Rosemount
1958-65
Roseville
1958-65
Rossford
1958-65
Roxana
1958-65
Rush Run
1958-65
Russell
1961-65
Sabina
1958-65
Saint Clairsville
1955-57
1961-65
Saint Paris
1958-65
Saint Stephens
1958-65
Salem
1946-49
1950, 4/30-9/30
1951-65
Salineville
1956-65

Sandusky
1948-49
1956-63
1964, 5/30-9/7
1965
Saybrook
1948-49
Scio
1954-58
1959, 4/26-9/27
1960, 4/24-9/25
1961, 4/30-9/24
1962, 4/29-9/30
1963, 4/28-9/29
1964, 4/26-9/27
1965
Sebring
1954
1956-65
Selma
1958-65
Seven Hills
1963-65
Seven Mile
1958-65
Seventeen
1958-65
Seville
1955-57
1960-65
Shadyside
1956-57
1960-65
Shaker Heights
1955-65
Sheffield Lake
1965
Sherrodsville
1960-61
Shinrock
1949

Shreve
1960, 4/24-9/25
1961-65
Silver Lake
1959-65
Slicks
1961-65
Solon
1948-65
Somerville
1958-65
South Charleston
1958-65
South Euclid
1955-65
South Lebanon
1958-65
South Olive
1958-65
South Russell
1961-65
South Zanesville
1958-65
Spencer
1956-57
1961-65
Spencerville
1956
1961-65
Springfield
1920
1921, 4/3-9/25
1922-26
Spring Valley
1958-65
Stanleyville
1958-65
Stelvideo
1958-65
Sterling
1956-57
1961-65

Steubenville
1941
1946-47
1948, 4/25-9/6
1949-55
1956, 4/29-10/28
1957, 4/28-10/27
1958, 4/27-10/26
1959-65
Stockton
1958-65
Stone Creek
1957-65
Stoutsville
1958-65
Stow
1958, 4/27-10/26
1959-65
Strasburg
1955-58
1959, 4/26-9/27
1962-65
Stratton
1957
1965
Streetsboro
1957-65
Strongsville
1956-57
1959-65
Struthers
1956-57
1958, 4/27-10/26
1959-65
Summit Station
1958-65
Summitville
1958-65
Sunbury
1958-65
Swander
1958-65

OHIO (cont.)

Tallmadge 1949-65	Union City 1958-65	Warsaw 1958-65	Westview 1963-65	Woodly 1958-65
Terrace Park 1963-65	Uniontown 1965	Warwick 1958-65	Westville 1958-65	Woodsfield 1960, 5/1-9/4
Tiffin 1961-65	Union Village 1958-65	Washington Court House 1958-65	Weyers 1958-65	1961-65
Tiltonville 1957-65	Unionville 1958-65	Washington Hills 1965	Whipple 1958-65	Woodstock 1958-65
Timberlake 1960-65	University Heights 1955-57	Watakomika 1958-65	Wickliffe 1948-49	Woodville 1958-65
Tobias 1958-65	1959-65	Wayne 1959, 4/26-9/27	1951	Wooster 1958-65
Toledo 1960-65	Urbana 1958-65	1960, 4/24-9/25	1955-65	Worthington 1958-65
1920	Valley View 1961-65	1961, 4/30-9/24	Wilberforce 1958-65	Yorkville 1956-65
1921, 4/2-9/25	Vermilion 1948-58	Waynesburg 1958-65	Williamsfield 1951	Youngstown 1946-49
1948	1959, 4/26-9/27	Waynesville 1958-65	1959, 4/26-9/27	1950, 4/30-9/30
1961-65	1960, 4/24-9/25	Wellington 1951	1960, 4/24-9/25	1951-65
Toronto 1955	1961, 4/30-9/24	1955-65	1961, 4/30-9/24	Zanesville 1958-65
1956, 4/29-10/28	1962-65	Wellsville 1949-65	Willoughby 1948-65	Zoar 1963-65
1957, 4/28-10/27	Vienna 1958	West Alliance 1958-65	Willowick 1957	Zoarville 1958-65
1958, 4/27-10/26	1959, 4/26-9/27	Westerville 1958-65	1960-65	
1959-65	1960, 4/24-9/25	West Jefferson 1958-65	Wilmington 1958-65	
Townsend 1958-65	1961, 4/30-9/24	Westlake 1956-57	Wilmot 1958-65	
Trinway 1965	1965	1958, 4/27-10/26	Windham 1949-65	
Trotwood 1958-65	Wadsworth 1949-65	West Loudonville 1959-65	Windsor 1965	
Troyton 1958-65	Walbridge 1958-65	West Manchester 1958-65	Wintersville 1959, 4/26-9/27	
Tunnel Hill 1958-65	Waldo 1956-57	West Salem 1961-65	1960, 4/24-9/25	
Tuscarawas 1957	1958, 4/27-10/26	West Sonora 1958-65	1961, 4/30-9/24	
Twinsburg 1957	Walton Hills 1961		1965	
1959-65	Warner 1957		Winton Place 1959-65	
Tyner 1946-65	1958-65		Wolf 1958-65	
Uhrichsville 1957-65	Warren 1946-65		Woodington 1958-65	
	Warrensville Heights 1961			

OKLAHOMA

1752	9/14	Gregorian (NS) Calendar adopted in U.S.A.
1883	11/18	Noon, Central Standard Time (90°W) adopted except along western boundary. ** (1)
1889		Area settled
1907	11/16	State entered the Union
1921	3/4	Entire State included in CST zone. (2)

DAYLIGHT (OR WAR) TIME OBSERVED:
(Changes at 2 A.M.)

1918	3/31 – 10/27	World War I
1919	3/30 – 10/26	World War I
1920	To 1941	Not observed
1942	2/9 – 9/30/45	World War II
1946	To 1966	Not observed state-wide. See Local Ordinance Listing.
1967	To 1979	For dates, see Table, page 181.

OBSERVATION BY LOCAL ORDINANCE:
(Refer to Table for Month & Day)

Bartlesville
1962

TABLE

1918		War Time
1919		War Time
1942–45		War Time
1962		5/28–11/13

MO.

ARK.

KANS.

Tulsa

96°w

TEX.

COLO.

N. MEX.

MST **CST**

** Check with local authorities
(1) See dotted line on map
(2) See heavy line on map

TABLE

1918	War Time		1956	4/29-9/30
1919	War Time		1957	4/28-9/29
1942-45	War Time		1958	4/27-9/28
1949	4/24-9/25		1959	4/26-9/27
1950	4/30-9/24		1960	4/24-9/25
1951	4/29-9/30		1961	4/30-10/1
1952	4/27-9/28		1962	4/29-10/28
1953	4/26-9/27		1963	4/28-10/27
1954	4/25-9/26		1964	4/26-10/25
1955	4/24-9/25		1965	4/25-10/31

WASH. PST MST IDAHO. Malheur Co. Salem CALIF. NEV. 123°W46' PACIFIC OCEAN

OREGON

1752	9/14	Gregorian (NS) Calendar adopted in U.S.A.
1838		Area settled
1859	2/14	State entered the Union
1883	11/18	Noon, Pacific Standard Time (120°W) adopted, except Ontario (MST 105°W)

DAYLIGHT (OR WAR) TIME OBSERVED:
(Changes at 2 A.M.)

1918	3/31 - 10/27	World War I
1919	3/30 - 10/26	World War I
1920	To 1941	Not observed
1942	2/9 - 9/30/45	World War II
1946	To 1950	Not observed state-wide. See Local Ordinance Listing.
1951		Observed state-wide, except Malheur County, which observed MST (105°W) year round.
*1952	To 1962	Not observed state-wide. See end of State Listing.
1963	To 1965	Observed state-wide. Refer to Table for dates.
1966		See Chapter VII
1967	To 1979	For dates, see Table, page 181.

NOTE: Much of Southeast Oregon observes Mountain Standard Time (105°W) year round due to its economic tie to Idaho. Time for communities on that state border should be investigated thoroughly.

OBSERVATION BY LOCAL ORDINANCE
(Refer to Table for Month & Day)

*See note, page 136

OREGON (cont.)

Abernethy 1950
Ada 1950
Ady 1950
Albany 1950
Algoma 1950
Aloha 1952
Alpine 1950
Alvadore 1950
Amity 1950
Anlauf 1952
Armitage 1950
Ashland 1950
Astoria 1950 1952
Aurora 1950
Baker 1950
Balm 1950
Bandon 1950
Banks 1950
Barlow 1950
Bar View 1950

Batton 1950
Bay City 1950
Bear Creek 1950
Beavercreek 1950
Beaverton 1950
Bedding 1950
Beecher 1950
Belfort 1950
Bend 1950
Betzen 1952
Blodgett 1950
Bonanza 1950
Booth 1952
Brandt 1950
Braymill 1950
Brenham 1950
Brewster 1950
Briedwell 1950
Brighton 1950
Broadacres 1950

Broadbent 1950
Brockway 1950
Brooks Downs 1950
Brownsville 1950
Bruce 1950
Byers 1950
Buchanan 1950
Bufo 1950
Buman 1950
Bunting 1950
Butterfield 1950
Buxton 1950
Calimus 1950
Calloway 1950
Calon 1950
Canary 1950
Canby 1950
Canyonville 1950
Carlton 1950
Carman 1950
Carnes 1950

Carstens 1950
Carter 1950
Cartney 1950
Cascade Locks 1950
Cascade Summit 1950
Cedar Point 1950
Central Point 1950
Chelsea 1950
Chemawa 1950
Chemult 1950
Cheshire 1950
Chiloquin 1950
Chinchalo 1950
Clatskanie 1950
Clawson 1950
Claxtar 1950
Cleo 1950
Coburg 1950
Cochrane 1950
Colestin 1950
Columbia City 1950

Comstock 1950
Coos 1950
Coos Bay 1950
Coquille 1950
Cornelius 1950
Cornut 1950
Corvallis 1950
Cottage Grove 1950
1952
Cove Orchard 1950
Crabtree 1950
Crescent Lake 1950
Creswell 1950
Crowley 1950
Cruzatte 1950
Curtin 1950
Cushman 1950
Dallas 1950
Davis Slough 1950
Dayton 1950
Deady 1950

Delake 1950
Deter 1950
Devitt 1950
Diamond Lake 1950
Dillard 1950
Dilley 1950
Divide 1950
Donald 1950
Dothan 1950
Drain 1950
Dundee 1950
Eagle Point 1950
Eastside 1950
Eddyville 1950
Elam 1950
Elkton 1950
Elrus 1950
Empire 1950
Enid 1950
Enright 1950
Estabrook 1950

OREGON (cont.)

Estacada 1950
Eugene 1950, 1952
Eula 1950
Falls City 1950
Fanno 1950
Fawn 1950
Fensler 1950
Fields 1950
Florence 1950
Forest Grove 1949, 1952
Foss 1950
Fox Valley 1950
Frazier 1950
Fuego 1950
Gaines 1950
Gardiner 1952
Gaston 1950
Gas Works 1950
Gaylord 1950
Gearhart 1950, 1952

Georgetown 1950
Gervais 1950
Gladstone 1949
Glendale 1950, 1952
Globe 1950
Gold Hill 1950
Gooch 1950
Goshen 1950
Grants Pass 1950
Gray 1949, 1952
Green 1950
Greenberry 1950
Greer 1950
Gregory 1950
Gresham 1950
Griggs 1952
Halsey 1950
Harrisburg 1950
Hauser 1950
Hayden Inlet 1950

Heather 1950
Helloff 1950
Helon 1950
Hillsboro 1949
Hipp 1950
Hito 1950
Hood River 1950, 4/30-9/4 1952
Hoskins 1950
Hubbard 1950
Hugo 1950
Hulbert 1950
Independence 1950
Irving 1950
Isadore 1950
Ivan 1950
Jacksonville 1950
Johnson 1950
Junction City 1950
Juno 1950
Kingston 1950

Kirk 1950
Klamath Falls 1950
Knudson 1950
Kotan 1950
Kroll 1950
Lafayette 1950
Lake Lytle 1950
Lakeside 1950
Lakeview 1952
Landax 1950
Latham 1950
Lawler 1950
Lebanon 1950
Leland 1950
Lenz 1950
Leona 1950
Liberal 1950
Linn 1950
Linslow 1950
Lobert 1950
Lonroth 1950

Lookout 1950
Lowell 1950
Lumberton 1950
Lynbrook 1950
Lyons 1950
Lystful 1950
Macleay 1950
Malin 1950
Manhattan 1950
Manning 1952
Mapleton 1950
Marcola 1950
Marshfield 1950
Martin 1950, 1952
Mayo 1950
Maywood 1950
Mazama 1950
McCormack 1950
McCredie Springs 1950
McGlinn 1950
McKee 1950

McMinnville 1950, 1952
Medford 1950, 1952
Merlin 1950
Merrill 1950
Midland 1950
Mill City 1950
Millwood 1950
Milwaukie 1949-50, 1952
Mistletoe 1950
Modoc Point 1950
Mohawk 1950
Molalla 1950, 1952
Monet 1950
Monitor 1950
Monmouth 1950
Monroe 1950
Mount Angel 1950
Mowick 1950
Mulloy 1950
Myrtle Creek 1950

OREGON (cont.)

Myrtle Point	1950
Nashville	1950
Natron	1950
Nehalem	1950
Nekoma	1950
Newberg	1950
Newport	1952
North Bend	1950
Nortons	1950
Norway	1950
Noti	1950
Oakland	1950
Oakridge	1950, 1952
Oceanlake	1950
Odell Lake	1950
Oregon City	1949, 1950, 1952
Orville	1952
Oswego	1950
Ouxy	1950
Overland	1950
Paygold	1950
Parker	1950
Paunina	1950
Peck	1950
Pelican	1950
Philomath	1950
Phoenix	1952
Pirtle	1950
Pine Ridge	1950
Plainview	1950
Pollard	1950
Portland	1949, 4/24-9/11; 1950-53; 1955-62
Potter	1950
Powers	1950
Pratum	1950
Prineville	1950
Pryor	1952
Ranier	1950
Reckards	1950
Rector	1950
Redmond	1950
Reedsport	1952
Reedville	1950
Reliance	1950
Reserve	1950
Rice Hill	1950
Riddle	1950
Ripples	1950
Rivero	1950
Rockaway	1950
Rockpoint	1950
Rogers	1950
Rogue River	1950
Roseburg	1950
Round Prairie	1952
Rowland	1950
Roy	1950
Ruckles	1950
Saginaw	1950
Saint Helens	1950
Saint Joseph	1950
Saint Paul	1950
Salem	1950
Salmonberry	1952
Sandy	1950
Scappoose	1950
School	1950
Scio	1950
Seaside	1950
Seltners	1950
Seven Oaks	1950
Shaw	1950
Shedd	1950
Shelburn	1950
Sheridan	1950
Sherwood	1950
Shipley	1950
Signal	1950
Silverton	1950
Siskiyou	1950
Sitcoos	1950
Springfield	1950
State School	1950
Steinman	1950
Sublimity	1950
Summit	1952
Sutherland	1950
Sutherlin	1950
Sweet Home	1950
Swisshome	1952
Switzerland	1950
Taft	1950
Talent	1950
Talman	1950
Tangent	1950
Texum	1950
Tharp	1950
The Dalles	1950
Tiernan	1950
Tillamook	1950
Tigard	1952
Timber	1950
Tola	1950
Toledo	1950
Tonquin	1950
Townsend	1950
Troutdale	1950
Tualatin	1950
Tulsa	1950
Tunnel	1950
Turner	1950
Twin Buttes	1950
Umli	1950
Union Creek	1950
Veatch	1950
Veneta	1950
Vernonia	1950
Voorhies	1950
Waconda	1950
Wakefield	1950

OREGON (cont.)

Walker	1950
Wallace	1950
Walton	1950
Wapato	1950
Winch	1950
Warko	1950
Warner	1950
Warrenton	1950 1952
Weaver	1950
Wells	1950
Westfir	1950
West Linn	1949 1950 1952
Westimber	1950
Wheeler	1950
White Point	1950
Whiteson	1950
Wilbur	1950
Wilkesboro	1950
Willaminia	1950
Willard	1950
Willamette	1950

Williams	1950
Wilson	1950
Wilsonville	1950
Winchester	1950
Wocus	1950
Wolf Creek	1950
Woodburn	1950
Worden	1950
Wren	1950
Yamhill	1950
Yarnell	1950
Yoncalla	1950
York	1950

1952 - 1962 OREGON DAYLIGHT TIME

1952 DST observed in Portland from 4/30 to 9/28, changes at 2:00 a.m.

1953 - 1960 DST not observed

1961 DST observed in Multnomal, Clackamas, Washington, Columbia and Hood River Counties from 5/7 @ 1:00 a.m. to 9/24 @ 2:00 a.m.

1962 DST observed in the same five counties, as well as in Eugene, Albany, Corvallis, Newberg, McMinnville, The Dalles, Bend, Redmond, Madras, Prineville, and the Northern Oregon Beaches from 4/29 to 9/29, changes at 2:00 a.m.

DST observed in Baker from 5/27 to 9/29, changes at 2:00 a.m.

PENNSYLVANIA (see Pennsylvania, p. 190)

1682		Area settled
1752	9/14	Gregorian (NS) Calendar adopted in U.S.A.
1787	12/12	State entered the Union
1887	1/1	Pittsburgh and suburbs adopted Eastern Standard Time (75°W)
1887	4/13	Eastern Standard Time (75°W) adopted state-wide except Erie
1887	7/1	Erie adopted EST (75°W)

DAYLIGHT (OR WAR) TIME OBSERVED:
(Changes at 2 A.M.)

*1918	3/31 - 10/27	World War I
*1919	3/30 - 10/26	World War I
1920	To 1941	Observed in parts of State. See Local Ordinance Listing.
*1942	2/9 - 9/30/45	World War II
1946	To 1964	More and more communities began to observe DST until in 1964 only one small village (Yatesville) remained on Standard Time. By 1964 all communities save Yatesville began DST on the last Sunday in April and with one exception ended DST on the last Sunday in October. LaJose ended DST on the last Sunday in September.
1965	4/25 - 10/31	Observed state-wide.
1966	To 1979	For dates, see Table, page 181.

OBSERVATION BY LOCAL ORDINANCE:
(Refer to Table for Month and Day if not shown)

NOTE: In 1920, DST was discontinued as a State ordinance, but continued by local ordinances as noted below. This information is incomplete; however, it may be used as a key to DST observance. Information on all communities is not known, and therefore not all years are included.

TABLE I

Year	Dates	Year	Dates
*1918	War Time	1950	4/30-9/24
*1919	War Time	1951	4/29-9/30
1920	4/25-9/26	1952	4/27-9/28
1921	4/24-9/25	1953	4/26-9/27
1922	4/30-9/24	1954	4/25-9/26
1923	4/29-9/30	1955	4/24-10/30
1924	4/27-9/28	1956	4/29-10/28
1925	4/26-9/27	1957	4/28-10/27
1926	4/25-9/26	1958	4/27-10/26
1927	4/24-9/25	1959	4/26-10/25
1928	4/29-9/30	1960	4/24-10/30
1929	4/28-9/29	1961	4/30-10/29
1930	4/27-9/28	1962	4/29-10/28
1931	4/26-9/27	1963	4/28-10/27
1932	4/24-9/25	1964	4/26-10/25
1933	4/30-9/24	1965	4/25-10/31
1934	4/29-9/30		
1935	4/28-9/29		
1936	4/26-9/27		
1937	4/25-9/26		
1938	4/24-9/25		
1939	4/30-9/24		
1940	4/28-9/29		
1941	4/27-9/28		
*1942-45	War Time		
1946	4/28-9/29		
1947	4/27-9/28		
1948	4/25-9/26		
1949	4/24-9/25		

TABLE II

Year	Dates
1955	4/24-9/25
1956	4/29-9/30
1957	4/28-9/29
1958	4/27-9/28
1959	4/26-9/27
1960	4/24-9/25
1961	4/30-9/24
1962	4/29-9/30
1963	4/28-9/29
1964	4/26-9/27

*see Pennsylvania, page 196

PENNSYLVANIA (cont.)

Place	Dates	Class
Adamstown	1940–41	I
Akron	1940–41	I
	1950–64	I
Aladdin	1954–64	I
Albany	1950–64	I
Albion	1953–64	I
Alburtis	1950–64	I
Alexandria	1953–64	I
Alford	1951–64	I
Aliquippa	1930–41	I
	1946–64	I
Allentown	1930–46	I
	1958–64	I
Allenwood	1950–64	I
Altoona	1941	I
	1946–54	I
	1955–60	II
	1961–64	I
Alva	1953–64	I
Alverton	1953–64	I
Amasa	1951–64	I
Ambler	1931–41	I
	1946–64	I
Ambridge	1930–41	I
	1946–64	I

Place	Dates	Class
Analomink	1938–41	I
Andalusia	1958–64	I
Andersontown	1954–64	I
Annville	1953–64	I
Antes fort	1940–41	I
	1950–64	I
Apollo	1950–64	I
Ararat	1947–64	I
Archbald	1951–64	I
Ardara	1946	I
	1948	I
	1953–64	I
Ardmore	1954–56	I
	1958–64	I
Arnold	1931–41	I
	1947–54	I
	1958–64	I
Arona	1941	I
Ashland	1946–54	I
	1958–64	I
Ashley	1953–64	I
Ashmore	1951	I
	1956–64	I
Ashtola	1953–64	I

Place	Dates	Class
Aspinwall	1956	I
	1958–64	I
Atglen	1938–41	I
	1958–64	I
Athens	1951–54	I
	1955	II
	1956–64	I
Atlantic	1951–64	I
Auburn	1941	I
	1946–64	I
Audenried	1951–64	I
Avalon	1954	I
	1956	I
	1958–64	I
Avoca	1951–64	I
Avon	1950–64	I
Avondale	1946–64	I
Avonmore	1953–64	I
Baden	1954–64	I
Baldwin	1946–47	I
	1954–64	I
Bally	1941	I
Bandersville	1950–64	I
Bangor	1949–64	I
Barking	1954–64	I

Place	Dates	Class
Barnesville	1956	I
Barto	1950–64	I
Bath	1938–41	I
	1951–64	I
Beaver	1938–41	I
	1946–54	I
	1955–56	II
	1957–64	I
Beaver Falls	1938–41	I
	1946–64	I
Beaver Falls, New Brighton	1951–64	I
Beaver Valley	1946–54	I
	1955	II
	1956–64	I
Bedford	1950–51	I
	1951–64	I
Beech Creek	1946–64	I
Beechwood	1953–64	I
Belfast	1951	I
	1956–64	I
Bellefonte	1946–64	I
Belle Vernon	1949–52	I
Bellevue	1947	I
Bellwood	1947–64	I

Place	Dates	Class
Ben Avon	1954–64	I
Bentleyville	1949–64	I
Benton	1950–64	I
Berne	1938–41	I
	1951–64	I
Bernice	1950–64	I
Bernville	1951	I
	1956–64	I
Bertha	1941	I
Berwick	1953–64	I
Berwyn	1946–64	I
Bessemer	1947–64	I
Bethlehem	1950–64	I
Biglerville	1930–41	I
	1946–64	I
Bird-in-Hand	1950–64	I
Birdsboro	1940–41	I
Birmingham	1938–41	I
	1946–64	I
Black Creek Junction	1953–64	I
Blacklick Station	1951	I
	1956–57	I
Blackwood	1950–64	I

Place	Dates	Class
Blairsville	1941	I
	1953–64	I
Blanchard	1953–64	I
Blandburg	1953–64	I
Blawnox	1954	I
	1956	I
Bloomsburg	1947–64	I
Blossburg	1951–64	I
Blue Ridge	1947–54	I
	1955–61	II
	1962–64	I
Boiling Springs	1950–64	I
Bolivar	1953–64	I
Boothwyn	1941	I
Boston	1941	I
Bowanstown	1951	I
	1956–64	I
Bowers	1950–64	I
Boyertown	1938–41	I
	1946–64	I
Brackenridge	1940–41	I
	1956–64	I
Braddock	1930–41	I
	1946–64	I

PENNSYLVANIA (cont.)

Bradford 1940 I / 1941, 4/27-9/1 I / 1946-64 I
Bradley 1956-64 I
Bradley Junction 1953-64 I
Braeburn 1954-64 I
Branchville 1956-64 I
Brandonville 1950-64 I
Brandt 1951-64 I
Brandywine Summit 1947-52 I / 1956-64 I
Brave 1956-64 I
Bridgeport 1949-64 I
Bridgeton 1953-64 I
Bridgeville 1947-52 I / 1956-64 I
Bristol 1925-41 I / 1946-64 I
Brockway 1949-64 I
Brookville 1947-52 I / 1956-64 I
Brownfield 1953-64 I
Brownsville 1946 I / 1949-64 I
Bryansville 1953-64 I

Bryn Mawr 1921-41 I / 1946-64 I
Buchanan 1951-64 I
Buck Hill Falls 1955 II / 1956-64 I
Buffalo Mills 1953-64 I
Bulger 1954-64 I
Burgettstown 1947-64 I
Burnham 1949-64 I
Bushkill 1941 I
Bustleton 1950-64 I
Butler 1941 I / 1946-64 I
Butler Junction 1956-64 I
California 1947-64 I
Cambridge 1956-64 I
Cambridge Springs 1941 I
Cameron 1956-64 I
Camp Hill 1940-41 I / 1946-64 I
Canadensis 1941 I / 1955 II / 1956-64 I
Canonsburg 1946-64 I

Canton 1946, 6/1-8/31 I / 1953-64 I
Carbondale 1946-64 I
Carlisle 1939-41 I / 1946-64 I
Carlisle Junction 1950-64 I
Carmichaels 1953-64 I
Carnegie 1931-41 I / 1946 I / 1950-64 I
Carrier 1951-64 I
Carrolltown 1953-64 I
Cassandra 1953-64 I
Catasauqua 1938-41 II / 1946-64 I
Catawissa 1947-64 I
Cedar Hollow 1950-64 I
Cementon 1951 I / 1956-64 I
Center Bridge 1941 I
Center Hall 1953-64 I
Centerville 1953-64 I
Center Valley 1950-64 I
Central City 1953-55 I / 1956 II / 1957-64 I

Centralia 1951 I / 1956-64 I
Cessna 1953-64 I
Chadds Ford Junction 1950-64 I
Chalfont 1950-64 I
Chambersburg 1946-54 I / 1955-57 II / 1958-64 I
Charleroi 1946-64 I
Cheltenham 1950-64 I
Cherry Tree 1956-64 I
Chester 1928-41 I / 1946-54 I / 1955-56 II / 1957-64 I
Chestnut Hill 1950-64 I
Cheswick 1946-64 I
Chewton 1951 I / 1956-64 I
Cheyney 1954 I
Christiana 1956-64 I
Churchtown 1938-41 I / 1953-64 I
Churchville 1953-64 I / 1950-64 I

Clairton 1940-41 I / 1946-64 I
Clarendon 1947-52 I
Clarence 1946 I / 1953-64 I
Clarion 1953-64 I
Clarks Summit 1941 I / 1956-64 I
Clearfield 1946-50 I / 1955 II / 1956-64 I
Clifton 1946-64 I
Cly 1947-64 I
Clymer 1954-64 I
Coalport 1948 I
Coatesville 1950-64 I
Coburn 1921-41 I / 1946-64 I
Cochranton 1948 I / 1953-64 I
Cogan Station 1931-41 I / 1951-64 I
Cokeburg 1956-60 II / 1961-64 I
Colebrook 1953-64 I
College 1949-51 I / 1953-64 I
Columbia 1940-41 I / 1946-64 I

Conboy 1947-48 I
Concordville 1947-52 I
Conemaugh 1953-64 I
Conewago 1953-64 I
Confluence 1948-57 II / 1958-60 I / 1961-64 I
Conklin 1956-64 I
Connellsville 1941 I / 1946 I / 1947, 4/27-9/15 I / 1948-64 I
Conshohocken 1931-41 I / 1946-64 I
Coopersburg 1941 I / 1950-64 I
Copeland 1954-64 I
Coplay 1951 I / 1956-64 I
Coraopolis 1931-41 I / 1946-55 I / 1956-60 II / 1961-64 I
Corliss 1954-64 I
Cornwells Heights 1954 I
Corry 1941 I / 1946-64 I

PENNSYLVANIA (cont.)

Place	Years	Zone
Coudersport	1956	II
	1957-64	I
Courtney	1953-64	I
Coxton	1951	I
	1956-64	I
Cranesville	1953-64	I
Crafton	1954-64	I
Cranville	1953-64	I
Creighton	1954-64	I
Cresco	1938-41	I
	1946-65	I
Cresson	1949-54	I
	1955	II
	1956-64	I
Cressona	1953-64	I
Creston	1953-64	I
Creswell	1956-64	I
Croydon	1954	I
Crum Lynne	1946-64	I
Culbertson	1947-54	I
	1955-60	II
	1961-64	I
Curtis Park	1954-64	I
Curwensville	1946-64	I
Dagusca bonda	1953-64	I
Dahoga	1953-64	I
Dallas	1956-64	I
Dallastown	1953-64	I
Dalmatia	1948-64	I
Dalton	1949-64	I
Danielsville	1938-41	I
Danville	1946-64	I
Darby	1949-64	I
Darlington	1954-64	I
Darragh	1953-64	I
Dauphin	1940-41	I
	1953-64	I
Davidsville	1956-60	II
	1961-64	I
Dawson	1950-52	I
Daylesford	1954-64	I
Dayton	1951-53	I
Deboistown	1953-64	II
Delabol	1956-64	I
Delano	1951	I
	1956-64	I
Delaware Water Gap	1938-41	I
	1946-52	I
Denver	1940-41	I
	1950-64	I
Deringer	1951	I
	1956-64	I
Derry	1953-64	I
Devault	1940-41	I
Devon	1954-64	I
Dewart	1946-64	I
Dickson	1949-64	I
Dickson City	1953-64	I
Dingmans Ferry	1946-48	I
Donaldson	1941	I
Donohoe	1958-60	I
Donora	1940-41	I
	1950-64	I
Dornsife	1954-64	I
Downingtown	1950-64	I
Douglasville	1931-41	I
	1946-64	I
Doylestown	1950-64	I
Dravosburg	1938-41	I
	1946-54	I
	1958-64	I
Drifton	1951	I
	1956-64	I
Driftwood	1954-64	I
Du Bois	1950-64	I
Dunbar	1949, 4/24-9/4	I
	1950-64	I
Duncannon	1948-64	I
Duncansville	1953-64	I
Dunmore	1951-64	I
Dunning	1953-64	I
Duquesne	1940-41	I
	1946-54	I
	1958-60	I
Duryea	1949-50	I
Dushore	1946	I
	1949-51	I
	1956-64	I
Dysart	1953-64	I
East Bloomsburg	1946-47	I
East Brady	1946-54	I
East Brookside	1950-64	I
East Earl	1940-41	I
East Freedom	1953-64	I
East Liberty	1940-41	I
	1955-60	II
	1961-64	I
Easton	1929-41	I
	1946-64	I
East Petersburg	1950-64	I
East Pittsburgh	1931-41	I
	1946-64	I
East Sandy	1953-64	I
East Stroudsburg	1940-41	I
	1946-64	I
Ebensburg	1947-64	I
Eddington	1954	I
Eddystone	1940-41	I
	1946-54	I
	1958-64	I
Edgely	1954-64	I
Edgewood	1938-41	I
	1954-64	I
Edgeworth	1941	I
	1954-64	I
Eldred	1946-47	I
	1954-64	I
Elgin	1953-64	I
Elizabeth	1938-40	I
Elizabethtown	1940-41	I
	1946-64	I
Elizabethville	1947-48	I
Elkview	1953-64	I
Ellsworth	1929-41	I
	1949-64	I
Elwood City	1920, 3/28-10/30	I
	1921-32	I
	*1933, 4/29-9/31	I
	*1934, 4/28-9/29	I
	*1935, 5/4-9/28	I
	*1936, 5/2-10/3	I
	*1937, 5/1-10/2	I
	*1938, 4/30-10/1	I
	*1939, 4/29-9/30	I
	*1940, 5/4-9/28	I
	*1941, 5/3-10/4	I
	1946-55	I
	1956-58	II
	1959-64	I
Elmhurst	1951-64	I
Elrama	1954-64	I
Elverson	1950-64	I
Elwyn	1954-64	I
Embreeville	1950-64	I
Emigsville	1953-64	I
Emlenton	1946-64	I
Emmaus	1938-41	I
	1946-54	I
	1955-60	II
	1961-64	I

* Change at 0:01 A.M.

PENNSYLVANIA (cont.)

Emporium
1947 — I
1948, 4/29-9/1 — I
1949-64 — I

Emsworth
1954 — I

Enola
1940-41 — I

Enon
1954-64 — I

Ephrata
1940-41 — I
1946-64 — I

Erie
1921, 4/17-10/23 — I
1922, 4/16-10/22 — I
1923, 4/15-10/28 — I
1924, 4/20-10/26 — I
1925, 4/19-10/25 — I
1926, 4/18-10/24 — I
1927, 4/17-10/23 — I
1928, 4/15-10/28 — I
1929, 4/21-10/27 — I
1930, 4/20-10/26 — I
1931, 4/19-10/25 — I
1932, 4/17-10/23 — I
1933, 4/16-10/22 — I
1934, 4/15-10/28 — I
1935, 4/21-10/27 — II
1936, 4/19-10/25 — I
1937, 4/18-10/24 — I
1938, 4/17-10/23 — I
1939, 4/16-10/22 — I
1940, 5/13-9/2 — I
1941 — I
1946-54 — I
1955-59 — II
1960-64 — I

Ernest
1954-64 — I

Etters
1953-64 — I

Evans
1949 — I

Evans City
1938-39 — I
1941, 5/1-10/1 — I
1951-64 — I

Everett
1954 — I

Excelsior
1950-64 — I

Export
1956-64 — I

Fairchance
1949-64 — I

Fairview
1946-64 — I

Falls Creek
1951-64 — I

Fallsington
1938-41 — I
1948-55 — I
1956-57 — II
1958-64 — I

Farrandsville
1953-64 — I

Farrell
1946-49 — I
1950, 4/30-9/30 — I
1951-64 — I

Federal Street
1955 — II
1956-64 — I

Felton
1953-64 — I

Ferndale
1941 — I
1950-64 — I

Finleyville
1949-64 — I

Fleetwood
1940-41 — I

Fleming
1953-64 — I

Flemington
1956-64 — I

Flinton
1953-64 — I

Florin
1941 — I
1946-64 — I

Folcroft
1954-64 — I

Ford City
1941 — I
1946-64 — I

Fordham
1953-64 — I

Forest City
1951-64 — I

Fort Belleville
1953-64 — I

Fort Pitt
1954-64 — I

Forty Fort
1956-64 — I

Foster
1949-50 — I

Foxburg
1946-52 — I
1956-64 — I

Frackville
1948-64 — I

Frankfort
1950-64 — I

Franklin
1941 — I
1946-48 — I
1949, 4/30-9/25 — I
1950-64 — I

Frazer
1953-64 — I

Freedom
1954-64 — I

Freeland
1946-47 — I
1951 — I
1956-64 — I

Freemansburg
1938-41 — I
1951 — I
1956-64 — I

Freeport
1938-41 — I
1946-64 — I

Frugality
1953-64 — I

Frystown
1941 — I

Fullerton
1951 — I
1956-64 — I

Gallitzin
1953-64 — I

Gap
1938-41 — I
1946-64 — I

Garland
1953-64 — I

Garvers Ferry
1954-64 — I

Geneva
1951-64 — I

Germansville
1950-64 — I

Gettysburg
1946-64 — I

Gilberton
1950-64 — I

Gillett
1953-64 — I

Girard
1946-57 — I

Girardville
1949-64 — I

Gladstone
1954-64 — I

Glassport
1940-41 — I

Glenburn
1951-64 — I

Gleneyre
1951-64 — I

Glenfield
1954-64 — I

GlenIron
1953-64 — I

Glen Lock
1938-41 — I
1954-64 — I

Glenlyon
1953-64 — I

Glen Mills
1954-64 — I

Glenolden
1954-64 — I

Glen Osborne
1954-64 — I

Glen Riddle
1954-64 — I

Glen Rock
1941 — I
1946-64 — I

Glenside
1940-41 — I
1950-64 — I

Glen Summit Springs
1951 — I
1956-64 — I

Glen Union
1953-64 — I

Glenville
1947-64 — I

Gordon
1958-60 — II
1961-64 — I

Gordonville
1953-64 — I

Gouldsboro
1947-64 — I

Grampian
1953-64 — I

Grandville Summit
1953-64 — I

Grapeville
1954-64 — I

Gravity
1951-64 — I

Great Belt
1953-64 — I

Great Bend
1951-64 — I

Greencastle
1946-64 — I

Green Dell
1956-64 — I

Greenock
1941 — I

Green Ridge
1946-48 — I

Greensboro
1956-64 — I

Greensburg
1941 — I
1946-64 — I

Greenville
1946-47 — I
1951-64 — I

Gregg
1954-64 — I

Grove City
1946 — I

Grover
1953-64 — I

Guilford Springs
1953-64 — I

Gwynedd
1950-64 — I

Halls
1950-64 — I

Hallstead
1947-64 — I

Hamburg
1938-41 — I
1946-64 — I

PENNSYLVANIA (cont.)

Place / Year	Type
Hamilton	I
1953-64	I
Hanlin Station	I
1953-64	I
Hanover	I
1946-64	I
Hanover Junction	I
1953-64	I
Harmony	I
1941	I
Harrisburg	I
1929-41	I
1946-64	I
Harrison Township	I
1940	I
Hastings	I
1953-64	I
Hatboro	I
1938-41	I
1949-64	I
Hatfield	I
1941	I
1950-64	I
Haverford	I
1938-41	I
1954-64	I
Hawkins	I
1956	II
Haysville	I
1954-64	I
Hazelton	I
1940-41	I
Hellam	I
1954-64	I
1946-64	I
Hellertown	I
1941	I
1950-64	I
(1) Henryville	I
1938-41	I
1949-50	I

Place / Year	Type
Hensel	I
1941	I
Hepburnville	I
1953-64	I
Herminie	I
1947	I
1953-64	I
Herndon	I
1948	I
1953-64	I
Herrick	I
1951-64	I
Hershey	I
1940-41	I
1946-64	I
High Spire	I
1940-41	I
1946-64	I
Hocks Mills	I
1938-41	I
1949-64	I
Hokendauqua	I
1951	I
1956-64	I
Hollidaysburg	I
1941	I
1946-64	I
Hollsopple	I
1956	II
1957-64	I
Holtwood	I
1940-41	I
1953-64	I
Homer City	I
1954-64	I
Homestead	I
1931-41	I
1946-64	I
Homets Ferry	I
1951	I
1950-64	I
Homewood	I
1954-64	I

Place / Year	Type
Homewood Junction	I
1953-64	I
Honesdale	I
1951-64	I
Honey Brook	I
1940-41	I
1953-64	I
Hop Bottom	I
1951-64	I
Horse Shoe Curve	I
1956-64	I
Houston	I
1953-64	I
Houston Junction	I
1953-64	I
Houtzdale	I
1946-50	I
Howard	I
1947-64	I
Hudson	I
1953-64	I
Hummelstown	I
1940-41	I
1950-64	I
Hunlock	I
1951-64	I
Hunlock Creek	II
1949-50	I
Hunter's Run	I
1950-64	I
Huntingdon	I
1953-64	I
Huntsville	I
1955-57	I
1958-60	II
1961-64	I
Huron	I
1946-64	I
Hutchins	I
1951-64	I

Place / Year	Type
Hydetown	I
1953-64	I
Hyndman	I
1949-64	I
Hyner	I
1953-64	I
Idamar	I
1953-64	I
Idlewood	I
1953-64	I
Imler	I
1953-64	I
Indiana	I
1933	I
1941	I
Indiantown Gap	I
1950-64	I
Ingram	I
1950-64	I
Intercourse	I
1941	I
Irvine	I
1953-64	I
Irwin	I
1939-41	I
1946-64	I
Ivy Rock	I
1954-64	I
Jamestown	I
1953-64	I
Jeannette	I
1941	I
Jenkintown	I
1946-64	I
Jermyn	I
1946	II
Jersey Shore	I
1946-54	II
1955-59	I
1960-64	I

Place / Year	Type
Jessup	I
1946	I
1953-64	I
Jessup-Peckville	I
1948	I
Joanna	I
1950-64	I
Johnetta	I
1953-64	I
Johnsonburg	I
1949-64	I
Johnsontown	I
1956-64	I
Johnstown	I
1921-41	I
1946-54	I
1955-59	II
1960-64	I
Jonestown	I
1950-64	I
Julian	I
1953-64	I
Juniata	I
1953-64	I
Kane	I
1946-54	I
1955-56	II
1957-64	I
Kato	I
1953-64	I
Kaylor	I
1953-64	I
Keating	I
1953-64	I
Keating Summit	I
1953-64	I
Kempton	I
1950-64	I
Kennard	I
1951-64	I
Kennett	I
1953-64	I

Place / Year	Type
Kennett Square	I
1931-41	I
1946-64	I
Kimberton	I
1950-64	I
King of Prussia	I
1950-64	I
Kinglsey	I
1951-64	I
Kingston	I
1946-64	I
Kiskimetos Junction	I
1954-64	I
Kittanning	I
1938-41	I
1946-64	I
Kittanning Point	I
1953-64	I
Knox	I
1941	I
Kobute	I
1956-64	I
Koppel	I
1953-64	I
Kunkletown	I
1921-41	I
Kutztown	I
1938-41	I
1946-64	I
Laceyville	I
1951-64	I
Lackawaxen	I
1951-64	I
La Grange	I
1951	I
1956-64	I
Lahaska	I
1950-64	I
La Jose	I
1956-64	I

(1) Farmers did not observe DST in 1940

PENNSYLVANIA (cont.)

Column 1

Place	Years	Class
Lake Ariel	1951-64	I
Lake Carey	1951	I
	1956-64	I
Lake City	1955-56	I
	1957-64	I
Lakeville	1951-64	I
Lawrenceville	1953-64	I
Lawsonham	1956-64	I
Lambertville	1953-64	I
Leaman Place	1956-64	I
Lancaster	1921-41	I
	1931-41	I
	1946-64	I
Landisville	1932-41	I
	1950-64	I
Lanesboro	1951-64	I
Leechburg	1938-41	I
Lanes Mills	1951-64	I
Langdon	1953-64	I
Lees Cross Roads	1950-64	I
Longhorne	1932-41	I
	1950-64	I
Lansdale	1931-41	I
	1946-64	I
Landsdowne	1931-41	I
	1954-64	I
La Plume	1949-50	I
	1955	II
	1956-64	I
Larabee	1953-64	I
Larimer	1954-64	I
Latrobe	1941	I
	1946-64	I

Column 2

Place	Years	Class
Laurel	1953-64	I
Laureldale	1921-41	I
Laurys	1951	I
	1956-64	I
Lebanon	1931-41	I
	1946-64	I
Lee	1953-64	I
Leechburg	1938-41	I
Lemasters	1946-64	I
Lemont	1953-64	I
Lemont Fur	1953-64	I
Lemoyne	1940-41	I
Lenape	1950-64	I
Lenni	1954	I
Lenni Mills	1953-64	I

Column 3 — Leola

Place	Years	Class
Leola	1940-41	I
Letsdale	1954-64	I
Letty	1953-64	I
Level	1956-64	I
Levittown	1956-64	I
Levittown-Tullytown	1954-64	I
Lewisburg	1946-64	I
Lewistown	1931-41	I
	1946-54	II
	1955-59	II
	1960-64	I
Lickdale	1950-64	I
Logansport	1953-64	I
Ligonier	1947-49	I
	1950, 4/30-9/30	I
	1951-52	I
	1956-64	I
Lilly	1949-64	I
Limeridge	1953-64	I
Lincoln	1953-64	I
Lincolnville	1950-64	I
Linesville	1953-64	I
Linfield	1953-64	I
Lititz	1938-41	I
	1946-64	I

Column 4 — Littlestown

Place	Years	Class
Littlestown	1949-64	I
Livermore	1953-64	I
Lloydell	1953-64	I
Lloydville	1953-64	I
Lock Haven	1946-54	I
	1955	II
	1956	II
	1958	I
	1959-64	I
Locksley	1954-64	I
Locust Gap	1950-64	I
Locust Summit	1949-64	I
Logansport	1951-64	I
Lorane	1953-64	I
Lorberry Junction	1950-64	I
Lovell	1956-64	I
Lovett	1953-64	I
Ludlow	1953-64	I
Lurgon	1953-64	I
Luzerne	1950-64	I
Lykens	1949-64	I
Lyndell	1946-64	I
Lyon Station	1941	I
	1950-64	I

Column 5 — Macungie

Place	Years	Class
Macungie	1950-64	I
Mahonoy City	1946-64	I
Mainville	1950-64	I
Malvern	1938-41	I
	1946-64	I
Mammoth	1956-64	I
Manchester	1941	I
	1953-64	I
Manheim	1938-41	I
	1950-64	I
Manor	1949-64	I
Mansfield	1951-64	I
Mapleton	1953-64	I
Marcus Hook	1938-41	I
	1946-64	I
Marianna	1953-64	I
Marietta	1940-41	I
	1946-64	I
Marion	1953-64	I
Mars	1941	I
Marsh Hill	1953-64	I
Martha Furnace	1953-64	I
Martinsburg	1949-64	I
Martins Creek	1940-41	I
	1950-64	I

Column 6 — Matamoras

Place	Years	Class
Matamoras	1941	I
Mauch Chunk	1947-64	I
Mayfield	1946-48	I
McAdoo	1951	I
	1956-64	I
McAuley	1950-64	I
McCartney	1953-64	I
McClure	1946-64	I
McConnellsburg	1956	II
	1957-64	I
McCourtney	1956-64	I
McDonald	1951-64	I
McElhattan	1949-64	I
McGees	1954-64	I
McKeesport	1956-64	I
McKees Rocks	1925-41	I
	1946-64	I
McSherrystown	1940-41	I
	1946-64	I
McVeytown	1953-64	I
Meadow Lands	1953-64	I
Meadville	1930-41	I
	1946	I
	1956-64	I

PENNSYLVANIA (cont.)

Mechanicsburg
1939-41 I
1946-64 I
Media
1924-41 I
1946-64 I
Mehoopany
1951-64 I
Mercer
1956-64 I
Mercersburg
1948-64 I
Mertztown
1950-64 I
Meshoppen
1951 I
1956-64 I
Marion
1941 I
1954-64 I
Mexico
1953-64 I
Meyersdale
1947-54 I
1955-58 II
1959-64 I
Middletown
1932-41 I
1946-64 I
Midland
1938-41 I
1946-52 I
Midway
1953-64 I
Mifflin
1948-64 I
Mifflinburg
1947-64 I
Milan
1951 I
1956-64 I
Milesburg
1953-64 I

Milford
1938-41 I
Mill Creek Junction
1950-64 I
Millers
1951-64 I
Millersburg
1946-64 I
Millerstown
1953-64 I
Millersville
1940-41 I
Millhall
1953-64 I
Millmont
1953-64 I
Millsboro
1956-64 I
Millvale
1956-64 I
Millville
1953-64 I
Mill Village
1951-64 I
Millwood
1953-64 I
Milroy
1953-64 I
Milton
1946-54 I
1955-60 II
1961-64 I
Miners Mill
1953-64 I
Minersville
1948-64 I
Miquon
1954-64 I
Mohnton
1941 I
1946-64 I
Mohrsville
1932-41 I
1950-64 I

Monaca
1938-41 I
1946-54 I
1955-58 II
1959-64 I
Monessen
1946-64 I
Monocasey
1950-64 I
Monongahela
1946-64 I
Monroeton
1951 I
1956-64 I
Mont Alto
1953-64 I
Montandon
1954-64 I
Montgomery
1946-54 I
1955-58 II
1959-64 I
Montoursville
1951-64 I
Montrose
1951 I
1956-64 I
Moore
1954-64 I
Mooresburg
1950-64 I
Moravia
1953-64 I
Morgantown
1941 I
Morrisdale
1953-64 I
Morrisville
1940-41 I
1946-64 I
Morton
1954-64 I
Moscow
1947-64 I

Mosgrove
1953-64 I
Mountaindale
1953-64 I
Mountainhome
1951-64 I
Mount Bethel
1939-41 I
Mount Carmel
1950-64 I
Mount Carmel Junction
1946-64 I
1950-64 I
Mount Gretna
1941 I
Mount Hope
1953-64 I
Mount Holly Springs
1940-41 I
1950-64 I
Mount Jewett
1941 I
1950-64 I
Mount Joy
1941 I
1946-64 I
Mount Pleasant
1946-48 I
1949, 4/27-9/25
1950-54 I
Mount Pocono
1938-41 I
1946-54 I
Mount Union
1938-39 I
1953-54 I
1955-59 II
1960-64 I

Mountville
1938-41 I
1954-64 I
Mount Wolf
1953-64 I
Moylan
1956-64 I
Moylan-Rose Valley
1954-64 I
Moyer
1953-64 I
Muhlenberg
1932-41 I
1946-64 I
Muncy
1946-54 I
1955-60 II
1961-64 I
Muney
1956-64 I
Munhall
1940-41 I
1946-64 I
Munson
1953-64 I
Myerstown
1939-41 I
1946-64 I
Nanticoke
1946-48 I
Nanty Glo
1950-54 I
Narbeth
1938-41 I
1946-54 I
Natrona
1955
Nazareth
1938-41 I
1953-54 I
Nemacolin
1955-59 II
1960-64 I

New Albany
1951 I
1956-64 I
Newberry
1950-64 I
Newberry Junction
1950-64 I
New Bethlehem
1941 I
1946
1956-64 I
New Brighton
1938-41 I
1946-64 I
New Britain
1950-64 I
New Buffalo
1955-60 II
1961-64 I
New Castle
1953-64 I
1946-49 I
1950, 4/30-9/30 I
1951-55 I
1956-58 II
1959-64 I
New Castle Junction
1955-58 I
1959-64 II
New Columbia
1946-64 I
New Cumberland
1950-64 I
New Florence
1940-41 I
1946-64 I
New Freedom
1953-64 I
New Geneva
1953-64 I
New Holland
1956-64 I
1940-41 I
1946-64 I

PENNSYLVANIA (cont.)

Place	Years	
New Hope	1938-41	I
	1946-64	I
New Kensington	1938-41	I
	1946-64	I
New Kingstown	1950-64	I
New Milford	1947-54	I
	1955-60	II
	1961-64	I
New Oxford	1947-54	I
	1955	II
	1956-64	I
Newport	1946-64	I
New Providence	1953-64	I
Newton	1938-41	I
	1946-64	I
New Village	1956-64	I
Newville	1947-64	I
Nicholson	1949-54	I
	1955-57	II
	1958-64	I
Nisbet	1954-64	I
Noblestown	1953-64	I
Norristown	1928-41	I
	1946-64	I
Northampton	1938-41	I
	1946-64	I
North Bend	1953-64	I
North East	1946-54	I
	1955	II
	1956	I
	1957-59	II
	1960-64	I
North Girard	1946-64	I
North Philadelphia	1946-64	II
North Reading	1932-41	I
North Springfield	1948-49	I
North Trafford	1954-64	I
Northumberland	1947-64	I
North Wales	1940-41	I
	1950-64	I
Norwood	1954-64	I
Nottingham	1953-64	I
Oakburne	1954-64	I
Oakdale	1949-54	I
	1955-57	II
	1958-64	I
Oakland	1954-64	I
	1947	I
Oakmont	1954-64	I
Oaks	1940-41	I
Oakville	1953-64	I
Ogden	1941	I
Ohiopyle	1947-64	I
Oil City	1921-41	I
	1946-64	I
Old Forge	1947-64	I
Olyphant	1946-48	I
Oneida	1951	I
Ontelaunee	1924-41	I
	1946-64	I
Ore Hill	1956-64	I
Orelands	1950-64	I
Orrtanna	1947-64	I
Orviston	1953-64	I
Orwigsburg	1946-47	I
Osceola Mills	1947	I
	1956-64	I
Overbrook	1954-64	I
Oxford	1946-64	I
Oxford Furnace	1956-64	I
Palmerton	1938-41	I
	1946-64	I
Palmyra	1939-41	I
	1946-64	I
Palo Alto	1950-64	I
Panassus	1954-64	I
Paoli	1938-41	I
	1946-64	I
Paradise	1940-41	I
	1946-54	I
	1955-58	II
	1959-64	I
Paradise Valley	1951-64	I
Parkesburg	1938-41	I
	1946-64	I
Park Point	1951	I
	1956-64	I
Parsons	1953-64	I
Patton	1953-64	I
Paxinos	1950-64	I
Paxtang	1940-41	I
Peach Bottom	1953-64	I
Peale	1953-64	I
Peckville	1946	I
Pen Argyle	1938-41	I
	1946-64	I
Penfield	1953-64	I
Penn	1954-64	I
Penn Haven Junction	1951	I
Pennsburg	1938-41	I
Pennsville	1953-64	I
Pequea	1953-64	I
Perkasie	1938-41	I
	1949-64	I
Perkiomen Junction	1950-64	I
Petersburg	1953-64	I
Petroleum Center	1953-64	I
Philadelphia & Suburbs	1921-41	I
	1946-64	I
Philipsburg	1946, 4/28-10/31	I
	1947-64	I
Phillipston	1954-64	I
Phoenixville	1931-41	I
	1946-64	I
Pine Grove	1941	I
	1946-64	I
Pitcairn	1941	I
	1953-64	I
Pittsburgh & Suburbs	1920, 3/28-10/31	I
	1921-41	I
	1946-64	I
Pittsfield	1953-64	I
Pittston	1946-64	I
Pittston Junction	1951	I
	1956-64	I
Planebrook	1950-64	I
Platea	1953-64	I
Pleasant Gap	1953-64	I
Plymouth	1947-50	I
Plymouth Meeting	1940-41	I
Pocono Lake	1941	I
Pocono Manor	1938-41	I
	1946-54	I
	1955	II
	1956-64	I
Pocono Summit	1938-41	I
	1946-54	I
	1955-57	II
	1958-64	I
Point Marion	1953-64	I
Pomeroy	1932-41	I
	1953-64	I
Portage	1946-64	I
Port Allegany	1941	I
	1946-64	I
Port Clinton	1950-64	I
Porters	1947-54	I
	1955-56	II
	1957-64	I
Portland	1941	I
	1946-50	I

PENNSYLVANIA (cont.)

Location	Years	Class
Portland Mills	1951–64	I
Port Matilda	1953–64	I
Port Royal	1953–64	I
Pottstown	1931–41	I
	1946–64	I
Pottsville	1941	I
	1946–64	I
Powelton	1931–41	I
	1953–64	I
Preston Park	1951–56	II
	1956–57	I
Primos	1954–60	I
Primrose	1954–64	I
Prompton	1953–64	I
Providence	1924–41	I
	1946–48	I
Pulaski	1953–64	I
Punxsutawney	1949–64	I
Quakake	1950–64	I
Quakertown	1938–41	I
	1946–64	I
Quarryville	1940–41	I
	1949–64	I
Queen	1953–64	I
Raccoon	1946–54	I
	1955–59	II
Racine	1953–64	I
Radebaugh	1954–64	I
Radnor	1940–41	I
	1954–64	I
Ralston	1953–64	I
Rankin	1931–41	I
	1946–64	I
Rasselas	1941	I
	1951–64	I
Reading	1946–64	I
Red Bank	1954–64	I
Redington	1951	I
	1956–64	I
Red Lion	1953–64	I
Red Stone Junction	1956–64	I
Reedsville	1950–64	I
Reinholds	1950–64	I
Rennsylvania	1956–64	I
Rennerdale	1954–64	I
Reno	1953–64	I
Renovo	1960–64	I
Reynolds	1950–64	I
Reynoldsville	1947–52	I
	1956–64	I
Riceville	1953–64	I
Richland	1941	I
Richmond	1950–64	I
	1951–64	I
Ridgway	1931–41	I
	1947–54	I
	1955–56	II
	1957–64	I
Ridley Park	1958	II
	1959–64	I
Riegelsville	1941	I
Rimer	1953–64	I
Rimersburg	1946	I
Rimerton	1951–64	I
	1953–64	I
Ring Town	1954–64	I
Roaring Branch	1950–64	I
	1953–64	I
Roaring Spring	1946–64	I
Robersonia	1950–64	I
Rochester	1931–41	I
	1946–54	I
	1955–56	II
	1957–64	I
Rock Hill	1950–64	I
Rockland	1953–64	I
Rockwood	1947–54	I
Rohrerstown	1940–41	I
Rolfe	1953–64	I
Roscoe	1949	I
	1950, 4/30–9/30	I
Rosemont	1941	I
	1954–64	I
Roslyn	1954–64	I
Rothsville	1955–56	II
	1957–64	I
Rousch Creek	1950–64	I
Rouseville	1953–64	I
Royalton	1953–64	I
Rowland	1951–64	I
Royersford	1938–41	I
	1946–64	I
Ruffsdale	1953–64	I
Rummerfield	1951	I
Rupert	1956–64	I
Rushland	1950–64	I
Rutherford	1946–64	I
Ryde	1953–64	I
Sabula	1953–64	I
Saegerstown	1951–64	I
Saint Davids	1954–64	I
Saint Marys	1947–64	I
Saint Peters	1950–64	I
Saltsburg	1949, 4/30–9/25	I
	1951–64	I
Sanderton	1950–64	I
Sandy Ridge	1953–64	I
Sarver	1953–64	I
Satterfield	1951	I
Saxton	1949–52	I
Saybrook	1953–64	I
Saylorsburg	1941	I
Sayre	1946–64	I
Scalp	1956–64	I
Scenery Hill	1953–64	I
Schenley	1954–64	I
Schuylkill Haven	1941	I
	1946–64	I
Schwenk	1953–64	I
Schwenksville	1938–41	I
	1946–64	I
Scottdale	1946–50	I
	1951, 4/29–9/23	I
	1952–64	I
Scranton	1946–64	I
Secane	1954–64	I
Selinsgrove	1947–64	I
Sellersville	1940–41	I
	1946–64	I
Sergeant	1953–64	I
Seward	1953–64	I
Sewickley	1931–41	I
	1946–54	I
	1955–58	II
	1959–64	I
Shafton	1953–64	I
Shamokin	1946–64	I
Sharon	1946–49	I
	1950, 4/30–9/30	I
	1951–64	I
Sharon Hill	1954–64	I
Sharpsburg	1947	I
Sharpsville	1946	I
	1951–64	I
Shawmont	1954–64	I
Shawnee	1938–39	I
Shawnee–on–Delaware	1955–59	II
	1960–64	I

PENNSYLVANIA (cont.)

Place	Year(s)	Class
Sheffield	1941	I
	1946-64	I
Shellsville	1941	I
Shenandoah	1938-41	I
	1946-64	I
Shenango	1950-64	I
Sheppton	1951	I
	1956-64	II
Shields	1947	I
	1954-64	I
Shillington	1956-64	I
Shinglehouse	1940-41	I
Shippensburg	1950-54	I
	1955-57	II
	1958-64	I
Shippenville	1941	I
Ship Road	1954-64	I
Shiremanstown	1940-41	I
	1950-64	I
Shocks Mill	1953-64	I
Shoemakersville	1946-64	I
Shrewsbury	1953-64	I
Silverton	1961-64	I
Sinking Spring	1940-41	I
	1946-64	I
Sinnamahoning	1953-64	I

Place	Year(s)	Class
Sizerville	1953-64	I
Skytop	1941	I
Slatington	1938-41	I
	1946-64	I
Sligo	1956-64	I
Slippery Rock	1956-64	I
Smethport	1956-64	II
Smithfield	1941	I
	1953-64	I
Smyser	1947	I
Snedekerville	1953-64	I
Snowshoe	1953-64	II
Snyder	1950-64	I
Somerton	1950-64	I
Souderton	1938-41	I
	1949	I
South Danville	1946-64	I
South Duquesne	1954-64	I
South Heights	1941	I
South Sterling	1955-60	I
South Williamsport	1953-64	I
Spartansburg	1950-64	I

Place	Year(s)	Class
Split Rock Lodge	1955-59	II
	1960-64	I
Spring City	1941, 5/1-10/1	I
	1946-64	I
Spring Creek	1953-64	I
Springdale	1941	I
	1946-49	I
	1950, 4/30-9/30	II
	1951-64	I
Spring Grove	1921-41	I
	1946-56	I
	1957-58	II
	1959-64	I
Spring Mills	1954-64	I
Springville	1951	I
	1956-64	I
Spruce Creek	1953-64	I
Standing Stone	1951	I
	1956-64	I
	1959-64	I
Starrucca	1951-64	I
State College	1921-41	I
	1946-64	I
Steelton	1932-41	I
	1946-64	I
Steinsville	1950-64	I
Stevens	1950-64	I

Place	Year(s)	Class
Stockertown	1938-41	I
	1951	I
	1956-64	I
Stockton	1951	I
	1956-64	I
Strafford	1953-64	I
Strassburg	1921-41	I
	1953-64	I
Sterling Run	1953-64	I
Strickler	1954-64	I
Stroudsburg	1938-41	I
	1946-64	I
Sturgeon	1954-64	I
Suedburg	1951	I
	1956-64	I
Summerhill	1953-64	I
Sunbury	1946-54	I
	1955-58	I
	1959-64	I
Suplee	1950-64	I
Susquehanna	1951-64	I
Swanville	1948-64	I
Swarthmore	1932-41	I
	1946-64	I
Swatara	1950-64	I
Swedeland	1950-64	I

Place	Year(s)	Class
Swissvale	1940-41	I
	1946-64	I
Sycamore	1953-64	I
Tamanend	1950-64	I
Tamaqua	1946-64	I
Tarentum	1931-41	I
	1946-64	I
Tarrs	1953-64	I
Taylor	1947-64	I
Telford	1940-41	I
	1950-64	I
Temple	1932-41	I
	1950-64	I
Templeton	1921-41	I
	1953-64	I
Terre Hill	1940-41	I
Tetamy	1941	II
Thomasville	1946-54	I
	1955-58	I
	1959-64	I
Thompsontown	1953-64	I
Thorndale	1953-64	I
Throop	1953-64	I

Place	Year(s)	Class
Tiona	1953-64	I
Tionesta	1941	I
Tipton	1953-64	I
Titusville	1921-41	I
	1946-64	I
Tobyhanna	1946-64	I
Tomhicken	1951	I
	1956-64	I
Topton	1921-41	I
	1946-64	I
Torrance	1954	I
Torresdale	1955	II
	1956-64	I
Toughkenamon	1921-41	I
	1947-64	I
Towanda	1946	I
	1951-54	I
	1956-64	I
Tower City	1955-58	II
	1959-64	I
Trafford	1946-64	I
Trainer	1947-64	I
Treichler	1932-41	I
	1946-64	I
	1955-56	II
	1957-64	I
Tremont	1951	I
	1956-64	I
	1921-41	I
	1946-64	I

PENNSYLVANIA (cont.)

Trenton — 1941 I; 1946-47 I
Trevorton — 1932-41 I; 1946-64 I
Trevost — 1950-64 I
Trexler — 1950-64 I
Trexlertown — 1950-64 I
Tryonville — 1953-64 I
Trout Run — 1953-64 I
Troy — 1953-64 I
Tullytown — 1946-47 I; 1956-64 I
Tunkhannock — 1951-64 I
Turtle Creek — 1940-41 I; 1946-64 I
Turtle Point — 1953-64 I
Twin Oaks — 1941 I
Tyler — 1953-64 I
Tyrone — 1921-41 I; 1946-54 I; 1955-61 I; 1962-64 I
Ulster — 1951 I; 1956-64 I
Union City — 1921-41 I; 1946-64 I

Union Dale — 1951-64 I
Uniontown — 1946-64 I
Upper Black Eddy — 1921-41 I
Upper Darby — 1931-41 I
Utica — 1951-64 I
Vail — 1953-64 I
Valley Forge — 1953-64 I
Vandergrift — 1946-47 I; 1956-64 I
Vandling — 1951-64 I
Van Voorhis — 1953-64 I
Verona — 1947 I; 1954-64 I
Versailles — 1921-41 I
Vicksburg — 1953-64 I
Victory — 1953-64 I
Villanova — 1954-64 I
Vintondale — 1953-64 I
Wago Junction — 1953-64 I
Wagontown — 1950-64 I
Walker's Mill — 1954-64 I
Wallaceton — 1953-64 I

Walnut Bottom — 1950-64 I
Wampum — 1950-55 I; 1956-58 II; 1959-64 I
Wapwallopen — 1953-64 I
Ward — 1953-64 I
Warnersville — 1950-64 I
Warren — 1939, 6/3-9/4; 1940-41 I; 1946-50 I; 1951, 4/29-9/23; 1952-54 I; 1955 II; 1956-64 I
Washington — 1941-46 I; 1946-64 I
Waterford — 1953-64 I
Watsontown — 1946-54 I; 1955-59 II; 1960-64 I
Watsonville — 1956-64 I
Wawa — 1954-64 I
Waymart — 1953-64 I
Wayne — 1931-41 I; 1946-64 I
Wayne Junction — 1947-64 I

Waynesboro — 1946-56 I; 1957-59 II; 1960-64 I
Waynesburg — 1946-64 I
Weedville — 1953-64 I
Weikert — 1953-64 I
Wellsboro — 1956-64 I
Wernersville — 1938-41 I; 1946-49 I
West Brownsville — 1953-64 I
West Chester — 1930-41 II; 1946-64 I
West Elizabeth — 1954-64 I
West Fairfield — 1940-41 I
West Grove — 1946-64 I
West Homestead — 1940-41 I
West Leesport — 1950-64 I
West Middlesex — 1940-41 I; 1953-64 I
West Milton — 1950-64 I
West Nanticoke — 1949-50 I
West Newton — 1946-64 I
1941; 1946; 1950-64 I
Westover — 1953-64 I

West Pittsburgh — 1938-41 I
West Pittston — 1946-64 I
West Plymouth — 1951-64 I
West Point — 1950-64 I
Westport — 1953-64 I
West Reading — 1931-41 I; 1946-54 I; 1955 II; 1956-57 I; 1958 II; 1959-64 I
Westtown — 1954-64 I
West Willow — 1938-41 I; 1946
West Winfield — 1956-64 I
Westwood — 1950-64 I
Wetmore — 1953-64 I
Wheatland — 1953-64 I
White Deer — 1950-64 I
White Haven — 1951; 1956-64 I
Whiteland — 1954-64 I
White Mills — 1951-64 I
Whitford — 1938-41 I; 1946; 1950-64 I; 1953-64 I

Wilcox — 1954-64 I
Wilkes-Barre — 1946-64 I
Wilkinsburg — 1931-41 I; 1946-64 I
Williamsburg — 1950-64 I
Williamson School — 1954-64 I
Williamsport — 1946-54 I; 1955-58 II; 1959-64 I
Williamstown — 1946-64 I
Willow Grove — 1938-41 I
Wilmerding — 1920, 3/28-10/31; 1921-41 I; 1946-64 I
Wilmore — 1953-64 I
Wilson — 1954-64 I
Wimmers — 1951-64 I
Windber — 1950, 4/30-9/30; 1951-64 I
Winburne — 1953-64 I
Winfield — 1950-64 I
Windgap — 1938-41 I
Wingate — 1953-64 I

149

PENNSYLVANIA (cont.)

Wingerton
1953-64 I
Winton
1946-48 I
1953-64 I
Wolfsburg
1953-64 I
Womelsdorf
1950-64 I
Woodland
1953-64 I
Woodlane
1950-64 I
Wormleysburg
1940-41 I
Wrightsville
1941   I
1946-64 I
Wyalusing
1951   I
1956-64 I
Wynnewood
1954-64 I
Wyoming
1949-64 I
Wysox
1951   I
1956-64 I
Yardley
1921-41 I
Yates
1953-64 I
Yeagertown
1953-64 I
Yellow House
1921-41 I
Yocumtown
1921-41 I
Yoe
1953-64 I

York
1932-41 I
1946-56 I
1957-58 II
1959-64 I
York Haven
1921-41 I
1954-64 I
Youngsville
1950-64 I
Youngwood
1949-64 I
Zelienople
1956-64 I
1950-64 I
1938-41 I

RHODE ISLAND

1636		Area settled
1752	9/14	Gregorian (NS) Calendar adopted in U.S.A.
1790	5/29	State entered Union
1883	11/18	Noon, Eastern Standard Time (75° W) adopted

DAYLIGHT (OR WAR) TIME OBSERVED:
(Changes at 2 A.M.)

1918	3/31-10/27	World War I
1919	3/30-10/26	World War I
1920	To 1922	Not observed
1923	4/29 - 9/30	** Observed state-wide except in ten towns: Foster, Scituate and eight villages in southern section.
1942	2/9 - 9/30/45	World War II
1946	To 1948	** Optional, but generally observed throughout the State. Refer to Tables for dates.
1949	To 1965	Observed state-wide. Refer to Table for dates.
1966	To 1979	For dates, see Table, page 181.
1973	11/1-1974 4/29	Observed DST to conserve energy.

** Check with local authorities

TABLE

Year		Year	
1918	War Time	1946	4/28-9/29
1919	War Time	1947	4/27-9/28
1923	4/29-9/30	1948	4/25-9/26
1924	4/27-9/28	1949	4/24-9/25
1925	4/26-9/27	1950	4/30-9/24
1926	4/25-9/26	1951	4/29-9/30
1927	4/24-9/25	1952	4/27-9/28
1928	4/29-9/30	1953	4/26-9/27
1929	4/28-9/29	1954	4/25-9/26
1930	4/27-9/28	1955	4/24-10/29
1931	4/26-9/27	1956	4/28-10/28
1932	4/24-9/25	1957	4/28-10/27
1933	4/30-9/24	1958	4/27-10/26
1934	4/29-9/30	1959	4/26-10/25
1935	4/28-9/29	1960	4/24-10/30
1936	4/26-9/27	1961	4/30-10/29
1937	4/25-9/26	1962	4/29-10/28
1938	4/24-10/1	1963	4/28-10/27
1939	4/30-9/24	1964	4/26-10/25
1940	4/28-9/29	1965	4/25-10/31
1941	4/27-9/28	1973	11/1-1974 4/29
1942-45	War Time	1965	War Time

151

TABLE	
1918	War Time
1919	War Time
1941	8/1-12/31
1942	1/2-2/9
1942-45	War Time

SOUTH CAROLINA

1670		Area settled
1752	9/14	Gregorian (NS) Calendar adopted in U.S.A.
1788	5/23	State entered the Union
1883	11/18	Noon, Eastern Standard Time (75°W) adopted

DAYLIGHT (OR WAR) TIME OBSERVED:
(Changes at 2 A.M.)

1918	3/31 - 10/27	World War I
1919	3/30 - 10/26	World War I
1920	To 1940	Not observed
1941	8/1 - 2/9/42	Observed by State Offices Only.
1942	2/9 - 9/30/45	World War II
1946	To 1966	Not observed
1967	To 1979	For dates, see Table, page 181.

SOUTH DAKOTA

1752	9/14	Gregorian (NS) Calendar adopted in U.S.A.
1794		Area settled
1883	11/18	Noon, Mountain Standard Time (105°W) adopted in western portion. Central Standard Time (90°W) adopted in eastern portion. Borderline places using CST: Mackenzie, Mobridge, Murdo and Pierre; others on MST.
1889	11/2	State entered the Union

DAYLIGHT (OR WAR) TIME OBSERVED:
(Changes at 2 A.M.)

1918	3/31 – 10/27	World War I
1919	3/30 – 10/26	World War I
1920	To 1941	Not observed
1942	2/9 – 9/30/45	World War II
1946	To 1965	Not observed state-wide. See Local Ordinance Listing.
1966		See Chapter VII
1967	To 1979	For dates, see Table, page 181.

OBSERVATION BY LOCAL ORDINANCE:
(Refer to Table for Month & Day)

Jefferson
** 1964
Vermillion
** 1964
Yankton
** 1964

TABLE

1918	War Time
1919	War Time
1942-45	War Time

** Check with local authorities

TABLE	
1918	War Time
1919	War Time
1920	3/28-10/31
1940	5/12-9/29
1942-45	War Time
1946	5/8-9/29
1947	4/27-9/28
1948	4/25-9/26
1956	4/29-10/28

TENNESSEE

1752	9/14	Gregorian (NS) Calendar adopted in the U.S.A.
1757		Area settled
1796	6/1	State entered the Union
1883	11/18	Noon, Central Standard Time (90°W) adopted, except borderline communities of Bristol, Elizabethton, Erwin and Johnson City, on EST (75°W)
1941	7/21	All State offices on CST (90°W); compliance voluntary for citizenship.
1946		EST adopted year round for 1946 only in:

Alcoa	Jefferson City	Morristown
Bristol	Johnson City	Newport
Chattanooga	Jonesboro	Norris
Clinton	Knoxville	Oak Ridge
Dandridge	Lenoir City	Rogersville
Gatlinburg	Loudon	Sevierville
Greeneville	Maryville	Sweetwater

1947	9/28	Official EST boundary moved west to include additional portions of Eastern Tennessee**
1949	10/14 2:00 AM	EST adopted in the Chattanooga area, embracing Hamilton County on 8/14, and extended to include Rhea County on 8/28
1960	4/3	EST (75°W) effective in a portion of Northern Tennessee, including Scott, Morgan and Roane Counties.**

DAYLIGHT (OR WAR) TIME OBSERVED:
(Changes at 2 A.M.)

1918	3/31 - 10/27	World War I
1919	3/30 - 10/26	World War I. Perhaps not observed East of Knoxville.**

** Check with local authorities

TENNESSEE (cont.)

1920	To 1940	Not observed state-wide. See Local Ordinance Listing.
1941	8/1-9/28	Not observed statewide. See observation by Local Ordinanc
1942	2/9-9/30-45	World War II
1946	To 1965	Not observed state-wide. See Local Ordinance Listing.
1966	See Chapter VII	
1967	To 1979	For dates, see Table, page 181.

OBSERVATION BY LOCAL ORDINANCE:
(Refer to Table for Month & Day if not shown)

Chattanooga
1941, 7/19-9/28 (0 hr)
1949, 8/9-9/25
1974, 5/5-10/27 (power crunch)

Clarksville
1941, 7/20-9/15 (0 hr)

Franklin
1941, 7/20-9/15 (0 hr)

Hamilton
1941, 7/20-9/28 (0 hr)
1949, 8/9-9/25
1974, 5/5-10/27 (power crunch)

Humboldt
1941, 7/20-9/15 (0 hr)

Murfreesboro
1941, 7/20-9/15 (0 hr)

Nashville
1941, 7/6-9/15 (0 hr)

Pulaski
1941, 7/20-9/15 (0 hr)

Shelbyville
1941, 7/20-9/15 (0 hr)

Trenton
1941, 7/20-9/15 (0 hr)

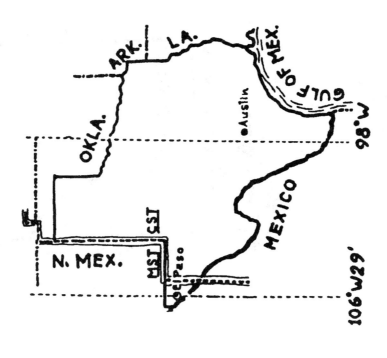

TABLE		
1918	War Time	
1919	War Time	
1942-45	War Time	

TEXAS

1686	Area settled	
1752	9/14	Gregorian (NS) Calendar adopted in U.S.A.
1845	9/29	State entered the Union
1883	11/18	Noon, Central Standard Time (90°W) adopted except in El Paso, Pecos and the westernmost part of the state, which through the years has observed Mountain Standard Time (105°W).
1918	10/27-3/7/21	The panhandle (greater Amarillo area) changed from Central (90°W) to Mountain (105°W) Standard Time.
1921	3/4	Official U.S. boundary of the CST zone was moved westward to include all of Texas; however, El Paso, Pecos and the surrounding area continued to observe MST all through the years..
1970	5/17	El Paso adopted Mountain Standard Time (105°W) at 2:00 A.M.

DAYLIGHT (OR WAR) TIME OBSERVED:
(Changes at 2 A.M.)

1918	3/31-10/27	World War I
1919	3/30-10/26	World War I
1920	To 1941	Not observed
1942	2/9-9/30/45	World War II
1946	To 1966	Not observed
1967	To 1979	For dates, see Table, page 181.

UTAH

1752	9/14	Gregorian (NS) Calendar adopted in U.S.A.
1847		Area settled
1883	11/18	Noon, eastern portion adopted Mountain Standard Time (105°W). Borderline places on MST: Bingham, Boulton, Brigham, Farmington, Garfield, Ogden, Lynndyl, Milford, Newhouse and Salt Lake City. Rest of communities in western portion adjoining Nevada adopted Pacific Standard Time.
1896	1/4	State entered the Union

DAYLIGHT (OR WAR) TIME OBSERVED:
(Changes at 2 A.M.)

1918	3/31 - 10/27	World War I
1919	3/30 - 10/26	World War I
1920	To 1941	Not observed
1942	2/9 - 9/30/45	World War II
1946	To 1965	Not observed
1966		See Chapter VII
1967	To 1979	For dates, see Table, page 181.

TABLE

1918	War Time
1919	War Time
1942-45	War Time

IDAHO WYO. COLO. NEV. ARIZ. PST MST Salt Lake City 111°W54'

VERMONT

1724		Area settled
1752	9/14	Gregorian (NS) Calendar adopted in U.S.A.
1791	3/4	State entered the Union
1883	11/18	Noon, Eastern Standard Time (75°W) adopted

DAYLIGHT (OR WAR) TIME OBSERVED:
(Changes at 2 A.M.)

1918	3/31 - 10/27	World War I
1919	3/30 - 10/26	World War I
1920	To 1941	Not observed state-wide. See Local Ordinance Listing.
1942	2/9 - 9/30/45	World War II
1946	To 1954	Not observed state-wide. See Local Ordinance Listing.
1955	To 1966	Observed state-wide. Refer to Table for dates.
1967	To 1979	

For dates, see Table, page 181.

OBSERVATION BY LOCAL ORDINANCE:
(Refer to Table for Month & Day if not shown)

Abnaki	1952-66
Albany	1941
	1946-66
Andover	1941
	1946-66
Arlington	1941
	1946-66
Alburg	1951-66

Ascutney	1946-66
Bakersfield	1941
Barnet	1940-41
Barre	1938-41
	1946-66
Barton	1940-41

Bartonsville	1941
	1951-66
Beecher Falls	1940
	1948-66
Bellows Falls	1938-41
	1946-66
Belvidere	1941

Bennington	1922-32
	1938-41
	1946-66
Berlin	1941
Bethel	1938-41
	1947-66
Bloomfield	1941

Bradford	1938-41
	1946-66
Braintree	1941
Brandon	1938-41
	1946-66
Brattleboro	1938-41
	1946-66
Bridgewater	1940-41

Bristol	1939-41
Brookfield	1940-41
Brookline	1941
Burke	1940-41
Burlington	1938-41
	1946-66

TABLE

Year	War Time	Year	War Time
1918	War Time	1942-45	War Time
1919	War Time	1946	War Time
1922	4/30-9/24	1947	4/27-9/28
1923	4/29-9/30	1948	4/25-9/26
1924	4/27-9/28	1949	4/24-9/25
1925	4/26-9/27	1950	4/30-9/24
1926	4/25-9/26	1951	4/29-9/30
1927	4/24-9/25	1952	4/27-9/28
1928	4/29-9/30	1953	4/26-9/27
1929	4/28-9/29	1954	4/25-9/26
1930	4/27-9/28	1955	4/24-10/30
1931	4/26-9/27	1956	4/29-10/28
1932	4/24-9/25	1957	4/28-10/27
1933	4/30-9/24	1958	4/27-10/26
1934	4/29-9/30	1959	4/26-10/25
1935	4/28-9/29	1960	4/24-10/30
1936	4/26-9/27	1961	4/30-10/29
1937	4/25-9/26	1962	4/29-10/28
1938	4/24-9/25	1963	4/28-10/27
1939	4/30-9/24	1964	4/26-10/25
1940	4/28-9/29	1965	4/25-10/31
1941	4/27-9/28	1966	4/24-10/30

VERMONT (cont.)

Cabot
1940
1941, 5/18-9/21
Cambridgeport
1940
1941, 5/18-9/21
Canaan
1938-41
1946-66
Castleton
1938-41
1948-66
Cavendish
1940-41
1946-66
Center Rutland
1946-66
Charlotte
1951-66
Clarendon
1940
1941, 5/1-10/1
1948-66
Chelsea
1941
Chester
1939-41
1947-49
Chester Depot
1951-66
Clarendon
1941
Colchester
1940-41
Concord
1940-41
1946-66
Craftsbury
1939, 5/28-9/10
1940, 5/26-9/8
1941, 5/25-9/14
1952
Cuttingsville
1947-66
Danby
1940-41
1946-66

Danville
1939-41
Deldens
1951-66
Derby Line
1938-41
Dorset
1940-41
Fairlee
1939-41
1946-66
Dover
1940-41
Dummerston
Station
1941
1946-66
East Alburg
1947
East Clarendon
1951-66
East Concord
1946-66
East Dorset
1946-66
East Northfield
1946
East Putney
1946-66
East Shoreham
1951-66
East Thetford
1946-66
East Wallingford
1946-66
Ely
1947-66
Enosburg Falls
1939, 5/28-9/10
1940, 5/26-9/8
1941, 5/25-9/14
1952
Essex Junction
1939-41
1946-66

Fairhaven
1938-41
1946-48
1949, 5/1-9/25
1954-66
Fairfax
1940-41
Fairlee
1939-41
1946-66
Ferrisburg
1947-66
Ferrisburg Station
1951-66
Florence
1940-41
1947-66
Gassetts
1940-41
1946-66
Gilman
1938-41
Grafton
1940-41
Grand Isle
1941
1947-66
Grand Isle Station
1951-66
Granville
1941
Greensboro
1941
Groton
1940-41
Grout
1946-66
Guildhall
1946-66
Guilford
1940-41

Halifax
1941
Hancock
1941
Hardwick
1939, 5/7-9/24
1940, 5/5-9/29
1941, 5/4-9/28
Hartford
1940-41
Hartland
1946-66
Healdville
1951-66
Highgate Springs
1939
Hinesburg
1940-41
Hyde Park
1940-41
Hydeville
1948
Irasburg
1941
Isle La Motte
Station
1949-66
Jamaica
1940-41
Jay
1941
Jeffersonville
1939-41
Johnson
1939-41
Kirby
1941
Lake Bomoseen
1939-41
Larrabees Point
1951-66

Leicester Junction
1949
1951
1953-66
Lewiston
1946-66
Lincoln
1941
Londonberry
1938-41
Lowell
1941
Ludlow
1939-41
1946-66
Lunenburg
1939-41
Lyndonville
1939-41
Maidstone
1946-66
Manchester
1938-41
1947-66
Manchester Depot
1951-66
Marlboro
1941
Mendon
1940-41
Middlebury
1939-41
1947-54
Middletown
1940-41
Middletown Springs
1939-41
Middlesex
1941-41
1946-66
Miles Pond
1946-66

Milton
1940-41
1946-66
Montgomery
1940-41
Montpelier
1938-41
1946-66
Montpelier Junction
1947-66
Moretown
1940-41
Morgan
1941
Morristown
1940-41
1946-66
Mount Holly
1949
1951-66
Newfane
1940-41
New Haven
1941
1947-50
New Haven Junction
1951-66
Newport City
1939-40
North Bennington
1946-66
North Clarendon
1951-66
North Concord
1946-66
North Dorset
1951-66
North Ferrisburg
1949-50
Northfield
1940-41
1946-66

VERMONT (cont.)

North Hartland 1946-66
North Hero 1941, 1947-66
North Hero Station 1951-66
North Pownal 1938-41, 1946-66
North Thetford 1946-66
North Troy 1940-41, 1946-66
Norton 1951
Norwich 1939-41, 1946, 1948-66
Old Chatham 1949
Orange 1941
Orleans 1939-41
Orwell 1947-50
Pawlet 1941
Peacham 1940-41
Peru 1940-41
Piermont 1946-66
Pittsfield 1941
Pittsford 1938-41, 1948-50

Plainfield 1939-41
Plymouth 1941
Pompanoosuc 1946-66
Pomfret 1941
Poultney 1938-41, 5/1-10/1, 1946-66
Pownal 1940-41, 1946-66
Proctor 1939-41, 1948-66
Proctorsville 1938-41, 1949-66
Putney 1940-41
Putney Station 1946-66
Queen City Park 1951-66
Randolph 1946-66
Randolph Village 1939-41
Readsboro 1940-41
Richford 1939, 5/26-9/3, 1940, 5/26-9/1, 1941, 5/25-9/7, 1948
Richmond 1940-41, 5/1-10/1, 1946-66
Rochester 1939-41

Rockingham 1939-41, 1951-66
Roxbury 1941, 1947-66
Royalton 1940-41
Rupert 1940-41
Rutland 1929-31, 1937-41, 1946-66
Ryegate 1941
Saint Albans City 1938-41, 1946, 1948-66
Saint Johnsbury 1938-41, 1946-66
Salisbury 1952-66
Saxton's River 1939-41
Searsburg 1941
Shaftsbury 1938-41, 1947
Shelburne 1940-41, 5/1-10/1, 1951-66
Sheldon 1940-41

Shoreham Center 1951-66
Shrewsbury 1940-41
South Burlington 1940-41
South Hero 1941, 1947-66
South Newbury 1946-66
South Royalton 1947-66
South Shaftsbury 1938-41, 1946-66
South Wallingford 1951-66
Springfield 1938-41
Stamford 1940-41
Stafford 1941
Stevens 1946-66
Stockbridge 1941
Stowe 1939-41
Sunderland 1951-66
Summit 1947-49
Sutton 1940-41
Swanton 1938, 5/29-9/11, 1939, 5/28-9/10, 1940, 5/26-9/8, 1941, 5/25-9/14, 1946-66

Thetford 1940-41
Topsham 1941
Townshend 1940-41
Turnbridge 1941
Vergennes 1938-41
Vernon 1951, 1953-66
Vershire 1940-41, 1946-66
Waitsfield 1941
Walburg 1951-66
Wallingford 1940-41, 1947-66
Wardsboro 1940-41
Warren 1940-41
Washington 1940-41
Waterbury 1938-41, 1946-66
Weathersfield 1940-41
Wells 1941
Wells River 1946-66
West Fairlee 1941

West Hartford 1940-41, 1947-50
Westminister 1941
Westminister Station 1940-41, 1946-66
Westmore 1941
Weston 1941
West Pawlet 1940-41, 1946-66
West Rutland 1948-66
West Windsor 1941
Weybridge 1951-54
White River Junction 1941, 1947-66
Whiting 1946
Whitingham 1952-66
Wilder 1940-41, 1946-66
Williamstown 1940, 4/28-10/27, 1941, 4/27-10/26
Williston 1941
Wilmington 1938 -41
Windham 1941

161

VIRGINIA

1607		Area settled
1752	9/14	Gregorian (NS) Calendar adopted in U.S.A.
1788	6/25	State entered the Union
1883	11/18	Noon, Eastern Standard Time (75°W) adopted, except west of Big Stone Gap (82W46) on CST (90°W)
1947		Entire State included in EST Zone.

DAYLIGHT (OR WAR) TIME OBSERVED:
(Changes at 2 A.M.)

1918	3/31 - 10/27	World War I
1919	3/30 - 10/26	World War I
1920	To 1941	Not observed
1942	2/9 - 9/30/45	World War II
1946	To 1961	Not observed state-wide. See Local Ordinance Listing.
1961	4/30-10/1	
1961		Until this year Northern Virginia (Fairfax County, Arlington County and Alexandria) observed DST, but by 1961 the whole state was in confusion. See Local Ordinance Listing.
1962	(1)	The Counties of Arlington and Fairfax, and the Cities of Alexandria and Falls Church, observed DST from the last Sunday in April to the last Sunday in October. See Local Ordinance Listing. The remainder of the State of Virginia observed DST from 5/30 to 9/3, except the City of Bristol. Changes at 24 hr.
1963		The Counties of Arlington and Fairfax, and the Cities of Alexandria and Falls Church, observed DST from the

(1) See map of Washington, D.C.

TABLE I

1918	War Time		*1959	4/26-10/25
1919	War Time		*1960	4/24-10/30
1942-45	War Time		*1961	4/30-10/29
1946	4/28-9/29		*1962	4/29-10/28
1947	4/27-9/28		*1963	4/28-10/27
1948	4/25-9/26		*1964	4/26-10/25
1949	4/24-9/25		*1965	4/25-10/31
1950	4/30-9/24			
1951	4/29-9/30			
1952	4/27-9/28			
1953	4/26-9/27			
*1954	4/25-9/26			
*1955	4/24-9/25			
*1956	4/29-9/30			
*1957	4/28-9/29			
*1958	4/27-10/26			

TABLE II

| 1961 | 4/30-10/1 |

ATLANTIC OCEAN

MD. D.C. W.VA. N.C. TENN.

Big Stone Gap 82°W46' KY.

VIRGINIA (cont.)

last Sunday in April to the last Sunday in October. See Local Ordinance Listing.

1964 — The remainder of the State of Virginia observed DST from 5/30 to 9/2, except the City of Bristol. Changes at 24 hr.

The Counties of Arlington and Fairfax, and the Cities of Alexandria and Falls Church, observed DST from the **last Sunday in April to the last Sunday in October.** See Local Ordinance Listing.

The remainder of the State of Virginia observed DST from 5/31 to 9/6 (changes at 24 hrs) except the Counties adjoining Kentucky and Tennessee, as follows:

Buchanan   Russell   Washington
Dickenson   Scott   Wise
Lee   Smyth

and the following cities also remained on EST:

Bristol   Norton

1965 — See 1964. Same, except DST observance dates which were from 6/6 to 9/5. Changes at 24 hr.

1966 — See Chapter VII

1967 To 1979 — For dates, see Table, page 181.

OBSERVATION BY LOCAL ORDINANCE:
(Refer to Table for Month and Day)

COUNTIES

Albemarle 1961	Charles City 1961	Goochland 1961 In schools only, not the courts.	King George 1961 4/30-10/1	Powhatan 1961	Stafford 1961 Schools only
Amherst 1961 5/3-10/29	Chesterfield 1961 4/30-10/1	Greene 1961	King William 1961	Prince George 1961 4/30-10/1	Warren 1961
Arlington 1948 5/2-9/26 1949-66	Dinurddie 1961 4/30-10/1	Greensville 1961 4/30-5/6	Nelson 1961	Prince William 1961	Westmoreland 1961 5/15 (0hr)-10/29
Augusta 1961 4/30-9/4 (0 hr)	Fairfax 1948 5/2-9/26 1949 1950 6/28-9/24 1951-66	Hanover 1961 4/30-10/1	New Kent 1961	Purcellville 1961	
Campbell 1961 5/3-10/29	Fauquier 1961 5/16 (0 hr)-10/29	Henrico 1961 4/30-10/1	Northumberland 1961 5/23-10/29	Rockbridge 1961	
Caroline 1961 4/30-10/1		James City 1961	Orange 1961	Rockingham 1961 4/30-10/1	
			Page 1961	Shenandoah 1961	

VIRGINIA (cont.)

<u>COMMUNITIES</u>

Alexandria (City)
1948 5/2-9/26   I
1949-1966
Altavista
1961   I
Ashland
1961   I
Berryville
1961   I
Buena Vista
1961   I
Charlottesville
1961   I
Colonial Beach
1961 5/15 (0hr)-10/29   I
Colonial Heights
1961   II
Culpepper (town)
1961   I
Elkton
1961   I
Emporia
1961   I
Falls Church
1961   I
Fredericksburg
1961   II
Front Royal
1961   I
Gordonsville
1961   I
Grottoes
1961   I
Hamilton
1961   I
Harrisonburg
1961   II
Hopewell
1961   I
Kilmarnock
1961   I
Leesburg
1961   I
Lexington
1961   I

Louisa (town)
1961   I
Luray
1961   I
Lynchburg
1961   I
Manassas
1950 5/5-9/24   I
Middleburg
1961   I
Mineral
1961   I
Norfolk
1946 4/28-9/30 (0hr)   I
1948 5/2-9/26
1949-1953
Orange (town)
1961   I
Petersburg
1961   II
Richmond (city)
1961 4/30 (0hr)-10/26   I
Richmond Heights
1961   II
Staunton
1961 4/30-9/4 (0hr)   I
Tappahannock
1961   I
Waynesboro
1961   II
Williamsburg
1961 4/30-10/15   I
Winchester
1961 5/2-9/26   I

164

Washington

<u>TABLE</u>

1918	War Time
1919	War Time
1933	5/7-8/27
1942-45	War Time
1948	6/1-9/25
1949	6/1-9/30
1950	4/30-9/24
1951	4/29-9/30
1952	4/27-9/28
1956	4/29-9/29
1961	4/30-9/24
1962	4/29-9/30
1963	4/28-10/27
1964	4/26-10/25
1965	4/25-10/31

* Change at 0:01 A.M.

(1) Observed at Washington State College, but not by the town.

(2) As Pasco and Kennewick remained on PST, the Hanford plant went back on PST 5/6, although Richland did not.

(3) Sultan observed PST, but the business district adopted PDST.

<u>WASHINGTON</u>

1752 9/14   Gregorian (NS) Calender adopted in U.S.A.

1811   Area settled

1883 11/18   Noon, Pacific Standard Time (120°W) adopted

1889 11/11   State entered the Union

<u>DAYLIGHT (OR WAR) TIME OBSERVED:</u>
(Changes at 2 A.M.)

1918 3/31 - 10/27   World War I

1919 3/30 - 10/26   World War I

1920 To 1941   Not observed state-wide. See Local Ordinance Listing.

1942 2/9 - 9/30/45   World War II

1946 To 1947   Not observed

1948 To 1952   Not observed state-wide. See Local Ordinance Listing.

1953 To 1955   Not observed

1956   Not observed except in Richland. See Local Ordinance Listing.

1957 To 1960   Not observed

1961 To 1965   Observed state-wide. Refer to Table for dates.

1966 To 1979   For dates, see Table, page 181.

<u>OBSERVATION BY LOCAL ORDINANCE:</u>
(Refer to Table for Month & Day if not shown)

WASHINGTON (cont.)

COUNTIES

Clallam
1950, 5/2-9/24
Cowlitz
1950
Island
1950, 5/2-9/24
King
*1949, 6/1-9/1
 (outside of Seattle)
1951
1952, 6/1-9/28
Lewis
*1949, 6/1-9/1
1950, 6/2-9/7
 (except rural areas)
Pierce
*1949, 6/1-8/31
 (in rural areas)
1950
Thurston
*1949, 6/1-9/1

COMMUNITIES

Aberdeen
1933
*1948, 6/3-9/25
*1949, 6/1-9/25
1950-51
Auburn
*1949, 6/1-9/25
1950, 5/2-9/24
1951
1952, 6/1-9/28
Battle Ground
1952
Bellingham
1933
*1948, 6/1-8/31
*1949, 6/1-9/1
1950

Bellingham
1933
*1948, 6/1-8/31
*1949, 6/1-9/1
1950-51
Bothell
*1949
1950-51
1952, 6/1-9/28
Bremerton
*1948-49
1950-52
Brewster
*1948, 6/14-9/25
1950
Buckley
*1949, 6/1-9/1
1950, 6/2-9/7
Camas
*1949, 4/24-9/1
1950
Castle Rock
1952
1950, 4/30-9/3
Centralia
1933, 5/10-8/21
*1948
*1949, 6/1-9/1
1950, 6/2-9/7
Chehalis
*1948
*1949, 6/1-9/1
1950, 6/2-9/7
Coulee Dam
*1948
Edmonds
*1948
1950-51
Ellensburg
1951
*1948, 6/6-9/25
Elma
*1948, 6/3-9/25
*1949, 4/24-9/11
1950-52
Enumclaw
1950-51
1952, 6/1-9/1

Everett
1933
*1948-49
1950
1952, 6/1-9/28
Fall City
1952, 6/1-9/28
Forks
*1949
Gig Harbor
1952, 6/1-9/28
Hood River
1949, 4/24-9/25
Hoquiam
*1948, 6/3-9/25
*1949
1950-51
Issaquah
1950
1952
Jefferson City
*1948
Kalama
*1949, 4/24-9/1
1950-52
Kelso
*1949, 4/24-9/1
1950-52
Kennewick
*1948, 6/20-9/25
Kent
*1948
1950
1952, 6/1-9/28
Kirkland
1950-51
La Center
1952
La Conner
*1948, 6/6-9/25
Longview
*1948
*1949, 4/24-9/11
1950-52

Marysville
1952, 6/1-9/28
McChord Airbase
1952
Montesano
*1948, 6/3-9/25
*1949, 6/1-8/31
1950
Mount Vernon
1950
Napavine
1950, 6/2-9/7
Nisqually
1950
North Bend
1952, 6/1-9/28
Oakville
1950-51
Okanogan
*1948, 6/14-9/25
Olympia
1933, 5/14-8/27
*1948
1950, 5/1-9/24
1951
1952, 6/1-6/28
Omak
*1948, 6/14-9/25
1950-52
Orting
1950
Pasco
*1948, 6/20-9/25
Port Angeles
*1948-49
1950, 5/2-9/24
1951
Port Townsend
*1949
Pullman
1952
(1) *1948, 6/20-9/25
Puyallup
*1949
1950-51

Raymond
*1948, 6/3-9/25
*1949, 5/30-9/1
1951
1952, 6/1-9/28
Redmond
1950-51
Renton
*1949
1950-51
Richland
1952, 5/5-10/5
1949, 4/24-9/25
(2) 1950, 5/2-9/24
1951, 6/10-9/2
Ridgefield
*1949, 4/24-9/1
1952
Ryderwood
*1949, 4/24-9/1
Seattle
1933
*1948-49
1950-51
1952, 6/1-9/28
Sequim
*1949
Shelton
*1948
1950-51
Snohomish
*1948
1950, 5/1-9/25
South Bend
*1948, 6/6-9/25
1951
1952, 6/1-9/28
South Tacoma
1950
Spokane
1933

Steilacoom
1950
Stevenson
1952, 6/1-9/28
Sultan
(3) 1950, 5/3-9/24
Summer
1950
Tacoma
1933
*1948
*1949, 6/1-9/1
1950-51
1952, 5/17-9/28
Tenino
*1949
1950
1952
Toledo
1950, 6/2-9/7
Vancouver
1933
*1949, 4/24-9/11
1950, 5/1-9/24
1951-52
Walla Walla
1933
Washougal
1952
Wenatchee
1933
*1948, 6/3-9/25
Winlock
1950, 6/2-9/7
Winslow
*1948
Woodinville
1951
Woodland
*1949, 4/24-9/1
1950-51

See footnotes above.

166

TABLE I

Year	Dates
1918	War Time
1919	War Time
1942-45	War Time
1950	4/30-9/24
1951	4/29-9/30
1952	4/27-9/28
1953	4/26-9/27
1954	4/25-9/26
1955	4/24-9/25
1956	4/29-9/30
1957	4/28-9/29
1958	4/27-9/28
1959	4/26-9/27
1960	4/24-9/25
1961	4/30-9/24
1962	4/29-9/30
1963	4/28-9/29
1964	4/26-9/27
1965	4/25-9/26

TABLE II

Year	Dates
1957	4/28-10/27
1958	4/27-10/26
1959	4/26-10/25
1960	4/24-10/30
1961	4/30-10/29
1962	4/29-10/28
1963	4/28-10/27
1964	4/26-10/25
1965	4/25-10/31

** Check with local authorities

WEST VIRGINIA

1727		Area settled
1752	9/14	Gregorian (NS) Calendar adopted
1863	6/20	State entered the Union
1887	3/31	Wheeling adopted EST (75°W)
1887	7/1	Eastern Standard Time (75°W) adopted state-wide

(EST used throughout the State by the B. & O. R.R. CST used by the Cleveland, Lorraine and Wheeling; Pittsburgh, C.G. & St.L.; Wheeling and Lake Erie R.R.)

DAYLIGHT (OR WAR) TIME OBSERVED:
(Changes at 2 A.M.)

1918	3/31 - 10/27	World War I
1919	3/30 - 10/26	World War I
1920	To 1941	Not observed state-wide. See Local Ordinance Listing.
1942	2/9 - 9/30/45	World War II
1946	To 1962	Not observed state-wide. See Local Ordinance Listing.
1963	To 1965	** Observed state-wide, varying dates. Daylight time is generally in effect on the same dates as in the nearest large city.
1966	To 1979	For dates, see Table, page 181.

OBSERVATION BY LOCAL ORDINANCE:
(Refer to Table for month & day if not shown)

167

WEST VIRGINIA (cont.)

Beckley	I
1957	I
1963-65	I
Beechbottom	I
1953-56	I
Benwood	I
1955-56	I
1957-65	II
Berkeley Springs	I
1954-61	I
1962-65	II
Bluefield	I
**1962, May-9/3	I
1963-65	I
Buckhannon	I
1963-65	I
Burnsville	I
1956-65	I
Cameron	I
1950, 4/30-10/29	I
1951-56	I
1957-65	II
Charleston	I
*1937, 4/25-9/5	I
1956-65	I
Charles Town	I
1948, 4/25-9/26	I
1949, 4/24-9/25	I
1950-61	I
1962-65	II
Cherry Run	I
1957-65	I
Chester	I
1953-56	I
Chiefton	I
1947, 4/27-9/28	I
1948, 4/25-9/26	I
1949, 4/24-9/25	I

Clarksburg	
1956-65	I
Colliers	I
1953-56	I
Congo	I
1953-56	I
Corinth	I
1962	II
Deep Water	I
1956-65	I
Durbin	II
1956-65	I
Elkins	I
1956-65	I
Fairmont	I
1946, 4/28-9/29	I
1949, 4/24-9/25	I
1950	I
1956-65	I
Fayetteville	I
1957	I
1963-65	II
Follansbee	I
1953-56	I
1957-65	II
Grafton	I
1956-65	I
Grantsville	I
1963-65	I
Hancock	I
1962	I
Harpers Ferry	I
1950-56	I
1957-65	II
Hinton	I
1956-65	I
Hoard	I
1953-56	I
Holidays Cove	I
1953-56	I
Hopemont	
1962	II

Hundred	I
1952	I
Huntington	I
1952-65	I
Hutton	II
1962	I
Independence	II
1962	I
Kenova	I
1951-56	I
1957-65	I
Keyser	I
1952-57	I
1958-65	II
Kingwood	I
1954-61	I
1962-65	II
Lewisburg	I
1963-65	I
Logan	I
1963-65	I
Loglow	I
1953-56	I
Madison	I
1957	I
1963-65	II
Mannington	I
1946, 4/28-9/29	I
Martinsburg	I
1948, 4/25-9/26	I
1949, 4/24-9/25	I
1950-57	I
1958	II
1959-60	II
1961-65	I
McMechen	I
1956	I
1957-65	II
Mingo Junction	I
1953-56	I
Montgomery	I
1957-65	II

Morgantown	I
1941, 4/27-10/28	I
1946, 4/28-9/29	I
1947, 4/27-9/28	I
1948, 4/25-9/26	I
1949, 4/24-9/25	I
1950-65	I
Moundsville	II
1951-56	I
1957-65	II
Mount Hope	I
1957	I
1963-65	I
Mullens	I
1963-65	I
Newburg	II
1962	I
New Cumberland	I
1953-56	I
Newell	I
1953-56	I
New Martinsville	I
1941, 4/27-10/28	I
1957-61	I
1962-65	II
Oak Hill	I
1957-65	I
Parkersburg	I
1963-65	I
Parsons	I
1963-65	I
Paw Paw	I
1962	II
Philippi	I
1963-65	II
Piedmont	I
1954-61	I
1962-65	II
Point Pleasant	I
1963-65	I
Power	I
1953-56	I

Princeton	I
1963-65	I
Ravenswood	I
1963-65	I
Richwood	I
1956-65	I
Ripley	I
1963-65	I
Ronceverte	I
1956-65	II
Rowlesburg	I
1962	I
Saint Albans	II
1957	I
1963-65	I
Sheperdstown	II
1949, 4/24-9/25	I
Short Creek	I
1953-56	I
Sistersville	I
1946, 4/28-9/29	I
1953-61	I
1962-65	I
South Charleston	II
1956-65	I
Spencer	I
1963-65	I
Star City	I
1953-56	I
Summersville	I
1963-65	I
Swanton	II
1962	I
Terra Alta	I
1962	I
Thornton	I
1962	I
Tunnelton	II
1962	I
Vanvoorhis	I
1953-56	I
Vienna	I
1963-65	I

Warwood	I
1954	I
Wayne	I
1963-65	I
Webster Springs	
1963-65	I
Weirton	I
1941, 4/28-10/28	I
1949, 4/24-9/25	I
1950-59	I
1960-64	I
1965, 4/25-10/24	II
Welch	II
1963-65	I
Wellsburg	I
1941, 4/27-10/28	I
1949, 4/24-9/25	I
1950-59	I
1960-65	II
Weston	I
1963-65	I
Wheeling	I
1937, 4/26-10/27	II
1941, 4/27-10/28	II
1946, 4/28-9/29	II
1947, 4/27-9/28	I
1948, 4/25-9/26	I
1949, 4/24-9/25	I
1950-57	I
1958-65	II
White Sulphur Springs	I
1956-65	I
Whitesville	II
1957	
Williamson	II
1963-65	II
Windsor Heights	II
1953-56	I

* Changes at 0:01 A.M.
** Check with local authorities

168

TABLE	
1918	War Time
1919	War Time
1921	4/24-10/30
1922	4/30-10/24
1923	4/29-9/30
1942-45	War Time
1955	4/24-9/25
1956	4/29-9/30
1957	4/28-9/29
1958	4/27-9/28
1959	4/26-9/27
1960	4/24-9/25
1961	4/30-9/24
1962	4/29-9/30
1963	4/28-9/29
1964	4/26-9/27
1965	4/25-10/31

WISCONSIN

1670		Area settled
1752	9/14	Gregorian (NS) Calendar adopted in U.S.A.
1848	5/29	State entered the Union
1883	11/18	Noon, Central Standard Time (90°W) adopted

DAYLIGHT (OR WAR) TIME OBSERVED:
(Changes at 2 A.M.)

1918	3/31 - 10/27	World War I
1919	3/30 - 10/26	World War I
1920	To 1941	Not observed state-wide. See Local Ordinance Listing.
1942	2/9 - 9/30/45	World War II
1946	To 1954	Not observed.
1955	To 1956	Not observed state-wide. See Local Ordinance Listing.
1957	To 1965	Observed state-wide. Refer to Table for dates.
1966	To 1979	For dates, see Table, page 181.

OBSERVATION BY LOCAL ORDINANCE:
(Refer to Table for day & month if not shown)

Fondulac
1921
Kenosha
1922-23
La Crosse
1921-23
Milwaukee
1921-22
1923, 4/29-5/11

Walworth
1955-56
Zenda
1955-56

TABLE	
1918	War Time
1919	War Time
1942-45	War Time

WYOMING

1752	9/14	Gregorian (NS) Calendar adopted in U.S.A.
1834		Area settled
1883	11/18	Noon, Mountain Standard Time (105°W) adopted
1890	7/10	State entered the Union

DAYLIGHT (OR WAR) TIME OBSERVED:
(Changes at 2 A.M.)

1918	3/31 - 10/27	World War I
1919	3/30 - 10/26	World War I
1920	To 1941	Not observed
1942	2/9 - 9/30/45	World War II
1946	To 1966	Not observed
1967	To 1979	For dates, see Table, page 181.

UNITED STATES POSSESSIONS, TERRITORIES AND TRUSTEESHIPS

AMERICAN SAMOA
Non-Self-Governing U.S. Territory

The seven eastern islands of the Samoan Group, located along the 14 degree S. Lat., and near 170°W Long., 2,300 miles S.W. of Hawaii in the South Pacific Ocean.

1872	Port Pago Pago, former U.S. Navy coaling station, was acquired by commercial treaty with the native king.
1899, 12/2	Under the Berlin convention, became a possession of the U.S.
1900, 2/16	Treaty ratified in which the U.S. was internationally recognized to have rights extending over the seven eastern islands of the Samoan group.
1900, 4/17	The chiefs of Tutuila and Annuu ceded these two islands to the U.S.
1904	The king and chiefs of the Manua Islands ceded Tau, Olosega and Ofu to the U.S.
1925, 3/4	Swain's Island annexed by the U.S.
1911	Standard Time Meridian of 172°W30' adopted
	In recent years the Standard Time Meridian was changed to 165°W00'
	No Daylight Savings Time observed

BAKER, HOWLAND and JARVIS ISLANDS
Non-Self-Governing U.S. Territory

Located in the South Pacific in a widely spread area, they are approximately 1,600 miles S. of Hawaii.

1832	Baker Island discovered
1857, 9/30	U.S. occupation
1936, 5/13	Extraterritorial plans of the U.S. allowed the perfection of its claim on these three islands.
1942	Although they have been uninhabited since 1942, Jarvis (a British possession) was used for the construction of radio towers.
	Standard Time Meridian: 165°W00'

CANAL ZONE
Non-Self-Governing U.S. Territory

A 50-mile strip bounded by the Atlantic and Pacific Oceans between North and South America

1899   A second French company failed to build a canal. The U.S. bought their rights and offered Columbia compensation for a canal zone, but Columbia failed to ratify the treaty.

1903, 11/3   Panama declared itself independent of Columbia

1903, 11/18   Canal strip granted to the U.S. by treaty

1904, 2/26   Treaty was ratified

                LMT of Colon (79°W54') to 1918

*1918, 4/22   Standard Time Meridian of 75°W00' adopted

                No Daylight Savings Time observed

CANTON AND ENDERBURY ISLANDS
Non-Self-Governing U.S. Territory

Canton is the largest of the Phoenix Group in the Central Pacific, about half-way between Hawaii and Australia. One of the U.S. manned Space Flight Tracking Stations is there.

Enderbury, which is about 32 miles S.E. of Canton, is uninhabited.

1939, 4/6   U.S. and Great Britain agreed on a system of joint control and administration to keep the islands available for communications and for use as airports for international aviation of both governments.

                Standard Time Meridians: 165°W00' and 180°E00'

CAROLINE ISLANDS. See Trust Territories.

CORN ISLANDS
Non-Self-Governing U.S. Territory

Great Corn and Little Corn are located in the Caribbean East of Nicaragua.

1914   Leased for 99 years from Nicaragua by the U.S.

                Standard Time Meridian: 90°W00'

ENDERBURY ISLAND. See Canton.

* Change at 0:01 A.M.

GUAM
Non-Self-Governing U.S. Territory

The largest of the Mariana Islands situated in the North Pacific.

1521, 3/6	Discovered by Magellan
1668	Colonized by Spanish Missionaries
1898, 12/10	Ceded to the U.S. by Spain
1941, 12/11	Seized by Japan
1944, 7/27	U.S. regained possession
	Standard Time Meridian $142^\circ 30'$ to 1912
1912, 10/1	Standard Time Meridian changed to $150^\circ E00'$
1978 4/3-8/26	**DST observed.**

HOWLAND ISLAND. See Baker.

JARVIS ISLAND. See Baker.

JOHNSTON ISLAND
Non-Self-Governing U.S. Territory

An island in the North Pacific about 1,200 miles S.W. of Hawaii

1807	Discovered by Capt. Charles James Johnston, a Britisher.
1858	Claimed by Hawaii
	Later became a U.S. possession
	Standard Time Meridian: $157^\circ W30'$

KINGMAN REEF
Non-Self-Governing U.S. Territory

The smallest land of U.S. sovereignty, it is located about 1,000 miles S. of Hawaii

185., Nov.	Discovered by Capt. W. E. Kingman
	Later became a U.S. possession
	Standard Time Meridian: $157^\circ W30'$

LADRONES ISLANDS. See Trust Territories.

MARIANA ISLANDS. See Trust Territories.

MARSHALL ISLANDS. See Trust Territories.

MIDWAY ISLANDS
Non-Self-Governing U.S. Territory

Two islands, Pearl and Hermes Reef, in the North Pacific, located 1,200 miles W.N.W. of Hawaii.

1859, 7/5	Discovered by N. C. Brooks for the U.S.
1867, 9/30	Formally declared a U.S. possession
	Former Standard Time Meridian: $157^{\circ}W30'$
1947, 6/8	Standard Time Meridian of $150^{\circ}W00'$ adopted

NAVASSA ISLAND
Non-Self-Governing U.S. Territory

An island in the Caribbean Sea between Jamaica and Haiti. Aids navigation with its lighthouse.

Standard Time Meridian: $75^{\circ}W00'$

PALMYRA ISLAND
Non-Self-Governing U.S. Territory

A small island just S.E. of Kingman Reef in the North Pacific Ocean

Standard Time Meridian: $157^{\circ}W30'$

PHILIPPINE ISLANDS
Former U.S. Territory

Located in the Western Pacific Ocean about 500 miles S.E. of Asia, they form an archipelago running 1,152 miles north and south.

1521	Discovered by Magellan
1565	Conquered by Spain
1572	Manila established
1600	Spain possessed most of the islands
1762	Brief British occupation
1763	Relinquished to Spain
1896	Strong insurrection

PHILIPPINE ISLANDS (Cont.)

1898, 12/10	Ceded to the U.S. by the Treaty of Paris, following the Spanish-American War, the U.S. paying for the territory.
1946, 7/4	The independent Republic of the Philippines was proclaimed in accordance with the Tydings-McDuffie Act passed by the U.S. Congress in 1934, providing for Philippine Independence in 1946.
	LMT to 1899
1899, 5/11	Standard Time Meridian of 120°E00' adopted

PUERTO RICO

Self-Governing Commonwealth

Located at the N.E. end of the Caribbean Sea

1493	Discovered by Columbus on his second voyage when it became a Spanish property
1898, 12/10	Spain ceded it to the U.S.
1952, 7/25	Elevated to the status of a free commonwealth associated with the U.S.
	LMT to 1899
1899, 3/28	Standard Time Meridian of 60°W00' adopted
1967, 11/25	Officially placed on Atlantic Standard Time (60°W) which had been observed in parts since 1899.
	No Daylight Savings Time observed

RYUKYU ISLANDS

Under U.S. Administration

Some 64 islands stretching in a 500-mile arc from Southern Japan to Taiwan (Formosa)

1874	Annexed by Japan
1945, 4/1	Okinawa seized by the U.S. and occupied ever since
1951, 9/8	U.S. Administration by Treaty of San Francisco
1952, 4/28	Administration of islands vested in U.S. by Japanese peace treaty (1951) with Japan retaining "residual sovereignty". Okinawa, the largest of these islands, is the site of a huge U.S. military base even though the Ryukyu is a State of Japan. It serves as a depot of war supplies slated for Vietnam (1966).
	Standard Time Meridian: 135°E00'

SAND ISLAND

Non-Self-Governing U.S. Territory

An island in the North Pacific near Johnston Island, about 1,200 miles S.W. of Hawaii

1857, 9/30	U.S. occupation
	Standard Time Meridian: 157°W30'

UNITED STATES POSSESSIONS

SWAN ISLANDS
Non-Self-Governing U.S. Territory

Two small islands in the Caribbean Sea about 100 miles N.E. of Honduras. Great Swan is used by the U.S. Weather Bureau and Federal Aviation Agency. Little Swan is uninhabited.

Standard Time Meridian: $90^{\circ}W00'$

TRUST TERRITORIES OF THE PACIFIC

2,000 islands (many only tiny coral reefs) in the Western Pacific Ocean, including the Caroline, Marshall and Mariana Islands (except Guam), formerly under Japanese Mandate.

1947, 4/2   The Security Council of the United Nations placed these islands under the trustee system.

1947, 7/18   Became trustee of the U.S.

MARIANA ISLANDS (LADRONES ISLANDS)

Located S. of Japan and E. of the Philippines. These islands include Guam (see above), Rota, Saipan, Tinian, Pagan, Guguan, Agrihan and Aguijan.

Standard Time Meridian: $135^{\circ}W00'$

CAROLINE ISLANDS

Located E. of the Philippines and S. of the Marianas, these islands include the Yap, Truk and the Palau Groups and the islands of Ponape and Kusaie, as well as many coral atolls.

Former Standard Time Meridian: $155^{\circ}E00'$

In recent years the Standard Time Meridian was changed to $150^{\circ}E00'$ for the Eastern Carolines and $135^{\circ}E00'$ for the Western Carolines

MARSHALL ISLANDS

Located E. of the Carolines. These islands are divided into two chains:

Western or RALIK group includes atolls of Jaluit, Kwajalein, Wotho, Bikini and Eniwetok. Bikini and Eniwetok have been the scene of several atomic-bomb tests.

Eastern or RATAK group includes the atolls of Mili, Majuro, Maloelap, Wotje and Likiep.

Standard Time Meridian: $150^{\circ}E00'$

VIRGIN ISLANDS of the U.S.
   Non-Self-Governing U.S. Territory

   A chain of islands straight E. of Puerto Rico separating the Caribbean Sea and the
   Atlantic Ocean

   1493   Discovered by Columbus

   1898, 12/10   Culebra and Vieques Islands ceded to the U.S. by Spain

   1917, 1/25   The three largest islands, St. Croix, St. Thomas and St. John and 50 or
                           so smaller islands (formerly Danish West Indies) purchased from Denmark
                           by the U.S.

   1967, 11/25   Standard Time Meridian: 60°W00' adopted.

                           No Daylight Savings Time observed

WAKE ISLAND
   Non-Self-Governing U.S. Territory

   With sister islands, Wilkes and Peale, lies in the North Pacific Ocean on the direct
   route from Hawaii to Hong Kong.

   1796   Discovered by the British

   1898, 7/4   The U.S. Flag hoisted over the Island

   1899, 1/17   Formal annexation from Spain

   1941, 12/23   Seized by Japan

   1945, 9/4   U.S. regained possession

                           Standard Time Meridian: 180°E00'

UNIFORM TIME ACT OF 1966

Public Law 89-387
89th Congress, S. 1404
April 13, 1966

An Act

To promote the observance of a uniform system of time throughout the United States.

Be it enacted by the Senate and House of Representatives of the United States of America in Congress assembled, That this Act may be cited as the "Uniform Time Act of 1966".

Uniform Time Act of 1966.

Sec. 2. It is the policy of the United States to promote the adoption and observance of uniform time within the standard time zones prescribed by the Act entitled "An Act to save daylight and to provide standard time for the United States", approved March 19, 1918 (40 Stat. 450; 15 U.S.C. 261-264), as modified by the Act entitled "An Act to transfer the Panhandle and Plains section of Texas and Oklahoma to the United States standard central time zone", approved March 4, 1921 (41 Stat. 1446; 15 U.S.C. 265). To this end the Interstate Commerce Commission is authorized and directed to foster and promote widespread and uniform adoption and observance of the same standard of time within and throughout each such standard time zone.

Sec. 3. (a) During the period commencing at 2 o'clock antemeridian on the last Sunday of April of each year and ending at 2 o'clock antemeridian on the last Sunday of October of each year, the standard time of each zone established by the Act of March 19, 1918 (15 U.S.C. 261-264), as modified by the Act of March 4, 1921 (15 U.S.C. 265), shall be advanced one hour and such time as so advanced shall for the purposes of such Act of March 19, 1918, as so modified, be the standard time of such zone during such period; except that any State may by law exempt itself from the provisions of this subsection providing for the advancement of time, but only if such law provides that the entire State (including all political subdivisions thereof) shall observe the standard time otherwise applicable under such Act of March 19, 1918, as so modified, during such period.

(b) It is hereby declared that it is the express intent of Congress by this section to supersede any and all laws of the States or political subdivisions thereof insofar as they may now or hereafter provide for advances in time or changeover dates different from those specified in this section.

(c) For any violation of the provisions of this section the Interstate Commerce Commission or its duly authorized agent may apply to the district court of the United States for the district in which such violation occurs for the enforcement of this section; and such court shall have jurisdiction to enforce obedience thereto by writ of injunction or by other process, mandatory or otherwise, restraining against further violations of this section and enjoining obedience thereto.

Violations.

Sec. 4. (a) The first section of the Act of March 19, 1918, as amended (15 U.S.C. 261), is amended to read as follows:

"That for the purpose of establishing the standard time of the United States, the territory of the United States shall be divided into eight zones in the manner provided in this section. Except as provided in section 3(a) of the Uniform Time Act of 1966, the standard time of the first zone shall be based on the mean solar time of the

80 STAT. 107.
Standard time zones.
80 STAT. 108.

Pub. Law 89-387   - 2 -   April 13, 1966

80 STAT. 108.

sixtieth degree of longitude west from Greenwich; that of the second zone on the seventy-fifth degree; that of the third zone on the ninetieth degree; that of the fourth zone on the one hundred and fifth degree; that of the fifth zone on the one hundred and twentieth degree; that of the sixth zone on the one hundred and thirty-fifth degree; that of the seventh zone on the one hundred and fiftieth degree; and that of the eighth zone on the one hundred and sixty-fifth degree. The limits of each zone shall be defined by an order of the Interstate Commerce Commission, having regard for the convenience of commerce and the existing junction points and division points of common carriers engaged in interstate or foreign commerce, and any such order may be modified from time to time. As used in this Act, the term 'interstate or foreign commerce' means commerce between a State, the District of Columbia, the Commonwealth of Puerto Rico, or any possession of the United States and any place outside thereof."

"Interstate or foreign commerce."

15 USC 262.

(b) Section 2 of such Act is amended to read as follows:

"Sec. 2. Within the respective zones created under the authority of this Act the standard time of the zone shall insofar as practicable (as determined by the Interstate Commerce Commission) govern the movement of all common carriers engaged in interstate or foreign commerce. In all statutes, orders, rules, and regulations relating to the time of performance of any act by any officer or department of the United States, whether in the legislative, executive, or judicial branches of the Government, or relating to the time within which any rights shall accrue or determine, or within which any act shall or shall not be performed by any person subject to the jurisdiction of the United States, it shall be understood and intended that the time shall insofar as practicable (as determined by the Interstate Commerce Commission) be the United States standard time of the zone within which the act is to be performed."

(c) Section 4 of such Act is amended to read as follows:

Designations.

"Sec. 4. The standard time of the first zone shall be known and designated as Atlantic standard time; that of the second zone shall be known and designated as eastern standard time; that of the third zone shall be known and designated as central standard time; that of the fourth zone shall be known and designated as mountain standard time; that of the fifth zone shall be known and designated as Pacific standard time; that of the sixth zone shall be known and designated as Yukon standard time; that of the seventh zone shall be known and designated as Alaska-Hawaii standard time; and that of the eighth zone shall be known and designated as Bering standard time."

60 Stat. 237.

Sec. 5. The Administrative Procedure Act (5 U.S.C. 1001-1011) shall apply to all proceedings under this Act, the Act of March 19, 1918 (15 U.S.C. 261-264), and the Act of March 4, 1921 (15 U.S.C. 265).

Effective date.

Sec. 6. This Act shall take effect on April 1, 1967: except that if any State, the District of Columbia, the Commonwealth of Puerto Rico, or any possession of the United States, or any political subdivision thereof, observes daylight saving time in the year 1966, such time shall advance the standard time otherwise applicable in such place by one hour and shall commence at 2 o'clock antemeridian on the last Sunday in April of the year 1966 and shall end at 2 o'clock antemeridian on the last Sunday in October of the year 1966.

Sec. 7. As used in this Act, the term "State" includes the District of Columbia, the Commonwealth of Puerto Rico, or any possession of the United States.

Approved April 13, 1966.

VII   1966 TIME PICTURE

Before the Uniform Time Act of 1966 became law, communities and states observing Daylight Saving Time did so on the months, days and hours that suited their own convenience. Formerly, the only periods when ALL of the States observed "fast time" was during the two World Wars. See TIME REFERENCE TABLES for dates.

Putting an end to the confusion of switchover dates, the 1966 Time Act stated that if Daylight Saving Time was observed that year, it must be observed from April 24 to October 30, with switchovers at 2:00 A.M. As the law reads, the option of observing or not observing Daylight Saving Time still remained a state and local matter during 1966. However, more uniformity is seen in the time picture beginning with 1967. See A LOOK INTO THE FUTURE.

The 1966 rundown of the Daylight Saving Time picture in the 50 States still revealed some confusion. Nevertheless, these time factors may be classified three ways:

(1) 14 States not observing Daylight Saving Time.
(2) 19 States and District of Columbia observing Daylight Saving Time state-wide.
(3) 17 States observing Daylight Saving Time in some portions.

States Not Observing Daylight Saving Time:

Alaska	Florida	Louisiana	Oklahoma
Arizona	Georgia	Mississippi	South Carolina
Arkansas	Hawaii	North Carolina	Texas
		North Dakota	Wyoming

States Observing Daylight Saving Time State-wide from April 24 to October 30:

California	Illinois	Nevada	Rhode Island
Colorado	Iowa	New Hampshire	Vermont
Connecticut	Maine	New Jersey	Washington
Delaware	Maryland	New York	West Virginia
District of Columbia	Massachusetts	Pennsylvania	Wisconsin

Portions of States Observing Daylight Saving Time from April 24 to October 30:

Alabama -- Communities in Chambers and Lee Counties, and Fort Rucker in Coffee and Dale Counties.

Idaho -- Communities north of Salmon River. Coeur d'Alene and Moscow and their surrounding communities.

Indiana -- Located in two time zones. Entire State was on equivalent of Eastern Standard Time. (49 Counties in the western part of the State which observe Central Standard Time switched to Central Daylight Saving Time.) See Indiana Map Section in TIME REFERENCE TABLES.

Kansas -- All or portions of 25 counties in northwestern part of the State.

Kentucky -- A number of communities in northwestern part of the State, including Owensboro.

Michigan -- Communities in Upper Peninsula, including Dickinson County and the City of Ironwood.

Minnesota -- State-wide, with the exception of a few communities on the western State border.

Missouri -- Some 50 communities in the eastern part of the State, including St. Louis.

Montana -- Butte and Anaconda Company and plant area in Anaconda.

Nebraska — Several counties in the southwest part of the State remain on Mountain Standard Time all year round.

New Mexico — Los Alamos County and some communities in Quay County.

Ohio — About 240 communities. In the northeastern part of the State in about 18 counties, including Akron, Canton, Cleveland and Youngstown; and some communities in the eastern and southeastern part of the State. In the residential community of Barnesville, only half of the residents observe Daylight Saving Time. This is because factory areas to its east go on "fast time" while those to the west stay on "slow time." Barnesville business and banks observe Daylight Saving Time. However, schools and the City government remain on Eastern Standard Time.

DAYLIGHT SAVING TIME AREA IN OHIO - 1966

Oregon   -- All of the State except a small area of communities at the eastern border, which
                   observe Mountain Standard Time.

South Dakota -- Portions of Mellette, Stanley, and Todd Counties, including half of the commun-
                   ity of Hayes.

Tennessee   -- A portion of Marion County.

Utah   -- Northwestern portion of State located in the Pacific Standard Time Zone.

Virginia   -- All but 8 counties in the southwestern portion of the State. These 8 counties
                   remain on Eastern Standard Time: Buchanan, Dickenson, Lee, Russell, Scott,
                   Smyth, Washington and Wise.

Local authorities may be consulted to determine the exact 1966 Daylight Saving Time status of
any community listed in this section.

"DAYLIGHT SAVING TIME IN REVERSE" is a phrase occasionally used by those who write or talk on
time. An explanation here will round out the list of popular terms applied to U.S. time changes.

VIII - A LOOK INTO THE FUTURE: 1967-2000

Starting in 1967, the Uniform Time Act of 1966 commenced automatic nationwide Daylight Saving Time from the last Sunday in April to the last Sunday in October with all switchovers, both beginning and ending dates, throughout the United States at 2:00 A.M. In this Public Law No. 89-387, the words "States" includes the District of Columbia, the Commonwealth of Puerto Rico, or any of the Possessions of the United States. For a listing see UNITED STATES POSSESSIONS, TERRITORIES AND TRUSTEESHIPS.

A state may vote to exempt itself and stay on standard time. But the entire state must go one way or the other. Failure of a state to take legal action puts it on daylight time automatically. If these conditions hold in the future, we will not be plagued with the numerous deviations which appear in the local ordinance exceptions listed in the TIME REFERENCE TABLES.

Newspapers and news magazines issued during late April each year usually feature an article covering time changes in the United States. They will undoubtedly list states which by legislative action exempt themselves from observing daylight saving time in a particular year. (By noting such information this book can be kept up to date.)

Unless a major change occurs in future years, simply consult the following table to learn the exact daylight saving time observance dates for any year from 1966 to 2000. The last Sunday in April and the last Sunday in October are given for each year.

DAYLIGHT SAVING TIME DATES: 1967-2000

Year	Sundays	Year	Sundays	Year	Sundays	Year	Sundays
1966	4/24-10/30	1975	2/23-10/26	1984	4/29-10/28	1993	4/4-10/31
1967	4/30-10/29	1976	4/25-10/31	1985	4/28-10/27	1994	4/3-10/30
1968	4/28-10/27	1977	4/24-10/30	1986	4/27-10/26	1995	4/2-10/29
1969	4/27-10/26	1978	4/30-10/29	1987	4/5-10/25	1996	4/7-10/27
1970	4/26-10/25	1979	4/29-10/28	1988	4/3-10/30	1997	4/6-10/26
1971	4/25-10/31	1980	4/27-10/26	1989	4/2-10/29	1998	4/5-10/25
1972	4/30-10/29	1981	4/26-10/25	1990	4/1-10/28	1999	4/4-10/31
1973	4/29-10/28	1982	4/25-10/31	1991	4/7-10/27	2000	4/2-10/29
1974	1/6-10/27	1983	4/24-10/30	1992	4/5-10/25		

The exception to daylight saving time dates for 1987-2000 are Alaska, American Samoa, Arizona, Hawaii, Puerto Rico, Virgin Islands and some counties in eastern Indiana (1986-90 Indiana DST maps s̶. the same time pattern as that for 1977 on page 70).

These new daylight saving time regulations eliminate some of the confusion out of the chaotic patchwork of time. But is our time schizophrenia a thing of the past? Maybe not! It all depends upon the states which opposed the new law. When they objected, they were advised that they could petition the Interstate Commerce Commission for a revision in their time zones. In the main, the objecting states are those which have the complication of being located either in two time zones or on a time zone boundary line. For some examples, see Michigan, Indiana, Kansas, Missouri, Minnesota and Alaska (with its arctic summer) in the TIME REFERENCE TABLES.

If these objections foreshadow time zone shifts, even with the new time act that insures uniform dates for daylight time, alertness will still be required by the time researcher to note changes in the U.S.A. time picture.

The shifts will be regulated by the Interstate Commerce Commission, and no longer will informal time of another time zone be observed on the whim of some local group. Should there be future time zone shifts, the I.C.C. reports may be found in the public library, and undoubtedly these changes will be reported in the press. Thus the standard time reference in this book can be kept abreast of the times.

As we approach the end of this century, mankind has come a long way in solving the riddle of time. His quartz-controlled clocks can accurately determine a 20-millionth of a second; his calendar is in pretty good shape; and he is to be congratulated for his late adoption of the uniform observance of Daylight Time.

***

IX   SUGGESTED TIME REFERENCE SOURCES:

Many sources were contacted to provide the vast amount of data upon which the TIME REFERENCE TABLES are based.   Space does not permit giving a complete bibliography.   That would require listing every State Attorney General, Secretary of State, Community and State Chamber of Commerce, etc.   Because there are omissions in the TIME REFERENCE TABLES, certain communities will require further investigation.   To save the time researcher endless hours in tracking down unknown factors, the following reference list is presented as a helpful aid.

Chamber of Commerce, State & Community
City or Town Clerks
Clippings from Magazines & Newspapers
Code of Federal Regulation
Committee for Time Uniformity, Wash., D.C.
Encyclopedias
Information Please Almanac
Interstate Commerce Commission, Wash., D.C. 20423
Library References: County, Law & Public
Municipal Community Leagues
National Railway Publication Co., 424 W. 33rd St., New York, N.Y. 10001
Newspaper Libraries
New York Times Index
Research Division of State Legislative Counsel Bureaus or Commissions
Road Maps, Atlases, State Maps
State Attorney Generals
State & Community Chambers of Commerce
State Legislative Council
State Secretaries
State Year Books
Tourist Organizations
Transportation Association of America, 1101 17th St. N.W., Wash., D.C. 20036
Travel Bureaus
U.S. Dept. of Agriculture
U.S. Dept. of Justice, Immigration & Naturalization Service
U.S. Government Publications
U.S. Interstate Commerce Commission
Western Union Time Charts
World Almanac
World Time Chart, Manufacturers Hanover Trust Company, International
        Division, 44 Wall Street, New York, N.Y. 10015

X   ABBREVIATIONS

AHST	Alaska-Hawaii Standard Time		N	North
B & O	Baltimore and Ohio		NE	North East
BST	Bering Standard Time		NS	New Style
CAT	Central Alaska Standard Time		NT	Nome Time
Co.	County		OS	Old Style
CDST	Central Daylight Saving Time		PDST	Pacific Daylight Saving Time
CST	Central Standard Time		PST	Pacific Standard Time
DST	Daylight Saving Time		S	South
E	East		SE	South East
EST	Eastern Standard Time		SW	South West
HST	Hawaiian Standard Time		U.S.	United States
I.C.C.	Interstate Commerce Commission		U.S.A.	United States of America
Jct.	Junction		W	West
Lat.	Latitude		WNW	West North West
LMT	Local Mean Time		WT	War Time
Long.	Longitude		Yr.	Year
MST	Mountain Standard Time		YST	Yukon Standard Time

°	Degree
'	Minute
"	Second
h	Hour
m	Minute
s	Second

Michigan World War II Addendum

1942 2/9 to 2/14   Entire state observed Eastern War Time. However, by legislative act, the state moved into the Central Time Zone at 2 AM on Monday, Feb. 15, 1942.

1943 1/29   State legislature approved an amendment to make Central Time legal within the state. Since they were already on War Time, this amendment (section 9087) changed legal time from Eastern War Time to Central War Time on Feb. 15, 1943.

This amendment also provided for the state to return to Eastern Time once the U.S. Congress repealed or terminated War Time. But the amendment also stated "Any municipality confronted by a war emergency which necessitates changing the time of such municipality to Eastern War Time ... shall have the power to do so."

Municipalities could pass local ordinances exempting themselves from state law. Detroit and some other cities, especially those in Eastern Michigan, did just that, and they remained on Eastern War Time until the end of the war and repeal of war time (September 30, 1945).

Grand Rapids and some other cities in Western and Central Michigan went along with the State and observed Central War Time.

Some confusion exists because certain cities voted to observe Eastern War Time, while the county in which they were located observed Central War Time. An opinion of the State Attorney General held that counties were not municipalities within the meaning of the amendment and could not exempt themselves from the state law.

The *Grand Rapids Press,* February 15, 1943, printed the following listing:

EASTERN WAR TIME	CENTRAL WAR TIME
Ann Arbor	Washtenaw County
Bay City	Bay County
Flint	Genesee County
Jackson	Jackson County
Detroit	Grand Rapids
Monroe (?)	Battle Creek
Mt. Clemens	Benton Harbor
Pontiac	Hillsdale County
Oakland County Towns	Saginaw
Roscommon	Owosso
Harbor Beach	Lansing
Port Huron	Ingham County
Selfridge Field	Ft. Custer
South Macomb County Towns	Hillsdale
Wayne County Towns	Most of Western Michigan Towns
Ypsilanti	

Since most cities and counties north of the straits (except for a few in the eastern portion) were already on Central Time, they were little affected by the change in State Law.

In general, Western and Central Michigan observed Central Daylight Time while Eastern Michigan was on Eastern Daylight Time. However, it is advisable to check local sources carefully.

SUPPLEMENT

TIME CHANGES IN U.S.A.

By
DORIS CHASE DOANE

I — ADDENDA AND NOTES

(Use this space to enter any new time information which has not been recorded in the body of this book.)

1974	1/6 to 10/27	Energy Crisis, DST observed nationwide except . . .
	2/3 to 10/27	Malheur County, Oregon and the southern half of Idaho

Exempt: Not observing DST were Alaska, American Samoa, Arizona, Hawaii, Puerto Rico, Virgin Islands, and the Eastern Time Zone of Indiana. (Part of Kentucky in 1974 only.)

1975	2/23 to 10/26	DST observed nationwide except:
	4/27 to 10/26	Eastern zone portion of Michigan.

Exempt: Same as 1974

1976	4/25 to 10/31	DST observed.

Exempt: Same as 1974

*1977	4/24 to 10/20	DST observed
*1978	4/30 to 10/29	DST observed
*1979	4/29 to 10/28	DST observed
*1980	4/27-10/26	DST observed**

** In 1980 in Alaska, Juneau observed DST

*Alaska, American Samoa, Arizona, Hawaii, Puerto Rico, Virgin Islands exempt. Possibly some parts of other states. such as Indiana.

II — RECORDING OF VITAL STATISTICS

According to the United States Department of Health, Education, and Welfare, the time of birth was included on all of the U.S. Standard Certificates of Live Birth recommended for adoption by the States from 1900 until 1949. This item was omitted from the 1949 and 1956 revisions of this certificate, but was added once again to the 1968 revision which is still in effect.

If all of the States had followed this procedure, we would find a uniform pattern. However, as the State list in this section shows, all States did not comply with this request.

Some State Legislatures have passed bills requiring the Board of Health to adopt specific forms for the recording of vital statistics, such as births, stillbirths and deaths. Other States have no legislation whatsoever. In still other States, the Board of Health is empowered to adopt their own forms. Not only that, in some instances, there have been changes in these forms from time to time. That is, for a certain number of years the birth hour was required and a space was provided for its recording. Yet, the failure to fill this requirement (birth hour) on the form did not prevent the recording of the birth. During a number of years there was no space for the birth hour, and later that space was returned to the forms. Finally, some States have never provided a space for the birth hour.

Persons who need to refer to birth certificates as part of their work or research would read with interest the various legislation regarding them. As an example of one State's regulations on records of vital statistics, the following is presented.

(Reproduced by the Colorado State
Department of Public Health)

CHAPTER 66
ARTICLE 8

VITAL STATISTICS

Article 8 of Chapter 66, Colorado Revised Statutes 1963, as amended in 1966, was Repealed and Reenacted, with Amendments — Senate Bill #383, 1967.

66-8-1.	Short Title.
66-8-2.	Definitions.
66-8-3.	Centralized registration system for all vital statistics.
66-8-4.	Registration of vital statistics.
66-8-5.	Vital Statistics, reports, and certificates — forms and information to be included.
66-8-6.	Reports of marriage.
66-8-7.	Reports of adoption, divorce, paternity and other court proceedings affecting vital statistics.
66-8-8.	Reports and certificates as to births and deaths.
66-8-9.	Local registration districts for processing of birth and death certificates.
66-8-10.	Certificates of death.
66-8-11.	Dead bodies — disposition, removal from state, records.
66-8-12.	Certificates of birth.
66-8-13.	New certificates of birth following adoption, legitimation, and paternity determination.
66-8-14.	Delayed registration of births and deaths.
66-8-15.	Alteration of reports and certificates; amended reports and certificates.

66-8-1. SHORT TITLE —

This article may be cited as the "Vital Statistics Act".

66-8-2. DEFINITIONS —

(1) As used in this article, unless the context otherwise requires:

(2) "Regulations" means regulations duly adopted pursuant to section 66-8-3.

(3) "Vital statistics report" means any report required by section 66-8-6, 66-8-7, or 66-8-8.

(4) "Vital statistics certificate" means any certificate required by section 66-8-10 or 66-8-12.

(5) "Institution" means any establishment which provides in-patient medical, surgical, or diagnostic care or treatment, or nursing, custodial, or domiciliary care, to two or more unrelated individuals, or to which persons are committed by law.

(6) "Fetal death" means death prior to the complete expulsions or extraction from its mother of a product of human conception, irrespective of the duration of pregnancy. The death is indicated by the fact that after such expulsion or extraction the fetus does not breathe or show any other evidence of life such as beating of the heart, pulsation of the umbilical cord, or definite movement of voluntary muscles.

(7) "Dead body" means a lifeless human body or parts of such body or bones thereof from the state of which it reasonably may be concluded that death recently occurred.

66-8-3. CENTRALIZED REGISTRATION SYSTEM FOR ALL VITAL STATISTICS —

In order to provide for the maintenance of a centralized registry of the vital statistics of this state, the office of state registrar of vital statistics is hereby created in the division of administration of the state department of public health. The state registrar shall be appointed by the state board, shall have such staff and clerical help as reasonably may be required in the performance of his duties, and the state registrar and his staff and clerical help shall be subject to the constitution and civil service laws of the state. The state board of public health shall adopt, promulgate, amend and repeal such rules and regulations and orders in accordance with the provisions of section 3-16-2, C.R.S. 1963, as are necessary and proper for carrying out the provisions of this article. The state registrar shall direct and supervise the operation of the vital statistics system, prepare and publish annual reports of vital statistics, and administer and enforce the provisions of this article and all rules and regulations issued hereunder. Federal, state, local, and other public or private agencies may, upon request, be furnished copies of records of data for statistical purposes upon such terms and conditions as may be prescribed by regulation. The state registrar may delegate such functions and duties vested in him to his staff and clerical help and to the local registrars as he deems necessary or expedient.

66-8-4. REGISTRATION OF VITAL STATISTICS —

Promptly upon receipt of each and every vital statistics report or certificate from a county clerk, a court clerk, or a local registrar, the state registrar shall examine it to determine that it has been properly completed. If the report has been properly completed the state registrar shall register the statistical event described therein by noting on the report the date the report has been accepted as having been properly completed, and certifying thereon that it is registered and placing the same in the permanent files of the office. If not properly completed the state registrar shall take such action with respect thereto as may be required by applicable regulations.

66-8-5. VITAL STATISTICS, REPORTS, AND CERTIFICATES—FORMS AND INFORMATION TO BE INCLUDED —

The state board shall specify the information to be included in each type of vital statistical report and certificate required by this article and the division shall provide the necessary forms, but in no event shall any information be required in reports of court decrees or reports of marriages, births, or deaths that is not contained in such decrees or in the certificates pertaining to such marriages, births, and deaths. In order to assist in the promotion and maintenance of uniformity throughout the various states, the state board shall give consideration to, but not be limited by the items recommended by the federal agency responsible for a national system of vital statistics.

66-8-6. REPORTS OF MARRIAGE —

Each county clerk and recorder shall prepare a report containing such information and using such form as may be prescribed and furnished by the state registrar, with respect to every duly executed marriage certificate that is returned in accordance with section 90-1-12 (2), C.R.S. 1963. On or before the tenth day of each month, or more frequently if so requested by the state registrar, such clerk and recorder shall forward to the state registrar all such marriage reports for all marriage certificates returned in the preceding period. Certified copies of marriage certificates may be issued by any clerk and recorder pursuant to section 90-1-20, C.R.S. 1963.

66-8-7. REPORTS OF ADOPTION, DIVORCE, PATERNITY AND OTHER COURT PROCEEDINGS AFFECTING VITAL STATISTICS —

The clerk of each court shall prepare a report containing such information and using such form as may be prescribed and furnished by the state registrar, with respect to every decree entered by the court with respect to paternity, legitimacy, adoption, change of name, divorce, separate maintenance, and

annulment of marriage, and every decree amending or nullifying such a decree, and also with respect to every decree entered pursuant to section 66-8-14. On or before the tenth day of each month, or more frequently if so requested by the state registrar, such clerk shall forward to the state registrar the reports for all such decrees entered during the preceding period as well as the sum of one dollar for each such report.

66-8-8. REPORTS AND CERTIFICATES AS TO BIRTHS AND DEATHS —

Each local registrar who receives a birth or death certificate shall prepare a report with respect thereto, using such form as may be prescribed by the state registrar, and shall keep all such reports as part of such local registrar's permanent files. On or before the tenth day of each month, or more often if so requested by the state registrar, each such local registrar shall forward to the state registrar all of the original birth and death certificates received during the preceding period.

66-8-9. LOCAL REGISTRATION DISTRICTS FOR PROCESSING OF BIRTH AND DEATH CERTIFICATES —

(1) In order to facilitate the processing of certificates and reports pertaining to births and deaths, the state board shall divide the state into local registration districts and from time to time may modify, consolidate, or subdivide the same. There shall be a local registration district. In the event the local registration district is coterminous with a district or county health department organized under either article 2 or article 3 of this chapter, the health officer of such district shall be the local registrar; otherwise the state registrar shall appoint and remove the local registrar in each district.

(2) The local registrar shall require that birth and death certificates be completed and filed in accordance with provisions of this article and rules and regulations issued hereunder, and shall maintain such records, make such reports, and perform such other duties as from time to time may be required. Records of local registrars shall be maintained in such manner and at such places as shall be specified by regulation.

(3) Deputy local registrars to assist local registrars in the performance of their duties may be appointed and removed. In the event the local registration district is coterminous with a district or county health department organized under either article 2 or article 3 of this chapter, appointment and removal shall be accomplished by the local registrar; otherwise by the state registrar.

(4) The state registrar shall certify quarterly to the treasurer of each county and name and address of each deputy local registrar and the number of birth and death certificates pertaining to such county and processed by each such person during the preceding quarter. Upon approval of the proper auditing official of such county, each such local registrar and deputy local registrar shall be entitled to the sum of fifty cents for each such certificate so processed and fifty cents if no certificate has been so transmitted, but no

compensation shall be paid under this section to any full-time employee of the state or of any political subdivision thereof.

66-8-10. CERTIFICATES OF DEATH —

(1) Within three days after a death of a person or delivery of a dead fetus, and within three days after discovery thereof if the time or place of such death or delivery is unknown, a death certificate with respect thereto shall be filed with the local registrar of the local registration district in which such death or delivery occurred or, if such facts are unknown, in the local registration district in which the body or fetus was found. If the death or delivery occurred in a moving conveyance, the certificate shall be filed in the local registration district in which the body or fetus was first removed from such conveyance.

(2) The funeral director or person acting as such who first assumes custody of a dead body or dead fetus shall be responsible for the filing of the death certificate required by subsection (1) of this section. He shall obtain the personal data required by the certificate from the next of kin or the best qualified person or source available. He shall obtain completion of the portion of the certificate pertaining to the cause of death within twenty-four hours after the death or delivery of the dead fetus by the physician in charge with respect to the illness or condition which resulted in the death or delivery of the dead fetus, but if the death or delivery occurred without such medical attendance, the county coroner shall be notified by the funeral director or any other person having knowledge of such death or delivery and the coroner shall complete the medical certification.

66-8-11. DEAD BODIES — DISPOSITION, REMOVAL FROM STATE, RECORDS —

(1) Any person requested to act as funeral director for a dead body or otherwise whoever assumes custody of a dead body shall, within seventy-two hours after death or discovery of such body, obtain a disposition or removal permit therefor from the local registrar of the local registration district in which the death occurred or the body was found and no body shall be buried, cremated, deposited in a valt or tomb, or otherwise disposed of, nor shall any body be removed from this state until such a disposition or removal permit has been obtained. The local registrar of a local registration district in which a death has occurred or a body been found shall issue either a disposition or removal permit as requested, but only upon receipt of a death certificate or a removal permit issued under authority of another state or under such other circumstances as may be specified by regulations.

(2) A disposition permit issued under the law of another state which accompanies a dead body or fetus brought into this state shall be authority for final disposition of the body or fetus in this state.

(3) Within five days following the final disposition of any dead body or fetus in this state the disposition

permit therefor shall be filed with the local registrar of the local registration district in which such disposition occurred.

(4) Any person who removes from the place of death or transports or finally disposes of a dead body or fetus, in addition to filing any certificate or other form required by this article, shall keep a record which shall identify the body, and such information pertaining to his receipt, removal, and delivery of such body as may be prescribed in regulations. Such record shall be retained for a period of not less than seven years and shall be made available for inspection by the state registrar or his representative upon demand.

66-8-12. CERTIFICATES OF BIRTH –

(1) A certificate of birth for each live birth which occurs in this state shall be filed with the local registrar of the district in which the birth occurs within seven days after such birth. When a birth occurs on a moving conveyance the birth certificate shall be filed in the district in which the child was first removed from the conveyance. Either of the parents of the child shall sign the certificate to attest to the accuracy of the personal data entered thereon in time to permit its filing within such seven day period.

(2) When a birth occurs in an institution, the person in charge of the institution or his designated representative shall obtain the personal data, prepare the certificate, secure the signatures required by the certificate, and file it with the local registrar; the physician in attendance shall certify to the facts of birth and provide the medical information required by the certificate within five days after the birth. When the birth occurs outside an institution, the certificate shall be prepared and filed by the physician in attendance at or immediately after birth, or in the absence of such a physician by any other person so attending, or in the absence of any person so attending by the father or mother, or in the absence of the father and the inability of the mother by the person in charge of the premises where the birth occurred.

(3) If the mother was married either at the time of conception or birth, the name of the husband shall be entered on the certificate as the father of the child unless paternity has been determined otherwise by a court of competent jurisdiction, in which case the name of the father as so determined shall be entered. If the mother was not married at the time of conception or birth, the name of the father shall be entered if, but only if, the mother and the person to be named as the father so request in writing or if paternity has been determined by a court of competent jurisdiction, in which case the name of the father as so determined shall be entered.

(4) Whoever assumes the custody of a living infant of unknown parentage shall report on a form and in the manner prescribed by the state registrar within seven days to the local registrar of the district in which the child was found, such information as the state registrar shall require, which report shall constitute the certificate or birth for the infant. The place where the child was found shall be entered as the place of birth and the date of birth shall be determined by approximation. If the child is identified and a certificate of birth is found or obtained, any report registered under this section shall be sealed and filed and may be opened only by order of a court of competent jurisdiction or as provided by regulation.

66-8-13. NEW CERTIFICATES OF BIRTH FOLLOWING ADOPTION, LEGITIMATION, AND PATERNITY DETERMINATION –

(1) A new certificate of birth shall be prepared by the state registrar as to any person born in this state when, ever he receives with respect to such a person any of the following: A report concerning adoption, legitimacy or paternity as required by section 66-8-7; or a report or certified copy of a decree concerning the adoption, legitimacy, or paternity of such a person from a court of competent jurisdiction outside this state; or a certified copy of the marriage certificate of the parents together with a statement of the husband, executed after such marriage, in which the husband acknowledges paternity; but with respect to adoptions no new certificate of birth shall be prepared if the state registrar is requested not to do so by the court that has decreed the adoption, by an adoptive parent, or by the adopted person. Each new certificate shall show all information shown on the original certificate of birth except information for which substitute information is included as a result of the report or decree which prompts the preparation of the new certificate.

(2) The state registrar shall register each new certificate of birth prepared pursuant to subsection (1) of this section, by marking thereon the words "new certificate", by marking thereon the date such certificate is completed, which date thereafter shall be the registration date, and by substituting such new certificate for the original certificate of birth for such person.

(3) Thereafter the original certificate and evidence concerning adoption, legitimacy or paternity shall be sealed and not be subject to inspection except as provided by regulation or upon order of a court of competent jurisdiction after the court has satisfied itself that the interests of the child or of the child's descendants or the parents will best be served by opening said seal. The information obtained from opening said seal may be withheld from public view or from being presented as evidence at the discretion of the judge.

(4) In the event the decree which formed the basis for the new certificate of birth is annulled and if the state registrar receives either a certified copy of such decree of annulment or a report with respect to such decree as required by section 66-8-7 the state registrar shall return the original certificate to its place in the files. Thereafter the new certificate and evidence concerning the annulment shall not be subject to inspection except upon order of a court of competent jurisdiction or as provided by regulation.

66-8-14. DELAYED REGISTRATION OF BIRTHS AND DEATHS —

(1) When a birth, foundling birth, death, or fetal death has occurred in this state but no certificate as to such event has been filed or registered in accordance with the provisions of section 66-8-10 or 66-8-12 a certificate as to such event may be accepted for filing or registration, or both, in accordance with applicable regulations concerning certificates that have not been timely or properly filed or registered. The state registrar shall endorse on the certificate a summary statement of the evidence submitted to substantiate the facts asserted in such certificate. If a certificate is not registered until more than a year after the event, the state registrar shall mark the word, "Delayed" on the face thereof.

(2) When the state registrar finds the certificate or such supplementary evidence as may be required by regulations to be deficient or invalid, the certificate shall not be registered and the person who requested the registration shall be advised in writing both as to the basis for the alleged deficiency or invalidity and also as to such person's right of appeal. Judicial review of the action of the state registrar may be had in accordance with the provisions of section 3-16-5, C.R.S. 1963, but an action for judicial review shall be commenced within sixty days after the date the state registrar gives his notice in writing of his decision. If no action for judicial review is commenced within said period, the state registrar shall return the certificate and all documents submitted in support thereof to the person submitting the same if registration of the certificate has been refused.

66-8-15. ALTERATION OF REPORTS AND CERTIFICATES; AMENDED REPORTS AND CERTIFICATES —

(1) No vital statistics report or certificate shall ever be altered in any way except in accordance with this article and applicable regulations. The date of alteration and a summary description of the evidence submitted in support of the alteration shall be endorsed on or made a part of each vital statistics certificate that is altered. Every vital statistics report or certificate that is altered in any way shall be marked "Amended" excepting the birth report or certificate of any illegitimate child altered by the addition of a father's name pursuant to section 66-8-12 (3), in which case, upon request of the parents, the surname of the child shall be changed on the report and certificate to that of the father, and also excepting additions and minor corrections made within one year after the date of the statistical event as may be specified by applicable regulations.

(2) Upon receipt of a certified copy of a court order changing the name of a person born in this state and upon request of such person, or upon the request of his parent, guardian, or legal representative if he be under a legal disability, the original certificate of birth shall be amended to reflect the new name thereon.

(3) In the event the state registrar alters a birth certificate or death certificate, he shall promptly forward a certified copy of the altered certifictae to the local registrar who holds a copy of the certificate as originally filed.

66-8-16. INSTITUTIONS TO KEEP RECORDS; PERSONS TO FURNISH INFORMATION—

(1) Every person in charge of an institution as defined in this article shall keep a record of personal particulars and date concerning each person admitted or confined to such institution. This record shall include such information as required by the standard certificate of birth, death, and fetal death forms issued under the provisions of this article. The record shall be made at the time of admission. The name and address of the person providing the information shall appear on the record.

(2) When a dead human body is released or disposed of by an institution, the person in charge of the institution shall record the name of the deceased, date of death, name and address of the person to whom the body is released, date of removal from the institution, or if finally disposed of by the institution, the date, place, and manner of disposition shall be recorded.

(3) Any person having knowledge of the facts shall furnish such information as he may possess regarding any birth, death, fetal death, adoption, marriage, or divorce, upon demand of the state registrar.

66-8-17. CERTIFIED COPIES FURNISHED—FEE —

Vital statistics records shall be treated as confidential, but the department of public health shall, upon request, furnish to any applicant having a direct and tangible interest in a vital statistics record a certified copy of any record registered under the provisions of this article. For the making and certification of such certified copy there shall be paid by the applicant a fee of two dollars, but no fee shall be paid for a certified copy given to another state agency. Any copy of the record of a birth or death, when properly certified by the department of public health to be a true copy thereof, shall be prima facie evidence in all courts and places of the facts therein stated. For any search of the files and records when no certified copy is made, there shall be paid by the applicant a fee of two dollars for each hour or fractional hour of time of search. The department of public health shall keep a correct account of all fees received by it under the provisions of this section, and turn the same over to the state treasurer to be credited to the general fund.

66-8-18. PENALTIES —

(1) Any person who knowingly and willfully makes any false statement in or supplies any false information for or for purposes of deception alters, mutilates, uses, attempts to use, or furnishes to another for deceptive use any vital statistics certificate and any person who knowingly and willfully and for purposes of deception uses or attempts to use or furnishes for use by another any vital statistics certificate knowing that such certificate contains false information or relates to a person other than the person with respect to whom it purports to relate shall be guilty of a misdemeanor and shall be punished by a fine of not more than one thousand dollars or

imprisoned not more than one year, or both.

(2) Any person who willfully violates any of the provisions of this article or refuses or neglects to perform any of the duties imposed upon him by this article shall be guilty of a misdemeanor and shall be punished by a fine of not more than one hundred dollars or imprisoned not more than thirty days or both.

66-8-19. TAX ON COURT ACTION AFFECTING VITAL STATISTICS —

In order to help defray the maintenance of vital statistics records there is hereby levied, in addition to the tax levied under section 135-4-29, C.R.S. 1963, a tax of one dollar upon each action for divorce, separate maintenance, annulment, paternity, adoption, legitimation, and change of name that is filed in the office of each clerk of a court of record in this state on or after the effective date of this section. Said tax shall be paid to such clerk at the time of the filing of such action by the party so filing the same, and shall be kept by said clerk in a separate fund and remitted to the state treasurer on the first day of each month for deposit to the state general fund.

Section 2. 37-13-4 (3), Colorado Revised Statutes 1963 (1965 Supp.), is amended to read:

37-13-4. ORIGINAL CIVIL JURISDICTION —

(3) The county court shall have concurrent original jurisdiction with the district court in petitions for change of name.
SEVERABILITY CLAUSE. —
SAFETY CLAUSE. —
EFFECTIVE DATE: January 1, 1968.

The following sections of the Colorado Revised Statutes, 1963 are pertinent to the laws covering Vital Statistics:

CHAPTER 35
ARTICLE 6

35-6-6. CORONER'S INQUEST — JURY — CERTIFICATE OF DEATH —

Whenever the coroner shall learn that any person in his jurisdiction has died from external violence from unexplained cause, or under suspicious circumstances, he shall: immediately notify the district attorney; proceed to view the body; and make all proper inquiry respecting the cause and manner of death.

The coroner shall, if he or the district attorney deem it advisable, cause a post mortem examination to be made, by a licensed physician, of the body of the deceased to determine the cause of death. When the coroner has knowledge that the body of any person who has died as above stated within his jurisdiction he may, if he deem it advisable, summon forthwith six citizens of the county to appear at a place named to hold an inquest to hear testimony and to make such inquiries that he deems appropriate. In all cases wherein the coroner shall have held an investigation or inquest the certificate of death shall be issued by the coroner or his deputy.

35-6-9. PHYSICIANS SUMMONED — COMPENSATION —

In any case wherein the coroner orders a post mortem examination he may summon one or more licensed physicians to make a scientific examination of the body of the deceased, and each such physician shall be allowed reasonable compensation for his services. The amount of such compensation shall be determined by the coroner within the limits prescribed by the county commissioners. Any person so summoned may rely on the coroner's act in ordering an examination, and it shall be legally presumed that he has acted with due legal authority.

CHAPTER 113
ARTICLE 1

113-1-12. PUBLIC RECORDS FREE TO SERVICEMEN —

Whenever a copy of any public record is required by the United States veterans administration or its successors or any other agency of the government of the United States, to be used in determining the eligibility of any person who shall have served in the armed forces of the United States or any dependent or dependents of such person, to participate in benefits for such person or persons made available by the laws of the United States in relation to such service in the armed forces of the United States, the official charged with the custody of such public records, without charge, shall provide the applicant or applicants for such benefits or any person acting on his or their behalf, or the representative of such bureau or other agency, with a certified copy of such record.

III - STATE LISTING

All fifty states of the Union were contacted and the information asked for was, briefly:

(1) When did you start to file birth certificates?

(2) When was the hour of birth item included on the forms?

(3) What kind of time is this hour recorded in?

(4) Has the above been standard practice since the inception of birth certificates, or were changes made through the years?

(5) Please send a copy of the legislation regarding same.

Not all of the states answered this query. Some states which answered sent incomplete information. However, the material available is given in the listing below. If any of this information seems nebulous, you may send queries to the State Registrar, Bureau of Vital Statistics, at the state capitol city in the state, or to the address given under the heading of the states listed below.

HEW: Year each state started to record birth certificates according to the U.S. Department of Health, Education and Welfare, Washington, D.C.

ALABAMA

Department of Public Health, State Office Bldg., Montgomery, AL 36104

HEW: 1908

Currently and for quite some years we have not included the time of day as a part of the birth certificate form. This item is included on death certificates. As to the "kind of time," it depends upon what kind of time is legal as of the date of the event. For example, during daylight saving time months that is the time used. Otherwise the conventional time is used. There is no legislation pertaining to "kind of time" used in recording vital events.

ALASKA

Department of Health and Welfare, Pouch "H," Juneau, AK 99801.

HEW: 1913

No answer.

ARIZONA

State Department of Health, Box 6820, Phoenix, AZ 85005

Hew: 1909

The only time daylight time has been used in the State of Arizona was in 1967. Otherwise we use standard time. We do not know what year all events show the time, although the records from 1909 have a place for this, many do not have this entered in the older records. We have no copies of any legislation on this matter and do not know if it would be included as such in any printings you could find.

ARKANSAS

State Department of Health, 4815 W. Markham St., Little Rock, AR 72201

HEW: 1914

The hour of birth item has been included on certificates since the bureau was established in 1914. Also, the time of birth is based on the time system being used, whether Central Standard or Daylight Saving Time. The format of birth certificates is not determined by legislative action. Therefore, there is no documentation.

CALIFORNIA

State Department of Public Health, 1927 13th St., Sacramento, CA 95814

HEW: 1905

Generally, the recording of the time of the event has been provided for since 1905. However, some of the early certificate forms were provided by local jurisdictions and did not have a requirement for the reporting of the hour of the event. Suggest that you contact a law library in the specific area for information on laws pertaining to this matter.

COLORADO

State Department of Health, 4210 E. 11th Ave., Denver, CO 80220

HEW: 1907

The hour of birth shown on birth certificates is the time in effect at the time of birth. During the summer months now, when daylight saving time is in effect, it is daylight time. During the winter months, it is standard time. We have no statutes pertaining to the time element of birth registration.

CONNECTICUT

State Department of Health, 79 Elm St., Hartford, CT 06115

HEW: 1897

Statute pertaining to time: Sec. 1-6. Standard of time. The standard of time for the seventy-fifth meridian west of Greenwich shall be the standard of time for this state, except that the standard of time of this state shall be one our in advance of such established time from two o'clock ante meridian on the last Sunday in April until two o'clock ante meridian on the last Sunday in October. The year that the State of Connecticut has been recording the hours of birth began in 1933.

DELAWARE

State Board of Health, Dover, DE 19901
HEW: 1881

On certificates of birth filed in the state of Delaware that time used as the time of birth is the prevailing time established by the Federal Government. As soon as daylight saving time is adopted in the spring the time of birth is entered according to the Daylight Saving schedule. It is presumed that this has been going on ever since the use of Daylight Saving Time and at least for many years.

DISTRICT OF COLUMBIA

Department of Public Health, 300 Indiana Ave. NW, Washington, DC 20001
HEW: 1871

Births are recorded as to the time of birth, be it standard or daylight at the time of birth. The hour of birth was first recorded in 1907. Our records start 1874.

FLORIDA

State Board of Health, P.O. Box 210, Jacksonville, FL 32201
HEW: 1917

No answer.

GEORGIA

Department of Public Health, 47 Trinity Ave., Atlanta, GA 30334
HEW: 1919

Georgia did not begin recording vital events until 1919, and since that time has followed the kind of time (standard or daylight) as was in effect at the date of the vital event. The time of the event was shown on the regular certificate from the beginning of our vital records program in 1919 through June 1945 and from January 19, 1959 to the present date; however, during the period from July 19, 1945 through December 16, 1958, the time of the vital event was shown in the confidential medical section of the certificates.

HAWAII

State Department of Health, P.O. Box 3378, Honolulu, HI 96801
HEW: 1853

Standard time is generally used in reckoning the time of occurrence in the preparation of vital records. Birth hours appear to have been recorded since July 1, 1909. No legislation specifically requires the entry of this time on birth certificates. This office generally follows the standard vital statistics forms recommended by the federal agency, the Division of Vital Statistics, National Center for Health Certificates, Public Health Service, Department of Health, Education and Welfare.

IDAHO

Department of Health, Statehouse, Boise, ID 83707
HEW: 1911

Mountain Standard Time is used in Idaho for preparation of certificates. The hour of birth has not been included on birth certificates for many years. There is no legislation on this matter.

ILLINOIS

Department of Public Health, Springfield, IL 62706
HEW: 1916

The hour of birth has been recorded on Illinois birth certificates ever since the state central registry was established in 1916. Prior to July 1, 1959, United States Standard Time was used in reckoning the date and time of occurrence in the preparation of official certificates of births, stillbirths and deaths, regardless of whether or not Daylight Saving Time, War Time, or any other advanced time, by whatever term known, was in effect.

On July 1, 1959, by Act of the General Assembly of the State of Illinois, the period between 2:00 a.m. on the last Sunday in April and 2:00 a.m. of the last Sunday in October, is known as State Standard Time, and is one hour in advance of the United States Standard Central Time. During the above period of time, the reckoning of the date and time of occurrence in the preparation of official vital records is on State Standard Time.

Before July 1, 1959, all the hospitals in Illinois were recording Standard Time on birth certificates except for the following: all Catholic hospitals, Swedish Covenant, Lutheran Deaconess, Lying-In Hospital, South Chicago Hospital, and Highland Park Hospital. For the above hospitals you will have to deduct one hour for births occurring during Daylight Savings Time or War Time. Births at other hospitals were recorded as Standard Time. After July 1, 1959, all hospitals in the state were recording clock time.

INDIANA

State Board of Health, 1330 W. Michigan St., Indianapolis, IN 46206
HEW: 1907

The hour of occurrence of all vital events has been an item on the standard certificate of these events since the time of recording. This time is and was recommended by the United States Public Health Service: however each state may make its own decision. I am reasonably sure that this item appears on the certificate of all the registration areas.

The time is recorded in the legal time in that area at the time of the event. There are no statutes in this state dealing with ''time.'' This item is covered by regulation which has the authority of law, without having been passed by the General Assembly of this State. The time of birth is considered confidential information (Chapter 157, Acts 1949) and may be released only by court order.

IOWA

State Department of Health, Lucas State Office Bldg., Des Moines, IA 50319

HEW: 1880

The item pertaining to the hour of birth on birth certificates was first included on the forms about 1905. Hour is recorded in the prevailing time at the date of the event.

KANSAS

State Department of Health, Topeka, KS 66601

HEW: 1911

The hour of occurrence of a vital event is registered on the basis of the official local time that's in effect at the time of each event, whether it be Standard or Daylight Time.

The hour of birth was recorded on Kansas Birth certificates from 1911 to 1948 but was not recorded from 1949 to 1967. Effective with the 1968 revision of the standard birth certificate the time of the hour of birth was restored, thus the information is currently being recorded.

The basic legislation regarding the content of a birth certificate is that included in K.S.A. 65-2415, which provides in part that, ''The forms of certificates shall include as a minimum the items required by the national office of vital statistics subject to approval of and modification by the board.'' On this basis the Kansas certificate forms and registration procedures have always been in close conformity with the prescribed national standards.

KENTUCKY

State Department of Health, 275 E. Main St., Frankfort, KY 40601

HEW: 1911

No answer.

LOUISIANA

State Board of Health, PO Box 60630, New Orleans, LA 70160

HEW: 1914

1790, New Orleans City Health Department

No answer.

MAINE

Department of Health and Welfare, Augusta, ME 04330

HEW: 1892

The kind of time used would be the prevailing time in effect at the time of the occurrence. No attempt would be made to convert from daylight to standard. Birth records established between 1892 and 1967 contain no provision for time (hour) of birth only date. Records established after January 1, 1968 have provision for hour of birth if the information is provided at time of filing. If not provided the record is accepted for filing provided date of birth is included.

MARYLAND

Department of Health, 301 W. Preston St., Baltimore, MD 21201

HEW: 1898

1895, Baltimore City Health Department

The hour of birth inserted on the birth certificate is the time of birth regardless of whether it is Daylight or Standard Time. The legality of this procedure is contained in Article 94, Section 3 of the Annotated Code of Maryland.

An item for the hour of birth has been contained in the Maryland birth certificates since 1914, at which time the standard size and format of the certificate was developed. Prior to 1914 the birth certificate was a 3"x5" card and did not contain the hour of birth.

MASSACHUSETTS

Secretary of Commonwealth, State House, Boston, MA 02133

HEW: 1841

The statues do not provide that the time of birth be recorded on the birth record. After approximately 1943, the time has become a matter of record on birth certificates. Whatever the time of the year governs whether it be standard of daylight savings time.

MICHIGAN

Birth Records Office, 1151 Taylor, Detroit, MI 48202

HEW: 1867

Records prior to 1905 at Wayne County Clerk's Office.

MINNESOTA

State Department of Health, 350 State Office Bldg., St. Paul, MN 55101

HEW: 1900

This office did not begin receiving the original certificates until the year 1908 so our records from 1900 to 1907 are typed 3x5 cards containing information taken from the original certificates on file in the county offices. These copies do not contain the exact time of birth or death.

Beginning with 1908 all certificate forms contain a space in which to enter the exact time of the event. There is no legal requirement that this item be completed, therefore a certificate could be accepted by this office for filing if the space for the exact time was left blank.

We find, however, that a majority of the certificates received by this office do contain the exact time of birth or death and indicate whether or not the event occurred during Central Standard Time or Central Daylight Time.

MISSISSIPPI

State Board of Health, Jackson, MS 39205

HEW: 1912

The time of day ''hour'' was placed on the birth certificates as an item as of November 1, 1912 and continued thereon until December 31, 1948, when new certificates were instituted. The time of birth was again placed on the certificate

January 31, 1968, and will remain thereon until the need appears to have been satisfied for recording this item. The time of day ''hour'' is for the prevailing time when the event occurs.

MISSOURI
Division of Health and Welfare, Jefferson, MO 65101
HEW: 1910
The time of the event has been requested on Missouri birth and death records since January 1, 1910. The time given is the official time in effect in the place where the event occurred.

MONTANA
State Department of Health, Helena, MT 59601
HEW: 1907
The Montana death certificates have consistently included an entry for hour of death. From 1919 through the middle of 1946, the Montana birth certificate contained an entry for hour of birth. The most recent revision of the Montana birth certificate which was placed in use January 1, 1968, also includes an item for hour of birth. The hour of birth would be entered in daylight time whenever this is in effect. No legislation regarding the entry of hour of birth.

NEBRASKA
Department of Health, State House Station, Box 94757, Lincoln, NE 68509
HEW: 1904
In 1912 the standard birth certificate form was adopted and this provided space for the time of birth. Persons completing these certificates have been instructed to note the time in effect at the time of birth. This in some instances would have been daylight savings time when in use in Nebraska.

NEVADA
Division of Health, Carson City, NV 89701
HEW: 1911
Birth hours have been put on Nevada birth certificates since July 1, 1911 when they were first centralized. The kind of time in effect would be the time on the record. No legislation on the matter.

NEW HAMPSHIRE
Department of Health and Welfare, 61 S. Spring St., Concord, NH 03301
HEW: All recorded
Our records of vital events are recorded by date according to the time schedule in use at the time of the event; either eastern standard time or daylight time. Exact hour of an event has been on the birth and death certificate since 1937. Prior to 1937, hour of birth and death was not collected as a standard practice. No legislation. Items to be included on the certificates are recommended by formerly the State Board of Health and now by the State Registrar.

NEW JERSEY
Department of Health, P.O. Box 1540, Trenton, NJ 08625
HEW: 1848
An item calling for the insertion of hour of birth first appeared on our report form in 1920. However, this is not to say that the item has always been completed. We do not query if it has been omitted.
The only item in this office concerning time is a copy of the Attorney General's letter of July 7, 1921. ''If standard time is not the time stated, the record should disclose what method of calculation of the time has been used to locate the event referred to.''
Some hours are stated as standard time even though daylight time was being observed.

NEW MEXICO
Health and Social Services Department, 118 Pera Bldg., Santa Fe, NM 87501
HEW: All recorded
No answer.

NEW YORK
State Department of Health, Albany, NY 12208
HEW: 1880
NYC Burroughs, various dates
No answer.

NORTH CAROLINA
State Board of Health, Box 2091, Raleigh, NC 27602
HEW: 1913
The time used is that which is in effect at the time of occurrence.

NORTH DAKOTA
State Department of Health, Division of Vital Statistics, Bismarck, ND 58501
HEW: 1908
It has been customary for the persons to prepare certificates using the time in effect in the community when the certificate was prepared. The certificates in this state have ben patterned after the recommended standard form, and since registration years ago did not receive the same emphasis as in recent years, there can be no guarantee of the accuracy with which certificates were completed.

OHIO
Department of Health, P.O. Box 118, Columbus, OH 43216
HEW: 1908
Records of birth began December 20, 1908. The certificates contained the time of birth occurred in 1908 through 1955. The years 1956 through 1967 do not contain the time the birth occurred. Beginning with the year 1968 the certificates again indicate the time the birth occurred.

The certificates do not indicate whether it was standard or daylight time. The time used to reckon the time of occurrence I believe would be the time used at the time of the birth. In most cases this would be standard time since the State of Ohio did not adopt daylight saving time as a state until the year 1968.

OKLAHOMA

Division of Vital Statistics, State Department of Health, Oklahoma City, OK 73105
HEW: 1908

Birth certificates have been issued since October, 1908, and the time of birth is shown if the doctor recorded same when delivering a child. Delayed certificates of birth do not show time of birth.

OREGON

State Board of Health, State Office Bldg., P.O. Box 231, Portland, OR 97207
HEW: 1903

This item (time of birth) has appeared on Oregon birth certificates from the early 1900s to the present date. Of course, on individual records this item may not be completed. The kind of time recorded (Standard or Daylight) is the official time in effect in the place of birth at the time of the child's birth.

PENNSYLVANIA

Department of Health, P.O. Box 90, Harrisburg, PA 17120
HEW: 1906

Original records of births and deaths in Pennsylvania have been filed with the state since January, 1906.

A space for the hour of birth has always been on the record. To the best of our knowledge there is no legislation on this subject.

Time on the certificates of birth, death and fetal death has been given as Eastern Daylight Time (or War Time) when it is being observed.

RHODE ISLAND

Department of Health, Providence, RI 02903
HEW: 1852

The time of birth has been recorded on birth records from 1933 to 1956 and from 1961 through the present. Item is recorded in accordance with the local time being used.

SOUTH CAROLINA

State Board of Health, L. Marion Sims Bldg., Columbia, SC 29201
HEW: 1915

The law requiring the filing of birth records in South Carolina became effective January 1, 1915. The hour of birth has been a standard item since that time. The hour of birth recorded according to standard or daylight, whichever is in existence at that particular time.

SOUTH DAKOTA

State Department of Health, Pierre, SD 57501
HEW: 1906
No answer.

TENNESSEE

Department of Public Health, Nashville, TN 37219
HEW: 1914

The time used in preparing certificates of birth and other actual records is the time that was in effect when the event occurred. Space has been provided on birth certificates for recording the hour since 1914.

TEXAS

State Department of Health, Austin, TX 78701
HEW: 1903

The first law requiring the registration of births in Texas was passed in 1903; however, it was not until 1917 that the standard form for registering births included an item calling for the hour of birth. Depending upon which is in effect, Standard and Daylight Saving Time are both used in determining the hour of birth as reflected in birth certificates. We have no specific statutory or regulatory measure relative to the hour of birth entry on birth certificates.

UTAH

Department of Health, Salt Lake City, UT 84111
HEW: 1905

Our records have the time of birth since 1905 when our records began. At that time we were on standard time but at the present we are on daylight savings time and the birth is recorded according to the time the state is on.

VERMONT

Secretary of State, Montpelier, VT 05602
HEW: All recorded.

The hour of birth was recorded on birth records about 1919 and this information would be found in the various Town and City Clerks' offices where the births were recorded. However, the records returned to this office didn't require the information until 1953 so the hour of birth from 1919 through 1953 is not on the birth records in this office. The hour was the kind of time in effect in the locality.

VIRGINIA

Department of Health, P.O. Box 1000, Richmond, VA 23208
HEW: 1912

The time of birth has been shown on birth certificate since June 14, 1912. However, we have no way of knowing whether this would be Standard Time. We would assume that it would be the time that was being used in the locality at the time of the birth.

WASHINGTON
Department of Health, Public Health Bldg., Olympia, WA 98501

HEW: 1907

Hour of birth appeared on the birth certificate forms in use from 1907 through 1948. The item was dropped from the form through 1967 and was re-established on the forms that went into use January 1, 1968. As for reckoning date and time by standard or daylight time, the instructions have been that the time in effect in the area where the event occurred should be used. There is no specific legislation relative to this matter.

WEST VIRGINIA
State Department of Health, State Office Bldg. #3, Charleston, WV 25311

HEW: 1917

No answer.

WISCONSIN
Wisconsin Division of Health, P.O. Box 309, Madison, WI 53701

HEW: 1914

No answer.

WYOMING
Department of Public Health, State Office Bldg., Cheyenne, WY 82001

HEW: 1909

The time of birth has been recorded on birth certificates since compulsory registration went into effect. The certificates do not reflect whether or not Daylight Savings Time is used in determining the date and time of occurrence. The time used is whatever time is in effect at the time of birth.

IV POSSESSIONS AND TERRITORY LISTING

AMERICAN SAMOA
Registrar of Vital Statistics, Pago Pago, American Samoa 96920

HEW: 1920

CANAL ZONE
Vital Statistics Clerk, Health Bureau, Balboa Heights, Canal Zone

HEW: May, 1904

GUAM
Public Health and Social Services, P.O. Box 2816, Agana, Guam, M.I. 96910

HEW: October 26, 1901

PUERTO RICO
Department of Health, San Juan, Puerto Rico 00908

HEW: July 22, 1931

TRUST TERRITORY OF THE PACIFIC IS-LANDS
Department of Medical Services, Saipan, Mariana Islands 96950

HEW: November 21, 1952

VIRGIN ISLANDS (U.S.)
St. Thomas: Registrar of Vital Statistics, Charlotte Amalie, St. Thomas, Virgin Islands 00802

HEW: July 1, 1906

St. Croix: Registrar of Vital Statistics, Charles Harwood Memorial Hospital, St. Croix, Virgin Islands

HEW: 1840

It should be mentioned that the previous information came from the State Registrars' office. Records at each community may be more complete and should be checked if doubt arises as to some item in the record of the event. Some states require a court order, a specified reason, or the native's own request to release information on vital events. Furthermore, the hour item is sometimes kept in a confidential medical section of the records. Other sources where the hour item may be found are the hospital records or the attending doctor's records.

CONVERSION OF LONGITUDE TO TIME*

°	h m	°	h m	°	h m	'	m s
0	0 00	60	4 00	120	8 00	0	0 00
1	0 04	61	4 04	121	8 04	1	0 04
2	0 08	62	4 08	122	8 08	2	0 08
3	0 12	63	4 12	123	8 12	3	0 12
4	0 16	64	4 16	124	8 16	4	0 16
5	0 20	65	4 20	125	8 20	5	0 20
6	0 24	66	4 24	126	8 24	6	0 24
7	0 28	67	4 28	127	8 28	7	0 28
8	0 32	68	4 32	128	8 32	8	0 32
9	0 36	69	4 36	129	8 36	9	0 36
10	0 40	70	4 40	130	8 40	10	0 40
11	0 44	71	4 44	131	8 44	11	0 44
12	0 48	72	4 48	132	8 48	12	0 48
13	0 52	73	4 52	133	8 52	13	0 52
14	0 56	74	4 56	134	8 56	14	0 56
15	1 00	75	5 00	135	9 00	15	1 00
16	1 04	76	5 04	136	9 04	16	1 04
17	1 08	77	5 08	137	9 08	17	1 08
18	1 12	78	5 12	138	9 12	18	1 12
19	1 16	79	5 16	139	9 16	19	1 16
20	1 20	80	5 20	140	9 20	20	1 20
21	1 24	81	5 24	141	9 24	21	1 24
22	1 28	82	5 28	142	9 28	22	1 28
23	1 32	83	5 32	143	9 32	23	1 32
24	1 36	84	5 36	144	9 36	24	1 36
25	1 40	85	5 40	145	9 40	25	1 40
26	1 44	86	5 44	146	9 44	26	1 44
27	1 48	87	5 48	147	9 48	27	1 48
28	1 52	88	5 52	148	9 52	28	1 52
29	1 56	89	5 56	149	9 56	29	1 56
30	2 00	90	6 00	150	10 00	30	2 00
31	2 04	91	6 04	151	10 04	31	2 04
32	2 08	92	6 08	152	10 08	32	2 08
33	2 12	93	6 12	153	10 12	33	2 12
34	2 16	94	6 16	154	10 16	34	2 16
35	2 20	95	6 20	155	10 20	35	2 20
36	2 24	96	6 24	156	10 24	36	2 24
37	2 28	97	6 28	157	10 28	37	2 28
38	2 32	98	6 32	158	10 32	38	2 32
39	2 36	99	6 36	159	10 36	39	2 36
40	2 40	100	6 40	160	10 40	40	2 40
41	2 44	101	6 44	161	10 44	41	2 44
42	2 48	102	6 48	162	10 48	42	2 48
43	2 52	103	6 52	163	10 52	43	2 52
44	2 56	104	6 56	164	10 56	44	2 56
45	3 00	105	7 00	165	11 00	45	3 00
46	3 04	106	7 04	166	11 04	46	3 04
47	3 08	107	7 08	167	11 08	47	3 08
48	3 12	108	7 12	168	11 12	48	3 12
49	3 16	109	7 16	169	11 16	49	3 16
50	3 20	110	7 20	170	11 20	50	3 20
51	3 24	111	7 24	171	11 24	51	3 24
52	3 28	112	7 28	172	11 28	52	3 28
53	3 32	113	7 32	173	11 32	53	3 32
54	3 36	114	7 36	174	11 36	54	3 36
55	3 40	115	7 40	175	11 40	55	3 40
56	3 44	116	7 44	176	11 44	56	3 44
57	3 48	117	7 48	177	11 48	57	3 48
58	3 52	118	7 52	178	11 52	58	3 52
59	3 56	119	7 56	179	11 56	59	3 56

EXAMPLE: Convert S. T. Meridian 112E30 to hours and minutes East of Greenwich (0°).

```
112° -  7h 28m
 30' -      2m 00s  add
        7h 30m  East of Greenwich
```

* From Time Changes in the World, AFA Tempe AZ 85282

Standard Time Zones of the World

Standard time zones were adopted by the International Time Conference on October 1, 1884. The prime meridian or zero degree point is the Greenwich Meridian, and the world is divided into 24 equal divisions of 15 degrees each.

Meridian	Hours	Standard Time Zone
0	00	Greenwich Mean Time
+15	+1	West Africa Time
+30	+2	Azores Time
+45	+3	Brazil Standard Time
+52.5	+3.5	Newfoundland Time
+60	+4	Atlantic Standard Time
+75	+5	Eastern Standard Time
+90	+6	Central Standard Time
+105	+7	Mountain Standard Time
+120	+8	Pacific Standard Time
+135	+9	Yukon Standard Time
+150	+10	Central Alaska Time
+157.5	+10.5	Hawaiian Standard Time
+165	+11	Nome Time/Bering Time
+180	+12	International Date Line West
-180	-12	International Date Line East
-165	-11	Not Named
-150	-10	Guam Standard Time
-142.5	-9.5	S. Australia Standard Time
-135	-9	Japanese Standard Time
-127.5	-8.5	Moluccas Time
-120	-8	China Coast Time
-112.5	-7.5	Java Time
-105	-7	South Sumatra Time
-97.5	-6.5	North Sumatra Time
-90	-6	USSR Zone 5
-82.5	-5.5	Indian Standard Time
-75	-5	USSR Zone 4
-60	-4	USSR Zone 3
-45	-3	Baghdad Time
-30	-2	Eastern European Time
-15	-1	Central European Time